0 4 -0 -

0 3 -12- 1998

Why I Am
A Reform Jew

Why I Am
A Reform Jew

by

Rabbi Daniel B. Syme

DONALD I. FINE, INC.　　NEW YORK

Library of Congress Cataloging-in-Publication Data

Syme, Daniel B.
Why I am a Reform Jew / Daniel B. Syme.
p.   cm.
ISBN 1-55611-157-6
1. Reform Judaism—United States—History.   2. Syme, Daniel B.
3. Rabbis—United States—Biography.   I. Title
BM197.S94   1989
296.8'346—dc20   89-45332
CIP

Designed by Irving Perkins Associates

Manufactured in the United States of America
10 9 8 7 6 5 4 3 2 1

All photographs from author's collection.
Photographs # 1, 2, 3, 4, 5, 6, 9, and 18: Courtesy of American Jewish
Archives, Cincinnati Campus, Hebrew Union College, Jewish Institute
of Religion.

To my parents,
Rabbi M. Robert and Sonia Syme

To my brother,
David Syme

To my wife,
Debbie

And above all to my son, Joshua,
and his generation, whose love for
Reform Judaism guarantees its future.

ACKNOWLEDGMENTS

I wish to express my thanks to the many friends and colleagues whose comments and suggestions strengthened and enriched this book:

Jan Epstein, Monty Hall, Jocelyn Rudner, Paul Uhlmann, Jr., Evely Laser Shlensky, Charles J. Rothschild, Jr., Elaine Merians, Richard Cohen, Edith J. Miller, B.J. Tanenbaum, Jr., Margery Rothschild, Aron Hirt-Manheimer, Albert Vorspan, Rabbis Bernard Zlotowitz, Steven Foster, Harold Loss and Gary Bretton-Granatoor.

I also extend thanks to Eppie Begleiter and Joann Michaels for their help in typing the manuscript in its various stages.

I offer heartfelt gratitude to the three people who made this book possible:

Michael Cohn, my agent and friend, who convinced me to tell the story;

Donald Fine, who believed in the project and afforded me the chance to complete it;
and
Susan Schwartz, my sensitive, wise and perceptive editor.

Above all, I thank my wife, Debbie, and my son, Joshua, who sustained me with their patience, encouragement and love.

Introduction

Only two generations ago, Reform Judaism in America had to draw its rabbis and educators primarily from the ranks of the other movements of Judaism—Conservative and Orthodox. Now, after a period of astonishing growth, Reform Judaism is generating and producing its own leadership. The male and female rabbinical students at the Hebrew Union College–Jewish Institute of Religion—the Reform seminary—are products of Reform Jewish education, youth programs, Israel exchange programs. These future leaders are not imports, alienated from the traditional modes of Judaism from which they sprang; they are, for the most part, proud, affirmative and integrated liberal Jews, comfortable with the institutions of the movement, in tune with its modern thrust, reflective of its values.

Rabbi Dan Syme is one such rabbi. Although he is himself the son of a Reform rabbi and undoubtedly was preconditioned by a warm and positive home environment, Syme was shaped by the education he received from Temple Israel in Detroit and especially by the exhilarating years he spent in NFTY—Reform's dynamic youth movement and by his influential time in Israel. Growing up Reform, this bright, socially conscious, talented and sentimental young man found in Reform Judaism answers to the deepest questions of faith and ethics—simmering questions which seemed to come to a boil in the sixties, the turning-point years of Dan Syme's youth.

Dan Syme was born to Reform Judaism in a nominal sense, but

he chose it and committed himself to it in a much deeper sense. Why? Why did Reform appeal to him? For many of the same reasons that Reform Judaism has become the fastest growing movement in American Jewish religious life—and decidedly the Judaism of choice for young Jewish families.

This deeply personal volume is also a guide to contemporary Reform Judaism—its institutions, its personalities, its values. What moves Dan Syme is also what has made Reform Judaism the most successful liberal religion in contemporary America. Right-wing fundamentalism has overpowered the traditional Protestant social gospel denominations, whose social action staffs have been decimated. Reform is a ringing exception to that trend; its liberalism is its essence and a major part of its appeal.

Dan Syme deals with the most positive qualities of Reform—its honest facing-up to controversy, its passion for egalitarianism, its commitment to racial justice and women's rights, its courageous outreach to intermarried couples and to unaffiliated Jews; its commitment to Israel and Zionism, its work in building interreligious and interracial understanding, and its ritual and ceremonial creativity. But he is not content with a kind of airy-fairy Jewish ethical culture. Theology is central to his definition of Judaism, and God is a—perhaps *the*—major force in Dan Syme's personal decision-making. Some more rationalistic Jews may be put off by Syme's encounter with the Divine at moments of life-and-death significance. So be it. Syme's account of why he is a Reform Jew has a searing and searching honesty about it. One senses that a nice, undemanding, inoffensive Reform Judaism—where the bland lead the bland—would not satisfy Dan Syme's search for a personal faith of meaning and purpose and belief.

In this sense, Syme is a paradigm for many searching, well-educated American Jews. The old perennial causes—anti-Semitism, charity, Zionism, the Holocaust—will not by themselves stir young Jews or shape a Jewish identity. Indeed, some 30 percent of them are now marrying non-Jews. But that is not the end of the matter, for many still want to be Jewish; many are serious about Jewish study and practice. For them and for many others— including those already settled in Reform synagogues—Dan Syme's unassuming, readable, moving and deeply personal book is a welcome response to the question: *Why be Reform?*—and to the implicit and even more fundamental question: *Why be Jewish at all?* What difference does it make?

Dan Syme is a vice-president of the Union of American Hebrew Congregations. He is already an important Jewish leader and will be one of those who will shape a vibrant, dynamic American Judaism of the twenty-first century. Rabbi Syme is known and respected as an eloquent champion of Reform Jewish pride.

This book is a celebration of life—of the author's triumph over life-threatening illness at the age of twenty, and of the remarkable power of family and faith to confront and transcend despair and danger. This is an important testament to the life-enhancing spirit of a liberal Jewish faith upon which to build a humane value system for life.

—Albert Vorspan

Why I Am
A Reform Jew

June 1972

Plum Street Temple in Cincinnati was filled as our class of thirty-six marched down the center aisle to our seats. The service was a long one, but to us it seemed to be rushing past. At last, the time arrived when we would ascend the steps of the bimah in that magnificent temple and receive the blessing of ordination.

There was and is a custom at the Hebrew Union College–Jewish Institute of Religion that when the son or daughter of a rabbi becomes a rabbi, the parent blesses the child at the moment of ordination. Therefore, I knew that just after Dr. Alfred Gottschalk formally pronounced me a rabbi in Israel, I would stand before the ark of the Torah to receive my father's blessing as well.

When my turn arrived, I walked up the stairs to Dr. Gottschalk. He asked me quietly if I was prepared to be a rabbi and serve the Jewish people. I nodded my head in assent. He placed his hands on my shoulders and then on my head, offering a blessing and proclaiming me a rabbi. He then turned me to face the ark, where my father stood waiting. I wondered what he would say, how he would express what was in his heart at this instant. He always had a gift of saying exactly the right thing at the right time.

This time, however, there were no words. He placed his hands on my head and we both began to cry. It was the ultimate blessing, the blessing that comes from one's innermost being. We embraced one another, and my father kissed me. Then, as in the biblical story of Abraham and Isaac after God's commanded sacrifice was revealed to be no sacrifice at all, we descended the bimah together, father and son, rabbi and rabbi.

CHAPTER I

Roots of the Journey

*W*hat we know today as Reform Judaism did not come into
being as a sudden revolution in Jewish life, but rather as a
gradual manifestation of the determination of Jews to enter a modern era.

When the effects of the French Revolution and the Enlightenment began to be felt across Western Europe, the doors to the
Jewish ghettos swung open. For nearly three centuries, European
rulers had confined the Jewish community, allowing it to rule itself
in its own way so long as the kings, tsars and emperors were not
disturbed. In almost every instance, self-rule meant governance by
the rabbis, who wedded civil and religious law in a classic theocratic
system. The Talmud and Joseph Karo's book of codified Jewish law,
the *Shulchan Aruch,* prescribed the routine of daily life in minute
detail, while a variety of sanctions, the most severe being excom-
munication, gave the rabbinic courts the authority they required to
govern. With the advent of civil freedom, however, Jews left the
ghetto, the structure of the Jewish community changed radically,
and Reform Judaism, a liberal and modern expression of an ancient
faith, began to take root.

The seeds of Reform were sown in the eighteenth century by a
brilliant Jewish philosopher named Moses Mendelssohn. Convinced that Jewish isolation from the larger society was unhealthy
and dangerous, Mendelssohn organized a movement that came to
be known as the *Haskalah* (Hebrew for 'enlightenment'). Approaching Judaism from a rationalistic and universalistic perspective, he

translated the Torah into German, written in Hebrew characters. This new form of the Torah enabled Jewish students to study the sacred text in the vernacular, equipping them at the same time with tools they would need for meaningful participation in German life.

For many Jews, however, the work of Mendelssohn was but a prelude to a much more profound change in Jewish life. Jews were abandoning their faith in large numbers, turning their backs on what they felt was the tyranny of Orthodoxy in favor of Christianity, citizenship and new opportunity. Heinrich Heine, the great poet, was only one of many Jews who converted viewing their baptismal certificates as tickets of entry into German culture. As the effects of the Enlightenment spread, Jews became more and more committed to full participation in the life of their homelands. Even after they had attained full citizenship, first in France and Germany during the 1790s and then elsewhere, the religious flight from Orthodoxy continued. Jews increasingly shed the distinctive garb, beards and earlocks that for so long had distinguished them from non-Jews. They ceased to observe many traditional customs that they viewed as outmoded. Many wished to remain Jews in practice as well as fact. Sadly, however, there was no available alternative to Orthodoxy.

In 1801, a wealthy German businessman-banker named Israel Jacobson began what would ultimately become a critical undertaking in Judaism. In his hometown of Seesen, he started a Jewish Free School for the teaching of secular subjects. He introduced radical reforms into his school's religious services, translating certain prayers and hymns into German, and invited guest preachers to deliver sermons in German. He insisted that decorum be maintained during the service, as opposed to traditional synagogues, where services were often boisterous.

As word spread about the school at Seesen, Jacobson's friends began to attend worship services there. Jacobson's reputation grew. In 1807, he was put in charge of Jewish affairs in Westphalia by Napoleon's brother, Jerome. He started a second Jewish Free School in 1808 and a college for rabbis and teachers two years later. Then, in 1810, spending more than the equivalent of one hundred thousand dollars of his own money, he built a new synagogue in Seesen, which was to become the first Reform congregation. The synagogue's reforms reverberated across Germany. The use of an organ, men and women sitting together, and a ceremony in place of bar mitzvah called confirmation—for both boys and girls—shocked traditionalists but attracted many new members in search of a modern Jewish religious experience.

First in Berlin, and especially in Hamburg, Reform congregations were established and flourished. In spite of intense political opposition by the Orthodox, which ultimately closed the Berlin congregation, the Hamburg congregation grew and thrived, committed to the intellectual integrity of the individual and to the dynamic potential of Judaism. By 1840, Reform had spread to England, where twenty-four Jews formed the West London Synagogue of British Jews. Again the Orthodox made strong resistance, but as before, Reform held fast.

In Wiesbaden, in Frankfurt, and elsewhere, the new reformers set about developing a rationale and a practical guide for members. Reform Judaism gained a foothold in Hungary and Austria, in addition to Germany and England. Each community made its own innovations, with the result that no one expression of Reform could be defined. While all reformers joined in affirming the validity of and the need for change, the details of that change—or at least an underlying philosophic platform—had yet to be articulated.

A rabbinical conference held in Brunswick, Germany, in 1844 yielded few tangible results. The following year, in Frankfurt, the same group approved the use of the organ and the vernacular in worship as well as a number of changes in certain specific prayers. A third conference in Breslau in 1846 affirmed the permissibility of riding to services on the Sabbath, shortened certain holidays and altered Jewish mourning customs. In 1871, in Augsberg, a synod of rabbis and lay leaders went on record as favoring the equality of women in religious matters. A true European Reform began to take shape. The flowering of that movement, however, was cut short by a number of factors.

Political unrest, growing anti-Semitism and government repression dampened the spirits of those who felt that emancipation had been but a first step toward total freedom and equality. Orthodox intercession with the government against Reform engendered a series of complex struggles that took time and drained energy. Conservative Judaism and neo-Orthodoxy, as well as socialism and

Jewish nationalism, competed for the loyalties of those who sought an alternative to traditional forms and philosophy. Finally, a lack of unity led to a fragmentation in Reform that effectively precluded sustained and meaningful growth. It was to be almost fifty years after the Augsberg Synod before European Reform regained its vitality. Meanwhile, Reform philosophy had been transplanted to a continent where Orthodoxy was not entrenched, where religious freedom was guaranteed by law, where change was a way of life. As the German Jewish immigration began in the 1820s, a number of the early reformers and their followers made their way to the United States.

In 1824, a group of members of an Orthodox synagogue in Charleston, South Carolina, petitioned the temple board for changes in the worship service. These members, led by a lay leader named Isaac Harby, had heard of the reforms instituted in the Hamburg synagogue, and were drawn to them. They desired, among other changes, decorum in services, prayers in the vernacular and a weekly English sermon. Their appeal denied, twelve members formed their own congregation, the Reform Society of Israelites, instituting the changes they had requested plus instrumental music, the elimination of head coverings, and a shorter service. In 1830, the congregation published its own prayerbook. Reform had come to America.

In a short period of time, Reform congregations sprang up across the country, in every major city where pioneer Jews came to settle; in Baltimore, New York, Philadelphia, Chicago, and elsewhere. By 1871, between forty and fifty congregations had been established in Detroit, Cleveland, Boston, Louisville, Milwaukee, Richmond, St. Louis, Memphis, Nashville, Pittsburgh and elsewhere. All of them concurred on the need for a progressive, liberal, dynamic expression of Judaism for a new age and a free democratic home. The real question to be answered now was whether or not American Reform could achieve the unity that had eluded its European predecessors.

This book is intended for any reader interested in the evolution and flowering of a liberal religious tradition within Judaism. Most specifically, however, this book is for people who are already—or who may soon become—part of the modern, liberal Jewish community of North America. Like me, perhaps the path that you and your parents took to Reform Judaism was a journey with many milestones along the way. And perhaps, in sharing the story of my metamorphosis from a traditional Jewish background to a Reform Jewish identity, you will come to feel the same unconditional pride in Reform that now permeates my being.

I believe that Reform Judaism is Judaism's best chance for the next generation, a Judaism that can live and thrive in a democratic, pluralistic society. This book is a call to action, a call to assertive Reform identity, a call to shed the insecurities of the past and move boldly into a future in which Reform Judaism will unquestionably be a dominant Jewish force on the North American and world scene.

CHAPTER II

Isaac Mayer Wise—The Builder

*I*srael Jacobson had been the first lay leader to stand up and be counted as a proponent of constructive change in Judaism for a new world, and is rightfully honored as the father of European Reform. The architect of American Reform Judaism was Isaac Mayer Wise, born in Bohemia in 1819. There is no evidence that Wise received formal rabbinic ordination. When he arrived in the United States in 1846, however, he presented himself as a rabbi, and was accepted as such.

Educated in Europe, Wise came to Albany, New York, at the age of twenty-seven to serve as the rabbi of an Orthodox congregation in that city. A strong proponent of the changes instituted by Reform in Europe, Wise attempted to implement those same changes in Albany. He quickly found, though, that Jews in America were not as open to religious change as he had imagined. The transplanted European Jews had brought their old-world outlook, Jewish customs and commitments with them. Only a few of their rabbis and cantors even spoke English or understood what it meant to live in a democracy. Wise quickly realized that resistance to change would have to be overcome through extensive education; otherwise his dream of a unified, organized Jewish community would remain elusive.

Wise held that there could be a uniquely American form of Judaism only if a school was established to train rabbis in America and for American Jews. Accordingly, only two years after his arrival, Wise launched a campaign for a rabbinical school in the United

States. Circumstances in Albany made it impossible for the dream to be realized there. Indeed, there was so much hostility to Wise's reforms that his tenure was controversial and short-lived.

Wise went to the Albany synagogue on the morning of one Rosh Hashanah, the Jewish New Year, to find a detractor, a prominent leader of the congregation, sitting in the rabbi's chair on the pulpit. Anxious to avoid any sort of confrontation, Wise took another seat. The tension was palpable, and the congregation sensed impending disaster. When the time arrived to read from the Torah, Wise stepped before the ark. Precisely at that instant, another synagogue member blocked his way, punched him in the head and sent his skullcap flying. The members of the congregation were stunned. A series of fistfights broke out, with some seeking to protect Rabbi Wise, others attempting to pummel him further. The police were summoned, and only their intervention ultimately stopped the near riot.

In light of these events, Rabbi Wise realized that prudence dictated a departure from Albany. Thus, in 1854, he came to Cincinnati, Ohio, as the rabbi of another congregation whose members welcomed his intended reforms.

Wise lost no time in implementing his grand design. He established two newspapers, *The Israelite* and *The Deborah,* which gave him a journalistic vehicle through which he might reach the English- and German-speaking Jewish population all over the country. From this platform he immediately began to promote the creation of a rabbinical school in Cincinnati. Many Jews questioned the choice of Cincinnati as the site for such an institution. Wise asserted that the presence of four large congregations in the city, its central location, and the fact that Cincinnati at that time had the largest number of Jews outside of New York made it the only possible choice. Chicago, the only alternative, was rejected by Wise on the grounds that it was too far west and that no one would ever go to live there!

Wise's success was due as much to his personal magnetism as to his relentless dedication. A handsome man, Wise was the father of twelve children by two wives. His learning, tenacity and charm served him well, especially in the early years when his patience was tested severely. Wise's first attempt at establishing a school came in

1855, an institution which he named Zion College. The college closed less than twelve months later, due to lack of financial support.

Sixteen years passed before Wise had another significant opportunity to create the school of his dreams. One failure after another during that decade and a half might have discouraged a lesser man, but not Isaac Mayer Wise. He continued to spread the message that America required American rabbis and teachers imbued with American principles and thoroughly acquainted with the ideals of democracy, not merely transplanted rabbinic leaders from Europe whose own political and cultural baggage rendered them unsuitable for the job.

Wise was rebuffed three times along the way by potential funders, who felt that it was more important to establish an orphan asylum than a rabbinical school. Finally, however, in 1871, a conference of congregations in Cincinnati declared that as soon as twenty congregations with a total of no less than two thousand members affirmed the desirability of a rabbinical school, it would come into being. Wise did not hesitate for an instant. On July 8-10, 1873, twenty-eight congregations joined to found the Union of American Hebrew Congregations, whose goal it was to create the rabbinical school envisioned by Wise.

It is important to note that the name of that congregational body, which exists to this day, does not include the word *Reform*. It is the Union of *American* Hebrew Congregations, reflecting Wise's determination that this entity would serve an entirely new manifestation of Judaism, fostered in America and responsive to the needs of America's Jews. Wise was not parochial. He believed that the Jews of the United States could be united in common purpose, pursuing ancient Jewish values, ethics and traditions fully and with dignity. In July 1874, a convention of the UAHC held in Cleveland decided upon a name for the new rabbinical school, the Hebrew Union College. Again, the word *Reform* does not appear. The determination was made that the school would open in 1875, with Wise as its first president.

Jewish leaders from the eastern United States did not yet trust the new plan. They harbored great personal animosity for Wise and criticized his choice of Cincinnati as the venue for the college. But Wise avoided personal conflicts with his critics, concentrating his efforts instead on assembling a distinguished faculty that ultimately would win the dissenters over to his cause.

Wise was by no means a radical in terms of his personal theology. He regarded the teaching of the revelation of the Torah at Mount Sinai as fact. He embraced the authenticity and the authority of the Bible, and accepted the Talmud as the standard by which all Jews must live. These principles placed him solidly within what was then the mainstream of American Jewry, with his master plan embodying a strategy of gradualism rather than revolutionary upheaval.

With this philosophy as his guide, Wise prepared to open HUC. Classroom space was made available in the basement of one of Cincinnati's temples. Wise referred to this first home of the college as "this little hole in the wall of a school, in its not too bright cellar, carrying the pompous name of a college." There was a library of sorts, wrote Wise, small enough to be locked up each evening in a two-and-one-half-foot box, not because of thieves, but because of mice!

On Sunday, October 3, 1875, the Hebrew Union College started classes, initially with nine students and a total of seventeen during the course of the first year. The first student body included one woman named Julia Ettlinger, who remained at the college for only two years. As the first woman rabbinical student in the history of the United States, she established a precedent that would lead to the ordination of the first woman rabbi—almost a century later.

The college faculty consisted of two professors, Rabbi Wise and Solomon Eppinger, a local scholar who received a salary of $700 per year. The curriculum developed gradually, a total of eight years of instruction in those early days. Students who aspired to the rabbinate began their studies in high school, meeting from four to six o'clock each afternoon at the college then studying full-time upon reaching university age. At its inception, the Hebrew Union College was not the favorite school of the wealthy elite. Most of the students came from indigent homes or from orphanages and were given free tuition, as well as free board, lodging and clothes.

The building process went on. For the first four years, students studied classic texts. Leading rabbis and lay scholars conducted public examinations of the students at the end of each academic year. Wise went out of his way to invite critics of the school to come and participate in these oral tests. More often than not, those who came to criticize left praising the college, its curriculum and its pupils.

In 1879, seven of the original seventeen students graduated from the Preparatory Department, receiving a Bachelor of Hebrew Letters degree. They then moved into what was known as the Collegiate Department. Its initial success apparent, the school moved first to Plum Street Temple in Cincinnati and then, in 1881, to a spacious mansion on West Sixth Street, purchased as the college's first 'permanent' home.

Finally, on July 11, 1883, the seed that Wise had patiently nurtured for so many years reached fruition. The first ordination service was held. What most American Jews once believed to be impossible had been accomplished. Isaac Mayer Wise ordained the first graduating class of four Reform rabbis, educated and trained in America: Israel Aaron, Henry Berkowitz, Joseph Krauskopf and David Philipson. The American Reform Movement had its first American-trained leaders, and the journey had moved yet another step along the way.

Unfortunately, however, history played a cruel joke on Isaac Mayer Wise that very night, transforming a day of triumph into a nightmare. An apparently inadvertent error by a caterer changed the future of Wise, the Hebrew Union College and American Judaism.

On the evening of ordination, a great banquet was scheduled at Cincinnati's Highland House restaurant. Knowing that there would be visitors from across the country who strictly observed kashrut, the Jewish dietary laws, the committee in charge of the dinner instructed the caterer to serve no meat. According to eyewitness accounts, the banquet hall was beautifully lit, with hundreds of guests seated at elegantly arranged tables. The blessing before the meal was pronounced, and the guests prepared for a festive dinner. The caterer, carefully instructed regarding the composition of the guest list, prepared a menu consisting exclusively of sumptuous fish delicacies. The waiters entered the hall and began to serve the first course—shrimp!

There was a tremendous uproar as numerous guests stormed

out of the hall in fury. The dinner became known as 'the Trefa Banquet' and for weeks was the subject of one scandalous article after another in the Orthodox press.

'The Trefa Banquet' marked the beginning of the end of Wise's dream of one American Jewish community. Yet, even in later years, Wise never offered a public apology for this blatant faux pas. Though there is no evidence that he took any pleasure in the Fellini-esque scenario, a number of historians assert that he was privately relieved to be rid of the traditionalists. Wise no longer had to look over his shoulder, constantly accommodating ultra-Conservative elements scrutinizing his every action. He could now move much more freely in developing Hebrew Union College as he saw fit. The college and Reform Judaism now began to build in new directions. But in some parts of North America, it would be many years before Jewish immigrants from Europe would have any sense of the significance of Reform in shaping the future.

CHAPTER III

My Father and Mother

*T*he city of Winnipeg lies in the far western Canadian province of Manitoba. Though no longer a major center of Judaism, at the turn of the twentieth century it was a bustling, thriving center of Jewish life and activity. The community produced many individuals of note, including comedian David Steinberg; Metropolitan Opera star Morley Meredith; and television personality Monty Hall, whose mother, Rose Halpern, is still revered as a distinguished former leader of Hadassah and a champion of Jewish and Zionist identity throughout the world.

There was no Reform Judaism in Winnipeg, at least not in the early twentieth century. Orthodoxy in its various forms was then virtually the sole expression of Judaism, due in part to the way in which Jews came to what was then an isolated settlement. In the aftermath of upheaval in the Soviet Union, which began in the 1880s and continued through the Russian revolution of 1917, millions of persecuted Jews left Russia, seeking freedom and a new start in the *goldene medina* of America. U.S. immigration quotas did not allow all Jews who wished to settle in the United States to do so, but the government of Canada opened its doors wide, manifesting humanitarian concern while at the same time sensing an opportunity to populate areas of the country essential to its future.

Upon entering Canada, many thousands of Jews were placed aboard trains and transported to their new homes. Governmental leaders knew that Jews were likely to work hard, establish themselves, then send for their families. They were, therefore, perfect candidates for settlement in sparsely populated areas, where their presence virtually guaranteed growth. And so it was that religiously observant Eastern European Jews patiently endured the long journey to Winnipeg and a chance to begin anew. My grandfather, Max Schnellnyekopf, then a young man in his twenties, was among that early group of settlers. An immigration officer recognized that such a complicated last name would not serve him well in North America and changed it to Syme. Together with his wife, Anna, Max alighted from the train in Winnipeg into a foreign environment, where his family and his Orthodox Judaism provided rootedness and stability.

My grandfather Max was a blacksmith, a man of humble means, but a man of enormous dignity and pride. He would not accept charity, and raised chickens in his backyard so that he, his wife, and five children would never want for food or have to live on the public dole. A deeply religious man, he attended the local Orthodox synagogue daily and on Shabbat.

My father was the youngest of Max and Anna's five children. Unlike his elder siblings, Dad plunged into the life of the local synagogue with great enthusiasm. He was a child prodigy, and his magnificent singing voice earned him the nickname 'the Boy Hazan [Cantor] of Winnipeg'. People from across Canada travelled many miles to hear him at the age of thirteen lead the high holiday services at his shul. Indeed, when he had just observed his bar mitzvah, in 1933, in the midst of the Depression, he earned the then awesome sum of $1,000 for his work during Rosh Hashanah and Yom Kippur, enough to sustain his family for many weeks. He served as the youth group director and choir leader of the synagogue, and his name and reputation spread across Canada and to the United States as well. During the late 1930s, Rabbi Stephen Wise (no relation to Isaac Mayer Wise), the rabbi of The Free Synagogue in New York City and the founder and president of the Jewish Institute of Religion, heard of Monte Syme, and decided to recruit this young man, whom he had never met, to enter the ranks of the American rabbinate.

The Jewish Institute of Religion, or JIR, was the second Reform rabbinical school in America (the first, of course, being the Hebrew Union College in Cincinnati). The goal of JIR was to ordain rabbis qualified to serve congregations of any branch of Judaism. The curriculum was demanding, oriented to the study of both modern and classic texts. Students could attend the school only if they passed a rigorous entrance exam, whereupon they were granted a full scholarship for a four-year course of study.

The four key principles of the school were scholarship, a commitment to intellectual freedom, the right of the individual to make choices, and Zionism, a political philosophy that advocated the creation of a Jewish homeland in Palestine, a Jewish state to which any Jew would have the right to come and live in freedom and without fear. As one of America's most prominent Zionist spokesmen, Stephen Wise was viewed with disdain by the Hebrew Union College hierarchy, for until the end of World War II, HUC remained a bastion of anti-Zionist sentiment.

When my father received an invitation to interview for one of the six available scholarships in 1942, he reacted with mixed emotions. Such an invitation was a great honor, but there were many factors to consider. Dad's mother had died when he was only fifteen years old. His two older brothers moved away from home. One became a lawyer and a friend and colleague of Supreme Court Justice Arthur Goldberg, while the other pursued a career in electronics in California. As the youngest child in the family and the only remaining son, Dad was reluctant to leave his widowed father, and Max also felt ambivalent about his 'little boy' moving so far away. Another 'complication' was Dad's romance with my mother, Sonia Hendin.

Mom was born in a small village in Russia named Klintsi. Her father, Abraham, one of ten brothers, was a wealthy merchant, known throughout the area as a kind, compassionate man. That quality of character probably saved his life. For when the Russian revolution came, his stableboy, now a 'people's judge,' testified to his kindness, and thus freed him to leave Russia with his family and a significant sum of money.

My mother was one of four children, the third child in a family of true achievers. The first-born son, my uncle Nate, became a prominent figure in the Canadian real estate world. My aunt Molly became a doctor at a time when few if any women entered the workplace at all. My uncle Sam became an optometrist. Had she not married Dad, my mother probably would have followed in her older sister's footsteps. Instead, after taking a number of premed courses, she worked in a laboratory and trained as a medical technician.

My mother was clearly her mother Edith's favorite, though she came close to causing the family untold tragedy. She was just four years old when the Russian revolution erupted and had no way of knowing that my grandfather's attempt to save a portion of the family's wealth by burying it near their home was a secret to be shared with no one. When the Russian troops arrived, they interrogated each member of the family separately. They were particularly friendly to the four-year-old Sonia and asked her to help them on their way by telling them where any valuables might be hidden. Mom, who had been taught to deal respectfully with adults, led them to the buried jewels and money. Exulting in their good fortune, the soldiers departed with the booty and spared the family's lives.

Now grown to adulthood, Sonia Hendin was one of the most popular young Jewish women in all of Winnipeg. A dark-haired beauty, she attracted many suitors, who flocked to her home. My grandparents wanted her to marry a wealthy man, which my father clearly was not. Determined to have her way, my grandmother even faked heart attacks in an attempt to break up the young couple. It was only after my grandfather, in an echo from Sholom Aleichem and long before *Fiddler on the Roof,* pretended to have a dream in which a messenger of God came and gave his blessing to the relationship that my grandmother accepted Dad into the Hendin home. Winnipeg and New York, however, were many thousands of miles apart, and Dad was fearful that his absence could provide an opportunity for another man to woo my mother and sabotage the love affair.

Finally, the JIR dilemma was resolved. My father's father gave his assent to this quest, though he could only provide one-way bus fare to New York. That settled, my father and mother went to the local Orthodox rabbi and were secretly married, with the understanding that my father would send for my mother as soon as possible.

The bus ride to New York took several days, and Dad therefore went into the entrance exam interview totally spent. More than forty candidates presented themselves, and each in turn was called in to meet the faculty and to demonstrate his facility with classic texts and suitability for the student body. After this exhausting process, the prospective students gathered in the school chapel on West Sixty-eighth Street in New York, where the names of those who were not accepted and could leave were read in alphabetical order. With virtually no money in his pocket and with no way to get home, Dad's entire future hung in the balance. He agonized as the registrar moved closer to the end of the alphabet. His name was not read. He breathed a sigh of relief. As one of six scholarship students accepted for the entering class of 1942, my father began a journey that was to shake the very foundations of his Orthodox upbringing and propel him into a knowledge of the origins of Reform and a steadfast advocacy of its principles.

Dad had barely heard of Reform Judaism prior to that day. In later years, he confessed to me that when he came to New York to the Jewish Institute of Religion, he genuinely believed that he was coming to study at an Orthodox institution. As he entered the room in which his entrance examination was to take place, he confronted a group of professors, none of whom wore a *kipa,* the skullcap worn by all observant Orthodox Jews. He had never seen a rabbi without a *kipa* (*yarmulka* in Yiddish). When they began to ask him questions in English, he answered each of them in Yiddish. One of the professors suggested that perhaps he should transfer to the more traditional Jewish Theological Seminary. But Dad wanted to study with the famous Rabbi Stephen Wise, and therefore remained at JIR, determined to learn more about this Reform Judaism that did not exist in Winnipeg, Canada.

Little did he realize the impact that the Jewish Institute of Religion would have on his life—and mine.

CHAPTER IV

New York, 1942—Looking Forward, Looking Back

*F*or a young man who had never been out of Winnipeg, Manhattan was a most imposing and awe-inspiring city. My father often walked the streets of New York, struck with a feeling of wonder at the great melting pot of humanity contained within such a small geographic area.

Once accepted at JIR, and with his tuition assured by scholarship, Dad still had to find a way to sustain himself on a day-to-day basis in order to pursue his studies. A professor at the school put him in touch with New York's Bellevue Hospital, where he secured a position as the assistant chaplain in residence. He received room, board and eight dollars a month, in exchange for which he was on call literally twenty-four hours a day, save for class time. He could be summoned to a bedside or to one of the critical-care wards at a moment's notice, and often came to class directly from an all-night vigil with the family of a dying patient. But he accepted these conditions, all the while hoping to save enough money to send for his wife, who waited patiently for him two thousand miles away. Dad initially supplemented his income by singing in a nightclub, but Stephen Wise heard about this entrepreneurial venture and summoned Dad to his office. There Rabbi Wise told my father that he had a choice to make. He could be either an entertainer or a rabbi, not both, and he had to choose then and there. Needless to say, that meeting concluded my father's show business career! About that same time, however, the senior Jewish chaplain at Bellevue left, and Dad was promoted. Now his salary was forty dollars a month, a significant sum in those days. He wrote to my mother with great excitement, sent her a bus ticket to New York and asked her to come right away.

During the late evenings at the hospital, my father had a great deal of time to reflect upon this strange new environment. He thought of what his father Max would think of the Jewish Institute of Religion. My great-grandfather was killed in a pogrom on Good Friday, and at the age of seven Grandpa Max became the sole support of his widowed mother and three younger siblings. He worked during the day and attended *cheder* at night. Although his formal schooling was meager, he had an amazing knowledge of Torah and Talmud, and could quote entire passages from memory. At the age of twenty, he managed to escape from Russia and came to Winnipeg, where he was employed by the Manitoba Government Telephone Company. They thought so highly of his ability that they not only paid him well, but also respected his religious commitments. He was never asked to work on Shabbat, and was kept on long after normal retirement age.

Max and Anna maintained a kosher and observant Jewish home. The neighborhood was almost entirely Jewish, and totally Orthodox, with a synagogue on almost every block. People walked to the synagogue on Shabbat and holidays, both in observance of Jewish law and because very few of them even owned a car!

Members of this Orthodox Jewish community at the north end of Winnipeg had heard of a synagogue in the suburbs, where the affluent Jews lived. They were shocked by the rumor that the rabbi there gave his sermons in English! It was a Conservative congregation, and people in my grandfather's neighborhood wanted nothing to do with it. My father went to the local Talmud Torah from 4:30 to 6:30 in the afternoon, four days a week. He often told me that the faculty was completely innocent of any training in pedagogy. One of the teachers, for example, was also a *shochet*, a ritual slaughterer of animals who ensured that they were Kosher. With a smile on his face, Dad told me that this teacher sometimes became confused in his duties. He would slaughter the students and teach the chickens!

Dad had many problems with his teachers as a child, primarily because he asked too many questions. When, for example, he was studying the biblical story of the ten plagues, he demanded to know why Pharaoh was punished by God when the biblical account said that 'God hardened his heart.' "Why," my father asked, "was Pharaoh blamed for something that God forced him to do?" The teacher rewarded this inquisitiveness by bringing his ruler down on the back of my father's neck. He was sent home in disgrace, and was permitted to return only after my grandfather came to the school and promised the teacher that Dad would refrain from posing any more troublesome inquiries.

The daily routine in Winnipeg among Jews was predictable; work or school, then home to a close, self-contained, fairly insular Jewish neighborhood to share the day's events before bedtime. But Manhattan in 1942 was so different, a teeming cross-section of people, colors, religions and creeds, and so many different kinds of Jews—even Jews who had regular social interaction with non-Jews. In Winnipeg, extraschool or afterwork Jewish contact with the non-Jewish world was minimal. In my father's school at Christmastime, the students were expected to sing Christmas carols. The Jewish children had an unspoken pact, however. Whenever they came to the name of Jesus, they substituted the name of Moses. They never discussed it with their parents or protested. That was just the way they dealt with a situation that made them feel uncomfortable. My father often reflected upon how surprised his father would be at the cordial and friendly day-to-day relationships between Jews and Christians in New York, accepted as a normal way of life.

Another revelation to my father early in his rabbinical training was the equality enjoyed by women in the Reform movement. As a child, he had been greatly troubled by the apparent second-class status of women within Orthodoxy. He could not understand, for example, why women weren't counted for a *minyan*, the group of ten male Jews that Orthodoxy requires for a religious service. He could not understand why his mother had to climb up to the balcony to sit with the other women in the synagogue, or why his sisters were never given a Jewish education. He wondered why he had to say a prayer thanking God each morning for not making him a woman. Now he worshipped in a synagogue where men and women sat together at services, where families prayed together, and it made a great deal of sense to him.

My mother arrived in New York in 1943. Because no student at the college was supposed to be married "without permission," my father maintained his residence at Bellevue but rented a small apartment for Mom a short distance from the hospital, a fifth-floor walk-up, cold water flat, with a Murphy bed that pulled down from the wall. The apartment was so small that when the bed was down you could not open the front door! But at last my parents were together. My father continued his studies and chaplaincy duties, and he and Mom often invited friends to their apartment, entertaining them as though their tiny home were a palace. A short time later, Stephen Wise met my mother, and gave his enthusiastic blessing to the marriage. Wise liked to meet the women who married his 'boys,' and my mother 'passed muster' with flying colors.

In 1943, my father also discovered how it was that Stephen Wise had heard about him and helped him to reexamine the wariness that he and other Winnipeg Jews harbored against non-Jews. It turned out that the individual who had championed Dad's invitation to the Jewish Institution of Religion was an Anglican college professor in Winnipeg, a minister by the name of Dr. William Perry. When Dad attended Wesley College, a branch of the University of Manitoba, he took a class in Hebrew taught by this professor. After the first class, Perry summoned him to his office and confessed that my father knew more Hebrew than he did. The professor offered to excuse my father from attending classes and give him an A in the course if he would meet with him once a week to discuss questions relating to the Bible, Hebrew and other subjects of a religious nature, a proposal to which Dad readily assented!

At the time, my father planned to practice law, following in the footsteps of his brother, Michael. Professor Perry, however, had other ideas. Having attended a number of scholarly conferences on the Bible, Perry developed a friendship with Stephen Wise. He wrote to Wise, and said in the letter: "If Monte Syme were of my faith, I would encourage him to enter the ministry." On the day that Rabbi Wise told Dad this story, Dad was transformed. From that day on, he became a champion of interreligious cooperation, and thus welcomed the universal thrust of Reform and its insistence that Jews and those of other faiths must work together to build a decent society.

Shortly after my mother arrived in New York, Rabbi John

21

Tepfer took my father under his wing. This kindly, brilliant teacher was filling in at a congregation in Plainfield, New Jersey. World War II was raging, and most of the students had gone off to the war as chaplains. Therefore, many JIR professors substituted for those abroad, with no thought of remaining in those positions after the chaplains returned home. Rabbi Tepfer didn't really like conducting services, and brought my father with him for one or two Friday nights. The congregation adored Dad, and eventually Professor Tepfer gratefully turned over the interim rabbinic assignment to him. The congregation, Temple Sholom in Plainfield, became my father's weekly congregation until ordination, and enabled him to leave Bellevue and move to Plainfield with my mother. Here, for the first time, Dad came face to face with a group of Reform Jews in a synagogue setting on a regular basis. He gave his sermons in English. Men and women sat together. Most members of the congregation prayed with heads uncovered. The congregation had an organ and a choir. Creative pedagogy was encouraged in the religious school. Above all, there was a great excitement among the members about this modern manifestation of Judaism in the democratic environment of the United States.

Slowly, gradually, my parents became more and more comfortable in their new milieu. To no one's surprise, Dad finished his course of studies in three years instead of the prescribed four, allowed to skip a full year as a result of his impressive background. But then a problem arose. Just before ordination, he was summoned to Rabbi Wise's office. Wise showed my father a petition submitted by the Plainfield congregation, asking that Monte Syme remain as their rabbi and that the incumbent be asked to find another position. My father flatly refused. His deep sense of ethics and fairness would not allow him to accept a position that would in any way compromise the right of a chaplain to return from the war to his post. My father therefore asked Rabbi Wise to send him to any available congregation. And so it was that my father was assigned to a congregation in Sharon, Pennsylvania, for the next step in his journey—and mine.

CHAPTER V

Reform and the Capacity to Change

*A*s my father concluded his studies at the Jewish Institute of Religion, he also began to grasp the essence of a way of looking at Judaism that he had long personally embraced in theory but that now at last had a name. Early in his rabbinic training, Dad asked what he felt was a simple question, an inquiry that many Jews pose to this day. He wanted to know what the difference was between Orthodox Judaism and this movement called Reform. The question was simple, the answer more complex.

The most important question that any religious system must answer is the question of authority. In other words, by what right does any religious group tell an individual man and woman what he or she must do? For Orthodox Judaism, the answer is clear, at least in principle. The Orthodox Jew believes that the Torah, the Five Books of Moses, was given directly by God to Moses at Mount Sinai, a divine revelation in its totality. The Torah is this immutable divine law, with any seeming contradiction actually a challenge for us to understand what God really "meant." This law was transmitted in turn by Moses to the elders of the Israelites, then passed down from generation to generation in an unbroken chain of authoritative tradition. Orthodoxy affirms that there was also an Oral Law, shared with Moses by God at Mount Sinai and every bit as binding as the written law. Over the centuries, this Oral Law was codified and committed to writing in the Mishnah, amplified by the Gemarah, with the two combined into the Talmud.

Orthodoxy even declares that the rules of deriving God's "in-tent" are fixed and immutable, and thus each successive codification of Jewish law, called Halacha, has divine authority. Whenever a believing Orthodox Jew is pressed for the source of authority for any action, then, ultimately the answer is that "God said so."

Within the Reform Movement, there was great dissatisfaction with the philosophy propounded by the Orthodox. Many Jewish scholars noted contradictions in the Torah, errors of fact, supposedly unchanging laws which simply did not make sense as the enduring revelation of a perfect God. In the nineteenth century, a theory of scientific literary analysis emerged, called the Graf-Wellhausen Hypothesis, asserting that the Torah was really a compilation of at least four different documents, written by humans, and woven together and canonized about the year 400 B.C.E. The declaration shook the very foundations of the religious community, especially in those quarters in which the source of authority depended upon an authentic divine revelation.

The early reformers embraced this hypothesis, and thus an unbridgeable gap was created between Orthodoxy and Reform. By asserting human authorship of the Torah, the Reform movement, in one fell swoop, abrogated an authority system of some two thousand years' duration. If the Torah was written by human beings, however divinely inspired, then the only ultimate source of authority was the individual, and the communal norms that the individual freely chose to adopt in terms of personal observance. Reform Judaism affirmed the right to choose. Nothing in all of Judaism was by definition foreign to Reform, but the principle of intellectual freedom, the right to select options for observance, the right to set aside customs and ceremonies deemed to be outmoded, and the right to create new rituals and new manifestations of celebration became the heart of Reform ideology.

From the time he was a young boy, my father had been troubled by some of the conflicts ultimately addressed by Reform. While his scholarly studies, particularly of the great commentator, Rashi, acquainted him with a number of suggested solutions to disturbing questions about the Torah itself, they were never fully satisfactory. He wondered why there were two creation stories in the Torah, two different accounts of Noah and the Flood, two separate narratives on the creation of the first woman. He could not understand some of the laws in the Torah, seemingly more appropriate to a primitive society than to a modern era. The biblical God was portrayed as commanding certain actions and making certain demands—for example, stoning a man to death who picked up sticks on Shabbat—that were in total conflict with Dad's own notion of what his God would "ask" of humanity.

The opportunity to choose, the knowledge that freedom was part of the Reform Jewish bill of rights, led him to dig more deeply into the history of Reform for more answers to lifelong questions. And so it was that my father, the product of an Orthodox home, encountered a document adopted in 1885 by a convention of Reform rabbis meeting in Pittsburgh, Pennsylvania.

Called 'the Pittsburgh Platform,' the document's principles remained the foundation of Reform Judaism for over five decades. In eight brief statements, the platform not only laid the groundwork for a liberal faith, but also affirmed by implication the right of each individual Jew to confront the tradition in an intellectually free, non-prescriptive fashion. While declaring the importance of belief in God, the platform makes no reference to a particular, mandatory God-idea. While stating that the Bible is a central text in Jewish life, the platform dismisses the notion of divine authorship, and thus embraces the possibility of examining any law, any teaching in the light of current experience. The platform rejects anachronistic legislation, dietary and dress codes as unnecessary for modern Jews; sets aside the traditional ideas of a personal Messiah, bodily resurrection and the fervent hope for a return to Palestine; and projects a universalistic sense of mission and a commitment to social justice.

The Pittsburgh Platform constituted a radical break with Orthodoxy. Compared by some scholars to a Reform Jewish Declaration of Independence of thought and deed, the document established the notion of the freedom of modern Jews to interpret, expand and enrich Judaism for their time. A careful reading of the Platform reveals a series of principles that were to guide Reform Judaism for fifty-two years:

1. Science and religion are not incompatible.
2. The laws of the Torah were legislation devised for the Israelites of ancient times. They are not necessarily binding on modern Jews.

The moral laws, however, and the ceremonies which continue to have meaning and significance today, are to be preserved. Those which do not may be set aside.

3. Jews are no longer a nation but a religious community and therefore have no aspiration to restore sacrificial worship as was practiced in biblical times or a national homeland.

4. Judaism must extend a hand of friendship to those of other faiths, affirming their validity for their adherents as vehicles for the spreading of monotheism and morality.

5. The notion of bodily resurrection, affirmed in Orthodox prayer each day, is now replaced by the notion of the immortality of the soul, and the image of a messianic age, rather than a personal Messiah, an age in which all human beings will work together for the perfection of society.

6. It is the duty of every Reform Jew to affirm and practice the values of social justice enunciated by the prophets. Indeed, this is the essence of Reform Judaism.

The Pittsburgh Platform would be altered and reinterpreted in subsequent decades. In 1885, however, it was perceived as both the most liberating and most threatening document ever promulgated by the reformers. As a student, my father studied this manifesto over and over again. He could not bring himself to fully embrace it, since much of it was at total variance with every value with which he had been reared. Particularly disturbing was the suggestion that a return to Palestine was no longer a Jewish value. How could this be? The dream of a return to Zion had been part of his entire Jewish upbringing, a centerpiece of his daily prayers, a devout and pious wish and hope articulated at every Passover seder. If this principle indeed held sway, how could Rabbi Stephen Wise, the president of this institution at which he studied, be so passionate a Zionist himself, one of the leading champions in all the world of a Jewish homeland? My father needed to learn more.

Nineteenth-century Reform based itself on rationalism. Among the traditional Jewish doctrines rejected by the early Reformers was the notion of a return to Zion. With a few notable exceptions, the great majority of early European Reform pioneers perceived Zionism solely as a response to anti-Semitism. They believed that if anti-Semitism could be eliminated there would be no need for a Jewish state. Therefore, when Theodore Herzl began his campaign for a Jewish homeland in the last decade of the nineteenth century, much of German Jewry not only rejected but actively opposed it. They feared the emergence of charges of divided loyalties and were also concerned about the dollars potentially lost to German-Jewish charities.

When Reform came to the United States, this abhorrence of Zionism was transplanted to American soil and embodied in the Pittsburgh Platform. In 1897, just a brief time before Herzl convened the first Zionist Congress in Basle, Switzerland, the Central Conference of American Rabbis endorsed a statement declaring:

> We totally disapprove of any attempt for the establishment of a Jewish state. Such attempts show a misunderstanding of Israel's mission.

One year later, in 1898, the Union of American Hebrew Congregations passed a similar resolution:

> We are unalterably opposed to political Zionism. The Jews are not a nation, but a religious community.

Clearly the Reform Movement of that era saw Zionism as a retrogressive step. They believed that anti-Semitism could be defeated in a free land, that Jews could live throughout the world alongside their Christian neighbors. Accordingly, the 1898 UAHC statement contained these words:

> America is our Zion. Here, in the home of religious liberty, we have aided in founding this new Zion, the fruition of the beginning laid in the old.

By 1920, a number of Reform rabbis, Stephen Wise and Abba Hillel Silver of Cleveland most prominent among them, had embraced Zionism, and began to effect a gradual shift among the members of their own congregations and their colleagues as well. Wise obviously had a tremendous impact upon the students of the Jewish Institute of Religion, which became a training ground for many of the great future Zionists of American Reform Judaism.

Hebrew Union College of Cincinnati, a bastion of German-Jewish thought, however, remained staunchly anti-Zionist.

By 1935, radical changes had occurred in the American Reform Jewish community. The Reform movement had grown, with nearly three hundred congregations, four hundred rabbis, and some two hundred thousand members, many of them from Eastern European backgrounds in which Zionist activist roots ran deep and strong. In part because of this influence, and especially as a response to the Nazi takeover in Germany, the Depression and growing anti-Semitism, growing numbers of Reform Jews, including fully fifty percent of all Reform Rabbis, began to embrace a Zionist or quasi-Zionist position.

In June 1937, the Central Conference of American Rabbis drafted a new statement of guiding principles, the Columbus Platform, with a new statement on Zionism:

> In the rehabilitation of Palestine, the land hallowed by memories and hopes, we behold the promise of renewed life for many of our brethren. We affirm the obligation of all Jewry to aid in its upbuilding.

In that same year, the UAHC declared:

> The time has now come for all Jews, irrespective of ideological differences, to unite in the activities leading to the establishment of a Jewish homeland in Palestine, and we urge our constituency to give their financial and moral support to the work of rebuilding Palestine.

My father read on with a growing sense of admiration for a movement that could reassess its positions so drastically in the light of current events, and with a new appreciation for the visionary leadership of Stephen Wise. It also gave him a context to understanding more fully the events of the prior year.

When Dr. Tepfer arranged for my father to serve as interim rabbi in Plainfield, New Jersey and my parents relocated there, my mother took a job at Merck Laboratories in New Jersey, putting her medical training to work and supplementing the family income. One of her colleagues at Merck, a German refugee, was most cordial to my mother until he discovered that she was Jewish. There after, he studiously avoided speaking to her, glared at her from afar and sometimes made derogatory remarks about her to others. My mother, mystified and certain that she had done nothing to offend this man, began to make inquiries about him to determine the root of his inexplicable hostility. At last she discovered the truth. The man had been a Nazi soldier in Germany, then fled the country as Hitler began to overreach himself and slide towards the abyss of defeat. He had confided to one or two individuals in the lab that the Jews of Germany were being systematically gassed, shot, eliminated from the face of the earth—and rightly so. When my mother heard this report, she compared notes with my father, and many pieces of a puzzle began to fall into place for both of them.

Stephen Wise had received a telegram from a young man named Gerhart Riegner. This now-famous message sent from Geneva begged for help for the Jews of Germany and all of Europe who, the telegram asserted, were now subject to plans for a "Final Solution." Riegner was aware that Rabbi Wise had a close relationship with President Franklin D. Roosevelt, and hoped against hope that Wise's influence might move the president to action on behalf of European Jewry.

Though Wise conveyed the magnitude of Riegner's message immediately and passionately to Roosevelt, the president refused to take action. The reports were unconfirmed. Allied troops simply could not be diverted from the larger campaign on the basis of unsubstantiated rumor. Wise pleaded with Roosevelt at least to bomb the railroad tracks leading to Auschwitz, so that the tens of thousands of Jews he knew were being murdered each day might be saved. But this request, too, was denied.

Tirelessly, with new urgency, Wise traveled the length and breadth of North America, sharing Riegner's communication and urging the immediate establishment of a Jewish state. When a ship called the *Struma*, loaded with hundreds of Jewish refugees, left Germany and was refused a safe haven in every country of the world, Wise struggled in vain to help these more-than six hundred people sailing from country to country on a boat intended for less than two hundred passengers. On the day the boat exploded and sank, and when all those aboard were lost at sea, Wise assembled the students of the Jewish Institute of Religion in the school's chapel, and asked them to take a vow that they would never allow such a tragedy to recur. My father was in the chapel, and on that day he moved beyond the passive religious yearning for Zion of his youth to a passionate political Zionist stance, a position he now knew had a place in Reform Judaism.

The Hebrew Union College
Gains Strength

*W*hile my father's life centered on the Jewish Institute of Religion in New York, the greatest innovations in Reform were taking place in Cincinnati, then the home of both the Hebrew Union College and the Union of American Hebrew Congregations. More faculty members had been engaged, the curriculum of the college enriched, and the emergence of the Central Conference of American Rabbis as a significant force in American Jewish life had begun in earnest. Wise was so enthused with the progress made that in 1899 he predicted that within fifty years "the faith of the rational world will be the faith of the rational Jew." His prediction proved overly optimistic, but the spirit behind it motivated the vision of Reform for many years thereafter.

After Isaac Mayer Wise died in 1900, two scholars, members of the faculty, succeeded him as leaders of the College for brief periods of time. Dr. Moses Mielziner, a Talmudic scholar, served as acting president for a period of three years. Dr. Gotthard Deutsch, an historian, served for only three months. Neither effected significant changes in either the curriculum or program. Their stewardship lasted until 1903, when HUC entered an era of ideological self-definition with the election of Kaufman Kohler to the presidency.

Kohler, a great theologian and scholar, was born in 1843 in the Bavarian city of Furth. He came to the United States as a young man, and first served in Temple Beth El in Detroit, Michigan. There, and in two subsequent positions, he made great innovations in ritual and liturgy. He fought for the revitalizing of Jewish holidays in a modern context, the equality of women in the home and synagogue, a universal thrust for modern Reform Judaism and a disavowal of the political doctrine of Zionism. He gained respect for his central role in drafting the Pittsburgh Platform of 1885 and his editorship of the Philosophy and Theology sections of the *Jewish Encyclopedia* before assuming the presidency of HUC.

There were many to whom the selection of Kohler came as a surprise, for he was part of the Eastern bloc of rabbis with whom Isaac Mayer Wise had clashed, and who denied Wise the support he so ardently sought during the early years of the college. He also went head-to-head with Wise on the issues of Darwin's theory of evolution and biblical criticism, and Wise had even denounced Kohler in one of his newspapers. It was in spite of strong opposition, then, that Kohler at the age of sixty attained his new office. The board's expectations were clear. Kohler was to bring the Hebrew Union College into the twentieth century.

Kohler embraced his charge with great vigor, expanding the rabbinical program to five years, adding biblical criticism and systematic theology to the curriculum, as well as Jewish ethics, education and applied sociology. He oversaw the historic move of the college to its present site on Clifton Avenue in Cincinnati, the dedication of new administration and library buildings, and the growth of HUC's library collection.

Throughout the eighteen years of his tenure, Kohler sought ideological self-determination for the college as well, and dealt harshly with faculty members who resisted his approach. By the time he retired as president in 1921, however, the college still lacked philosophic unity. Part of the problem lay in the fact that Kohler, though respected, did not enjoy the affection of his colleagues, as a result of his insistence that his way was the only way. As tensions grew it became increasingly clear to many that a new sort of president was required. Thus, the college board turned to a young American-born professor of Bible and a graduate of the college, Julian Morgenstern, as its leader for the difficult interwar period.

Morgenstern was born in Indiana in 1881 and ordained at the college in 1902, then left for Germany to pursue postgraduate studies. He served a congregation in Indiana for three years, then returned to HUC as a faculty member in the field of Bible and

Semitic languages. Fourteen years of teaching gained Morgenstern great esteem in many quarters for his scholarly and pedagogic ability. The students loved him and used to walk him home each night. When the time came to select a new president for the Hebrew Union College, Morgenstern was the candidate who most commanded the loyalty of the faculty and the younger graduates of the College. Barely forty years old and American-born, he brought a distinctively American approach to the school. During Morgenstern's presidency, the college grew most dramatically in physical terms. A gymnasium was erected in 1924, a dormitory in 1925, and a new library in 1931. Finally, Morgenstern proved to be an effective fundraiser, providing the college with a greater measure of financial security.

It was during the Morgenstern years that Stephen Wise's Jewish Institute of Religion in New York came into being. Morgenstern was very much opposed to the creation of this separate center of Jewish scholarship, seeing the JIR as an attempt to undermine the power and authority of the Hebrew Union College. He regarded JIR as colorless and nondescript, so broad and all-inclusive in its stated mission of training rabbis for all of American Jewry that it was prepared to sacrifice what he felt was essential Reform ideology in pursuit of an impossible unity. He gave it short shrift, dismissed it as a sort of glorified secondary school and thus charged a period of enmity between himself and Stephen Wise that endured for over two decades.

One of Morgenstern's most significant contributions to the growth of Reform was the initiation of programs reaching out to other faiths in the interests of understanding and the scholarly sharing of ideas. He initiated a program of exchange lectureships with several Christian institutions of learning, convinced that the Reform Movement had a responsibility to build bridges between major religions in the free environment of America, and laid the groundwork for a program of visiting Christian Fellows at the college, brought to fruition during the tenure of his successor, Dr. Nelson Glueck.

If there was one issue in which history will judge Dr. Morgenstern as shortsighted, it was his unalterable opposition to the creation of a Jewish state. He refused to assist the Joint Distribution

Committee in raising funds to aid refugees in Eastern Europe and considered the growth of Zionism a secondary issue, deserving of only the slightest attention by American Jews. Indeed, in spite of his great accomplishments, there are many Reform Jewish leaders today who remember Morgenstern primarily for his anti-Zionist stance, a product of his German-Jewish upbringing and world view.

By 1946, the Hebrew Union College was in deep financial trouble, its endowment fund totally depleted. In the aftermath of World War II and the Holocaust, it was clear that the United States would now become the central focus for the reconstruction of Jewish life, but only through building strong, secure institutions. Accordingly, seeking to consolidate scarce resources, a number of lay leaders raised the possibility of a merger between the Hebrew Union College in Cincinnati and the Jewish Institute of Religion in New York. Stephen Wise favored such a consolidation with HUC, but refused to consider a merger with an outspoken anti-Zionist such as Morgenstern as president of the joint institution. In light of the deteriorating financial circumstances of the college in Cincinnati, the pressures for a merger with JIR in New York and a clear understanding that he could not effect such a merger, Julian Morgenstern announced his retirement as president of the college on September 15, 1946.

The Reform movement had reached a crossroads in terms of its own future, and the HUC board of governors began a search for a new president, potentially the president of two institutions joined in common pursuit of academic excellence and dynamic leadership. If the right individual could be found, he would step into a position of great complexity. Facing a world Jewish community in shambles, a new Jewish state and a newly established American hegemony, he would have to shape the Hebrew Union College and the Jewish Institute of Religion into a viable institution for a truly new world. The next president had to be a scholar, a fundraiser, a diplomat and an ambassador to American Jews everywhere. In addition, he would have to ease the college in Cincinnati out of its anti-Zionist stance to deal with the reality of a modern Israel. The new president would have as great an impact on my life as Stephen Wise had had on my father's.

CHAPTER VII

Sharon and Butler, Pennsylvania— 1948—1954

*S*haron, Pennsylvania sits on the Pennsylvania-Ohio border, just a few miles from Youngstown, Ohio. It is a small community which in 1945 had approximately 150 Jewish families. Sharon could not support more than one congregation, and the Reform Temple Beth Israel was the only synagogue in town. Unable to build a home of their own, Sharon's Orthodox Jews arranged with the officers of the temple to use the synagogue basement for their own religious services.

When he arrived in Sharon, my father was appalled by this arrangement. Because there were so few Jews in Sharon, he felt strongly that there must be one united congregation for everyone's sake. He insisted that the Orthodox be given the dignity of a service in the temple sanctuary. On Friday night, therefore, he conducted a service utilizing the Reform prayer book, with an organ for the music of the service. But on Saturday morning he led a traditional service with no organ and using the Orthodox siddur.

Orthodox Jews do not use any instrumental music on Shabbat, for a number of reasons. First, playing an instrument is a form of work, and all work is prohibited on the Sabbath. This is especially true of an organ, which must be turned on and off, thus violating another proscription against using electricity. Secondly, instrumental music is forbidden as a form of remembrance of the destruction of the ancient Temple in Jerusalem. Finally, Orthodox and many Conservative Jews frown upon the organ in particular because of its widespread use in the church—its symbolic "un-Jewish" nature.

Reform Judaism has no such reservations about the organ, valuing its enhancement of the worship experience.

My parents maintained a kosher home, and Dad walked to services on Shabbat so that everyone in the city would know that he was the rabbi for every Jew in Sharon. Beth Israel thus became a model of Jewish unity in its time, a model that is almost impossible to find in contemporary Jewish life as a result of the tensions that divide Jew from Jew today.

As their new status within the temple became apparent, the Orthodox Jews of Sharon themselves underwent some remarkable changes. After several months of watching the evolution of Jewish unity in diversity at Beth Israel, they asked for an emergency meeting with my father to air a grievance. Dad was puzzled. After all, he had bent over backwards to assure that the traditional Jews would not feel disadvantaged. As he awaited the meeting, therefore, he could not imagine the nature of their complaint. When the delegation arrived, he was dumbfounded at the source of their unhappiness.

Now that they felt secure in the community, explained the Orthodox delegation, they also felt comfortable attending the Reform service from time to time. They found great beauty in parts of the service, especially in the use of the organ. They therefore came to inquire why it was that the Friday night service had beautiful organ music, but their service did not! In spite of normative Orthodox practice, they wanted an organ too. My father of course acceded to their request and that day learned an important lesson. As he related the story to me many times over the course of my lifetime, he always emphasized its moral: you can never stereotype any branch of Judaism. He saw first-hand what many Jews have yet to realize: there is nothing in Judaism that is inherently foreign to Reform, and there is nothing within Orthodoxy that is totally impervious to change.

Near the end of his second year in Sharon, the year in which I was born, my father realized that he had done about as much as he could do in that particular community. The Jews were unified, the temple strong. But Dad began to yearn for a larger congregation in which he and my mother might have greater challenges and a better standard of living. It was about this time that a famous rabbi from Pittsburgh, Solomon Freehof, came to lecture in Youngstown.

Dr. Freehof enjoyed international stature throughout all of Judaism as a scholar of the first rank. Born in London, England, in 1892 and ordained at the Hebrew Union College in Cincinnati in 1915, Rabbi Freehof first taught at the college, then entered congregational life. By 1946, he had acquired a reputation as one of the preeminent experts on responsa. The responsa literature is a body of Jewish questions and answers regarding the application of ancient Jewish legal decisions to modern circumstances, roughly equivalent to our legal case law.

To take an example from today's world: it is now possible to take the fertilized ovum from the body of one woman, implant it in the womb of a second woman, and bring the egg to term in her body. Since Orthodox law holds that the religion of the mother determines the religion of the child, the question arises as to the religious status of a child brought to term in the body of a *Jewish* woman, but with an ovum transplanted from the body of a *non-Jewish* woman. For many decades, Rabbi Freehof has been asked these and literally thousands of other questions, publishing the answers to those he found of greatest interest in a series of volumes that are used for study by Jews from all streams of Judaism. (By the way, the answer to the question is that the child's Jewish status is determined by the religion of the woman from whose body the fertilized egg was taken. Therefore, according to Orthodoxy, if the donor was Christian, the child would require conversion in order to guarantee its Jewish identity.)

Freehof was regarded as somewhat of an anomaly by many within the Reform movement. After all, Reform Judaism had set aside the notion of the Torah as divinely given, and thus the binding authority of Jewish law. Yet here was a Reform rabbi who himself rejected the Torah's divine authority, but who nevertheless devoted thousands upon thousands of hours in search of that which Jewish law would say about modern life! In fact, Freehof represented Reform Judaism at its finest, an exemplar of learning, decision-making, and choice based upon knowledge.

My father, intrigued by what he had heard of this remarkable and unusual Reform rabbi and scholar, went to hear him speak. Freehof was mesmerizing. He spoke for an hour without a single note, quoting section after section of the Torah, the Talmud and other legal codes from memory. After the lecture, my father remained behind, waiting for the crowd of admirers congratulating Rabbi Freehof to disperse, then asked if he might come to Pittsburgh to meet with him. Rabbi Freehof, always gracious, agreed.

One week later, Dad sat with Rabbi Freehof for several hours and discussed Jewish sources with him. Near the conclusion of the meeting, Dad asked Freehof if he might study with him on a regular basis. Rabbi Freehof was more than happy to grant this request, but pointed out to my father that Pittsburgh was a rather long drive from Sharon. Given that opening, my father poured out his heart and confessed that he was ready for a change. He felt that he had much more to give to Judaism than that which he could reasonably accomplish in Sharon, and yearned for a large congregation in which to continue his career. Rabbi Freehof listened attentively, then urged my father not to be in too much of a hurry to move to a big city. He pointed out that the years before one reached the pinnacle of one's professional career were a time to study, to learn and especially to acquire additional academic credentials.

Rabbi Freehof was first and foremost a scholar. He was by no means a pastor, and accepted congregational life only with the proviso that "If you want my head, I will come. If you want my feet, I will not come." He never learned to drive, and rarely if ever paid hospital or condolence calls. When a family suffered a loss, they came to his apartment to make the funeral arrangements. If they wished him to do so, he would take a cab to the home of the mourners, visit with them briefly with the taxi waiting outside, then return home. It was therefore no surprise when he suggested that my father, already possessed of an impressive Jewish scholarly background, should now consider obtaining a doctorate in education at the University of Pittsburgh while remaining in a small temple somewhat closer to Pittsburgh.

Freehof, who at the time chaired the Reform movement's Commission on Jewish Education, shared his conviction that the future of Reform Judaism would in large measure be determined by the success of its educational program. American Jews, he asserted, required a new kind of Jewish education, modeled on the American public school, which had the capacity to combine Jewish values with Jewish content in a manner heretofore unprecedented in Jewish life. Jewish children, he said, must study not only texts, as was the case in the Orthodox cheder, but Jewish history and ethics, and the books and teachings of the prophets as well as the Torah. Yes, he would be happy to have my father study with him, to share more of the knowledge and wisdom that he had gleaned from traditional Jewish sources and from his own experience. In order for that to happen, however, Rabbi Freehof repeated what my father knew. He would need the time that a small congregation afforded, and he would have to be closer to Pittsburgh.

That night, as Dad related the details of his remarkable day to my mother, he asked her if they might defer a move to a large community until he had a few more years to expand and enrich his Jewish knowledge, his credentials and his capacity to touch the lives of Reform Jews. My mother had never seen my father so excited. Though she dreamed of living in a big city filled with cultural possibilities, many more Jews and opportunities for her own self-fulfillment, she agreed to wait a bit longer. In fact, she too wanted to meet this man who had had such a profound impact on her husband.

The following day, my father informed the placement office of the Central Conference of American Rabbis that he wished to consider moving to a new post, but one in a small community close to Pittsburgh and his teacher. At the time, no congregations in suburban Pittsburgh were available. The closest opening was in a little town called Butler, approximately thirty miles from Pittsburgh. Butler was not much larger than Sharon, but it was forty miles closer to Rabbi Freehof and within a thirty-minute drive of the University of Pittsburgh and its masters program in education. Therefore, though another *very* small town was hardly what either of my parents had envisioned, Dad applied for the pulpit and was accepted.

Like the temple in Sharon, Butler's Congregation B'nai Abraham had 150 families, but was a liberal Conservative congregation. The leadership of the congregation were drawn to my father's dynamism, his depth of knowledge of tradition and his openness to change, which they too valued. B'nai Abraham had mixed seating, an organ and an embryonic Hebrew school, which the members hoped would be enhanced by my father's presence.

Although I was born in Sharon, I consider Butler my hometown, for it was there I first became aware of the world around me and my own identity as a Jew. In retrospect, the six years in Butler were among the most precious of my life, for I had my parents all to myself in a congregation that made limited demands on my father's time and few intrusions into our family life. We had dinner together every night and spent a great deal of time together as a family. Mom and Dad treated me as most parents treat a first-born, as something special, and I must confess that I loved it. When I was only two years old, I began to walk to the synagogue with my father every Friday night and every Saturday morning. Dad even took me with him to make condolence calls to those families who had lost a loved one. I can still remember telling the grieving families that I was sorry for their loss, and seeing the stunned expression on their faces to hear such words coming from a toddler. I realize now that even then, my father was preparing me for what he hoped would be a life in the rabbinate.

But my relationship with my father went much further than participation in Jewish events. There were two moviehouses in the city, the Majestic Theatre and the Butler Theatre. Every year, on Thanksgiving and Christmas mornings, one of the theatres would show fifty consecutive cartoons. And every year we were in Butler, my father would take me to the movies and sit with me through every one of those cartoons! Only now that I am a father myself can I appreciate what that meant, and the genuine devotion and love those hours embodied.

I attended Hebrew school faithfully twice each week, and even led a section of the Saturday morning synagogue service, along with other boys and girls in the Hebrew school who had acquired a sufficient degree of facility in Hebrew. Virtually everyone was Jewish in my pre-school world, and the temple was that world's center. Everything changed, however, with my entry into Butler Elementary School. I took an entrance exam to get into the first grade when I was five. All of a sudden, instead of being with a group of Jews, I found myself the only Jewish child in an entire class of Christians. It was then that I understood for the first time that Jews were different, a minority, and with some very special essence that made me different from all the other children in my class.

During my first year of school, I caused a real problem in Butler around the time of Christmas. I could not understand why all my friends were so excited about a holiday on which you only got gifts for *one* day. On Chanukah, I pointed out to them, Jewish kids received gifts for *eight* days. That was all my classmates needed to hear. They all went home and told their parents that they wanted to become Jews, whereupon the school and my home were flooded with ugly phone calls. The teachers took their 'revenge' for the havoc I had created just a few days later. Although first graders were not supposed to have parts in the annual Christmas play, I was 'honored' with a role two days before the presentation. My teacher explained to me that all I had to do was sit in the middle of the stage and say nothing. I asked my parents to attend the play, which they did, proud that their son had been singled out for such a unique shot at stardom. Only after the play concluded and we returned home did I learn that my part had been that of the baby Jesus! My father was enraged, though he never again mentioned the episode or exactly what he said the following day when he went to visit the superintendent of schools.

My Jewishness also became an issue when my parents left me with a friend during a trip out of town they had to make. My friend's parents, devout Christians, took me to their church on Sunday morning. I was fascinated by the music and the ritual, so different from anything I had ever experienced. At the conclusion of the service, my friend's mother asked me if I would like to become a member of their church. It sounded wonderful to me, and so today my name may still be on the membership roles of a Christian congregation in Butler, Pennsylvania. When my parents returned home and I told the story to them, they did not react visibly, but I never again was allowed to stay at my friend's home.

While I was growing up in Butler, relishing my childhood years, loving Judaism and understanding that there was something special about it, Dad was busy pursuing his studies at the University of Pittsburgh and studying with Rabbi Freehof. Twice a week, he left early in the morning and returned home at dinnertime, full of all the knowledge and advice he had gleaned from Rabbi Freehof and loaded down with the books and assignments he had to complete as part of his classwork. The combination of those two influences, the brilliant rabbinic mentor and the modern insights of education, transformed Dad gradually in ways that were evident even to me. I became a guinea pig for the teachings of Dr. Spock, as my father began to treat me like an adult, to reason with me. I really found the whole thing ludicrous in a way. After all, I was only a kid! But I remember deciding to humor him, because that made him happy.

The quality of Dad's sermons at the synagogue also began to change, due in large measure to Rabbi Freehof's instruction. Freehof taught my father sermon structure and gave my father insights into textual materials that Dad's Orthodox teachers had never shared. He also took time to acquaint my father with the importance of Jewish education within Reform Judaism, more specifically within the Union of American Hebrew Congregations. In Europe, prior to the establishment of Reform Judaism in the United States, most parents engaged teachers for their children on a private basis. When the mass German-Jewish immigration to America began, however, the German reformers encountered the common or public school, fostered by Thomas Jefferson and championed by Horace Mann as the great equalizer of opportunity among all new Americans.

The German Jews were eager to become part of the American scene. Coming out of the ghetto, free to become full participants in society, they quickly became the Jewish backbone of the public education system. Instead of engaging home tutors or creating private schools for Jewish learning, they established Sunday schools, supplementary classes that met one day a week for the purpose of basic Jewish instruction. The Sunday school model, patterned after the public school, spread across the United States. An occasional voice called out for day schools, but by 1879 there was no doubt that the day school had been set aside as a viable option for Reform Jewish education of that era. After the Union of American Hebrew Congregations solidified the future of the Hebrew Union College, a Department of Synagogue and School Extension began to publish selections from the Bible and from Jewish historical literature. In

1907, the UAHC launched a magazine for Jewish religious schools called *Young Israel* and then in 1909 established a small Teacher's Institute.

By the 1920s, however, the leadership of the UAHC came to grips with the diminishing literacy of the Jewish home and resolved to pursue enriched Jewish education for the children of Reform Jews in the United States. They embarked upon a nationwide search for an appropriate individual to lead this new undertaking. They sought a modern educator and found one in the brilliant Emanuel Gamoran. Gamoran, the product of a traditional home, had earned his doctorate at Columbia University Teachers College. For over thirty years thereafter, Gamoran built a structure for Jewish education modeled on the public school. He commissioned a series of graded textbooks, again on the public school model, and developed an entire religious school curriculum. Until the end of World War II, the UAHC was the only national organization publishing such texts and teaching materials. Gamoran found a receptive audience for his vision among some of the most influential rabbis of the age. In 1922, the UAHC established the first Commission on Jewish Education, directed by Gamoran and chaired by Rabbi David Philipson, one of the original graduates of the Hebrew Union College. Philipson was succeeded by Rabbi Freehof, who guided the commission with a sure and steady hand for close to three decades.

Congregation B'nai Abraham in Butler, therefore, was a prime beneficiary, not only of Freehof's knowledge in texts and homiletics, but also inasmuch as it was the first Conservative congregation to have the benefit of the full UAHC curriculum and all its supporting materials. As I watched my father pore over his educational texts while I sat in the religious school classes at the synagogue, as his stature in the community increased, I felt instinctively that we would leave Butler in the not-too-distant future. Dad was outgrowing this community. By 1954, I knew that a major change was at hand.

CHAPTER VIII

Coming to Detroit: Reform Culture Shock

*B*y 1954, great changes occurring in both the Hebrew Union College–Jewish Institute of Religion and the Union of American Hebrew Congregations laid the groundwork for their emergence as two of the most significant Jewish institutions on the international scene.

Rabbi Maurice Eisendrath was now president of the UAHC after years of distinguished service at Toronto's Holy Blossom Temple. Eisendrath, a fine orator and dynamic leader, had a special passion for social justice, and moved to establish the UAHC as a strong, assertive voice in this realm. His leadership in formulating UAHC positions calling for fair employment practices, decrying atomic warfare and forging the beginnings of the UAHC's historic advocacy of civil rights generated both controversy and excitement. He urged the Union to advocate adequate housing, quality education, universal medical care, and the first Jewish organizational recommendation for ratification of the Genocide Convention, formally accepted by the United States only in 1988. He spoke out against McCarthyism, exposing and denouncing attacks on public figures and public school teachers as communists, and staunchly defended freedom of the pulpit for all rabbis. He established the UAHC as the most significant Jewish voice for social justice in America.

Most importantly, however, Eisendrath convinced the board of the UAHC to move to New York City. He understood that if the UAHC was to become an international force, it had to be where the action was, and that meant Manhattan. By 1954, UAHC headquarters were based at Fifth Avenue and Sixty-fifth Street in Manhattan just across the street from its largest member temple, Congregation Emanu-El.

Hebrew Union College also had a new president, Dr. Nelson Glueck, himself a graduate of the school. Glueck's uncle, Dr. Bernard Revel, became the first president of Yeshiva University, an Orthodox institution, but Glueck chose the path of Reform Judaism. Ordained at the age of twenty-three, Glueck decided that he would not enter the congregational rabbinate. Over the protests of his family, he decided to pursue a life of scholarship in the field of Bible. After traveling to Germany and earning his Ph.D., he returned to HUC as a member of the faculty. In 1927, he traveled to Jerusalem to study archaeology, his passion since childhood years, under the guidance of Prof. William F. Albright, director of the American School of Oriental Research.

From then on, Glueck had two homes, Palestine and Cincinnati. He believed strongly that the Negev desert held many secrets, that the biblical accounts of great cities that once existed in the arid expanse were true. And so, using the Bible as a road map, Glueck became the first archaeologist to make a mile-by-mile examination of the Negev, discovering city after city mentioned in Scripture and becoming an instant media figure with his discovery of what then appeared to be King Solomon's copper mines. Glueck's international profile, dynamic personality, charm and stunning good looks were among the factors that led the HUC board to approach him. His scholarly credentials were impeccable and his administrative ability was amply demonstrated at the American School. Many referred to him as the "Jewish Charles Lindbergh" or the "Jewish Lawrence of Arabia." His persona as an explorer and discoverer of antiquities stirred the imagination of people everywhere. These qualities led the Hebrew Union College Board to offer him the presidency of what would become in 1950 the merged institution of the Hebrew Union College and the Jewish Institute of Religion, HUC-JIR.

By 1954, Glueck reshaped the college-institute, even as Eisendrath refocused the UAHC. He opened the campus to the general Jewish adult population, offered a bachelor of arts degree for lay leaders who wished to become more literate Jews and established graduate fellowships so that Christian scholars might pursue studies in Judaism and Semitics. He supported his good friend Dr. Jacob Marcus in founding the American Jewish Archives for the collection and preservation of American Jewish historical material, and created a School of Sacred Music in New York, an institution designed to train cantors for North America. In addition, he reached out across the continent, and established a pre-rabbinic branch of the college in Los Angeles, California.

Now American Jewry had two powerful institutions under Reform auspices; the Hebrew Union College–Jewish Institute of Religion and the Union of American Hebrew Congregations. Now the Reform movement had two spokesmen of both national and international stature. Now the Reform movement was poised to take advantage of one of the greatest explosions in Jewish identity and affiliation in American history.

As my father once again began to explore his options within the Reform rabbinate in 1954, the Reform movement had become much more than a midwest phenomenon. It was now not only a liberal expression of Judaism but a Zionist and social-justice-oriented family of congregations. My father, my mother and I were about to step into that new world of Reform, still not fully understanding that it had already become the wave of the future for United States—and perhaps international Jewry as well.

My father's decision to move to Detroit, Michigan, was influenced in large measure by Dr. Freehof. Freehof advised him that it was now time to leave Butler and go on to bigger things. He felt that he had given Dad about as much as he could in the way of advice and training in Jewish scholarship and speaking. With his masters degree in education in hand, my father could spread his wings and reach a much larger community of Jews.

Together with Freehof, Dad reviewed the list of openings provided him by the CCAR. There were two large congregations seeking assistant rabbis, one in Akron, Ohio, the other in Detroit. Dr. Freehof advised my father to take the position in Detroit, inasmuch as the rabbi there, Leon Fram, was a bachelor. In Freehof's opinion, Fram would welcome Dad as a son, a member of his family. Furthermore, Fram was sixty years old, and thus presumably only five years from retirement. Therefore, if Dad did a good job and earned the respect and affection of the membership, there was every reason to believe that he would become the senior rabbi within a very few years. Dad interviewed for both positions and was offered both. But in the end, following Freehof's counsel, he opted for Detroit. The congregation in Butler made every attempt to entice him to stay, even going so far as to offer to match the salary and benefits provided by the Detroit congregation. To understand the magnitude of this gesture, one need only consider that Temple B'nai Abraham in Butler had a membership of 150 families, while Temple Israel in Detroit numbered over 1,000. But Dad had made up his mind. We would go to Michigan. We piled into our car and set off for a new city and a dramatically different Jewish world.

In 1954, my brother David was five years old. Today I consider David my best friend. In those early years, though, he was my greatest nemesis. Unlike me, David was a very quiet and well-behaved child. Therefore, even when he became obnoxious and we fought, as all brothers do, the automatic presumption was that I was at fault. David, always a quick study, played upon this clear edge in parental perception at every opportunity. I was to have a measure of revenge a few years later, but at the time I knew that his pique was to be avoided at all costs. It could only cause me trouble. Unbeknownst to either David or me was the fact that our mother was pregnant at the time we left Butler. Just a few months after arriving in Detroit, we were presented with a baby brother, Michael. As is customary in many Jewish families, each of us was named after a person close to our family who had passed away. My middle name, Bailey, memorialized my father's mother, whose Hebrew name was Bayla. David was named after a close friend of my parents in Butler, and Michael after my father's brother, who died suddenly and tragically at the age of fifty.

We arrived in Michigan during January 1954, and pulled up to our new home on a street called Glendale in what was once the equivalent of the Detroit Jewish ghetto. It was situated in a part of Detroit known as the Dexter-Davison neighborhood, where for many decades Orthodox, Conservative and Reform Jews filled its streets. Our home was located in the 'upscale' section of the Dexter-Davison area, just a few blocks from MacCulloch Elementary

School. The house seemed like a palace compared to our home in Butler, and the neighborhood was filled with Jewish children. Family after family came to our door to introduce themselves. Within a few weeks I realized that some ninety percent of my school classmates were Jewish! It was quite a change.

By the time the movers left and I registered for school, Friday night rolled around and I prepared myself for my first visit to Temple Israel. As always, we had Shabbat dinner as a family. As always, my mother stood before the Shabbat candles, pronounced the blessing and said a special prayer for each of us in turn. As always, my father led the chanting of the Kiddush, with David and me singing along. As always, David and I tore off a piece of the warm, doughy challah and pronounced the blessing over the bread. And as always, my father then summoned the two of us to his side and blessed us softly with the traditional prayer with which Jewish parents bless their children on each Shabbat. In retrospect, Shabbat is one of my most treasured childhood memories. My parents invested that twenty-four-hour period with a sense of the sacred that remains with me to this day.

After dinner, dressed in a suit and tie, I asked my father when we were leaving for the synagogue. He hesitated. I asked how far the temple was from our house. He replied that it was several miles away. I asked him how long it would take to walk there. He looked at me and said "Danny, from now on we are going to drive to the temple." I was astonished! "On Shabbes?" I asked. My father gazed into my eyes. "Yes, Danny, but it's all right. In a city as big as Detroit, people can't always walk to the synagogue. If they are going to come to services, they have to drive. And it's better for people to come than not to come, wouldn't you agree?" I nodded, satisfied with that answer. But then Dad hesitated once again. "Danny, there is one more thing that I think I should tell you. At this temple, they do not wear yarmulkas, so you don't have to wear one anymore either."

Now I was sure something was wrong. "Dad," I asked, "where are you taking me?" This simply could not be a synagogue. This sounded more like my friend's church in Butler. Surely this could not be a Jewish place of worship. My father took me by the hand and led me to the car. "You will see for yourself, Danny. This is a Reform temple. They do things very differently from the way we did things in Butler. But they are wonderful people, and I will have the chance to touch their lives."

We drove to the temple in silence. I could not even begin to fathom what I was about to see. We entered a neighborhood filled with enormous houses, some of them mansions, then turned down a street called Manderson Road. There before my eyes was one of the largest buildings I had ever glimpsed, with a parking lot bigger than a baseball field! I was speechless. Dad parked the car and we entered the huge doors of the temple, or at least they seemed so to me. The lobby of the temple was enormous, with beautiful marble floors and ceilings that must have been twenty or thirty feet high. We walked into the social hall. I expected something like B'nai Abraham, with a small room that would seat perhaps one hundred people. Instead, here was a sprawling, theaterlike space that could easily accommodate seven hundred or eight hundred people, with a stage, a main floor and a balcony.

"Now let's go into the sanctuary," Dad said quietly. We walked out of the social hall, across the lobby and up a series of marble stairs. There were three entrances! I picked the middle set of doors and gently pushed them open. I stood stock still! For there before my eyes was a sanctuary with 1,200 seats, ringed by massive pillars, and with a bimah that seemed at least a quarter of a mile from the back of the sanctuary. The platform at its center was fully three times my height, with high-backed leather chairs in which the rabbis sat. Then I saw the ark, the repository of the Torahs, the sacred scrolls of the Jewish people. Designed to resemble the Ark of the Covenant described in the book of Exodus, the ark was positioned at the top of a stairway on each side of the bimah. One had to climb in order to get to it! Its gold color and intricate design were stunningly beautiful, one of the most exquisite pieces of synagogue architecture I have ever seen. I looked up. The ceiling contained a huge Jewish star, with recessed lighting that bathed the sanctuary in a soft glow. I took all of this in as my father watched. Finally he spoke.

"You see, Danny, this is a Reform temple. The members of this congregation have built this temple to insure that Judaism will live for them and for their children. They have asked me to be one of their rabbis, and they will love you too. You'll see. Just be a little patient. Take a little time to get used to the things that are different here. Very soon you will understand that Reform Judaism is making Jewish survival possible for thousands of people who would otherwise not be part of the Jewish people."

My father always used to talk to me that way, more like an adult than as a child. Especially as I got older, it was one of the parts of our relationship that I treasured most. I never felt patronized. I hung on every word, reflecting all the while on this tangible expression of Reform Judaism. Dad had spoken to me of Reform in Butler, but because my sole experience of Judaism had been more traditional, I had no real concept of what he meant. Now here it was undeniably before me, a new kind of Judaism that I did not yet fully comprehend.

My personal reverie was broken as two other men entered the sanctuary. The first was Cantor Robert Tulman, the other Rabbi Leon Fram. They welcomed me warmly. Rabbi Fram patted me on the head and told me that I could call him Uncle Leon. He then reached into his pocket and pulled out an autographed picture of the Cisco Kid, one of the most popular cowboy actors of the 1950s. I was very excited! I thanked him, grateful that he would make a gesture of this kind, but even more impressed that he knew the Cisco Kid well enough to get an autographed picture! Cantor Tulman placed his hands on my shoulders and told me how happy he was to meet me. He tugged my ear, a gesture by this beautiful, sensitive man that I later learned was his trademark expression of affection for the hundreds of young boys and girls who came under his care.

The rest of that Shabbat is a blur in my memory. I sat in silence for most of the service, listening to Cantor Tulman sing in a full baritone voice, with a volunteer choir of some fifty men and women. I struggled to find my way through a new prayer book, the siddur published by the Central Conference of American Rabbis. I listened to Rabbi Fram deliver the sermon. After services concluded, I walked with my father to a receiving line in which literally hundreds of members welcomed him to Temple Israel. After what seemed an eternity, we entered the social hall and participated in the Oneg Shabbat, with a sumptuous selection of cake and cookies. I remember thinking to myself that this was not so bad after all. Since Rabbi Fram had no children, I would be the center of attention, the rabbi's oldest kid. Reform Judaism was different, but it was going to be okay.

CHAPTER IX

Temple Israel

*A*s our family gradually settled in Detroit, I began to learn about this unusual place that was now my Jewish home. Temple Israel was the second Reform congregation established in Detroit, as often was the case with synagogues bearing this name. A number of scholars of American Reform Judaism have noted that one can usually chart the development of any Reform community by studying the names of its Reform congregations. The first Reform temple in a given city is almost always named Beth El, 'House of God,' or Emanuel, 'God is with us.' The second congregation in the area, generally the Zionist breakoff, calls itself Temple Israel. And, almost inevitably, the third congregation, usually resulting from a bitter political battle at one of the two established synagogues, is named Temple Shalom ('peace')!

Detroit served as a classic example of that evolutionary trend. The first Reform religious institution in Detroit, Temple Beth El, was founded in the nineteenth century and had a proud historic past as a classical Reform congregation. The term *classical Reform* is most frequently employed to designate a congregation devoted to the principles articulated in the Pittsburgh Platform of 1885. These congregations, few in number today, were resistant to any return to traditional norms of observance and most certainly to any embrace of Zionist ideology. Accordingly, when a significant number of members of Temple Beth El felt a need to express advocacy for a Jewish state in a public manner, conflict was inevitable.

During the 1930s Leon Fram had been an assistant rabbi at

Temple Beth El. Far earlier than most Reform rabbis, he took a strong assertive stance in favor of the formation of Eretz Yisrael. As a child of Eastern European parents, he understood only too well the importance of a Jewish homeland, even before the world as a whole was spurred to action. Along with Rabbis Abba Hillel Silver of Cleveland, Stephen Wise and a very few others, Fram proclaimed his support of Zionism for all the world to hear. He never received the press coverage enjoyed by Silver or Wise, but he was every bit as courageous.

Fram's views made him many enemies within the Beth El membership, since most of the leadership still viewed Zionism as a tacit capitulation to anti-Semitism. Therefore, when the incumbent senior rabbi retired, Fram was passed over as his successor. His outraged Zionist supporters within the congregation urged him to establish a new temple where his freedom of expression would not be stifled by internal politics and where the voice of Zionism within Reform would be a central component of the temple. In 1941, after long and careful discussion, Temple Israel was established. Initially, services were conducted at Detroit's Art Institute. A few years later, the magnificent structure on Manderson Road that had so impressed me was erected. The temple grew by leaps and bounds, and Rabbi Fram could no longer shoulder the entire burden alone. Dad was his first assistant, engaged to direct the Sunday school, invigorate the synagogue's youth program and add to the congregation's strength and influence.

Dad embraced these tasks with great enthusiasm. He taught in the Sunday school and worked with the high school youth group. He visited the sick. He became a presence throughout the general community. In the process, he drew many young couples into the temple who had previously been unaffiliated. Somewhat shocked by the general lack of Hebrew literacy among the members, he also received permission to start a Hebrew school, which met two afternoons each week in addition to regular Sunday school sessions. This was a dramatic departure in the Reform community. Until then in Temple Israel, those wishing their children to have a bar mitzvah engaged a private tutor to prepare them. Girls had no such ceremony, participating instead in the pomp and ceremony of ninth-grade confirmation.

Dad understood those ground rules but was determined to open up the option of bar mitzvah and extend it to as many young people as possible. Therefore, within a few months of his arrival, he initiated the first Temple Israel Hebrew school class. There were a dozen of us in that first group. I was the youngest, eight years old, with classmates ranging in age from ten to twelve. That class taught me another lesson in the capacity of Reform to change. It was a great adventure for those of us who participated, three hours each week when we had the rabbi all to ourselves. We read prayers, memorized vocabulary words, formed friendships that exist to this day, and had a very clear understanding that we were true pioneers in our temple's history. Above all, in "owning" more and more Hebrew skills and bigger and bigger pieces of the Torah and prayer book, our self-esteem as Jews grew immeasurably.

By the following year, the class had tripled in size, expanded by children of many new members for whom the lack of a Hebrew school was the only barrier to affiliation. Now there was a new problem. Growing numbers of parents wanted their sons to have a bar mitzvah, but Dad was the only person available to teach them. Rabbi Fram did not wish to become a Hebrew tutor, and very few members of the congregation had a Hebrew proficiency sufficient to the task. Dad sought out certain congregants with a reading knowledge of Hebrew and began to train them as bar mitzvah instructors. In the meantime, however, he needed help. He physically could not handle the number of hours required but was determined that no child who wished to have a bar mitzvah would be turned away for lack of a teacher. At last he realized how he could solve his problem. One night he came home from the temple and asked to see me privately in his study for a "meeting." He had a proposal to make. He asked me to become his assistant bar mitzvah teacher! He would pay me three dollars an hour, with the expectation that I would teach four hours each Saturday afternoon. I was only nine years old at the time, and at first thought that Dad was kidding. He assured me that he was serious, since I was the only person in the congregation who had enough Hebrew ability to do this important job. I quickly sized up the situation, mentally calculated all of the things I could buy with my earnings, decided I wanted to help my Dad and became Temple Israel's first lay bar mitzvah teacher.

My teaching career ended almost as suddenly as it had begun. Complaints came from parents who found their twelve-year-old sons being instructed by a teacher half their height and three years younger. In order to reassure them, Dad prepared me to read from the Torah in front of the entire congregation on a Friday night. To be sure, this was highly unusual. In Judaism, boys are not supposed to read from the Torah until bar mitzvah at age thirteen, but these were unusual times. I remember that night as if it were yesterday. The synagogue was filled. I read my portion perfectly. That settled the issue. My credentials were never again questioned.

Meanwhile I was adjusting to a whole set of new friends and a new school. There, too, all seemed to be going well. MacCulloch School went up to the sixth grade. By the time I was ten, I was elected president of the student council primarily on the strength of a newspaper I began on my own, called *The Glendale Mirror*. Once each month, after having interviewed significant teachers and individuals in the neighborhood and having culled the most important news of the month from the magazines I read on a weekly basis, I wrote a rough draft of the paper, typing it myself on a typewriter that had been a gift from my grandmother. Dad then took it to the temple, had it retyped by his secretary and mimeographed enough copies for the entire McCulloch student body. As time went on, I brought other reporters onto the staff. Soon the school began to hold regular *Glendale Mirror* assemblies, where 'staff' reporters presented an oral summary of their articles.

I did not know at the time that my father was continuing to guide me towards a career as a rabbi. It is only now that I look back and realize how subtly he exposed me to various rabbinic situations and trained me to handle them. The many hours of accompanying him on condolence calls was no accident. His "job offer" to teach Hebrew lessons was no coincidence. His encouragement of the development of my writing skills was carefully conceived. But most of all, Dad taught me how to speak. When I had a book report to write for school, he would sit with me for hours, tired as he might be, helping me structure lead paragraphs, utilize colorful adjectives, paint pictures with words. Likewise, when there were speaking occasions during my tenure as student council president, Dad did not simply sit by and let me scribble and deliver the words of the average ten-year-old. By that age I was delivering full-blown addresses, including words I had not ever heard until Dad inserted them into my first drafts and had me look them up in the dictionary.

I enjoyed the attention that my growing facility with writing and speaking brought, and worked hard in school to earn good grades. But my success was somewhat bittersweet because everyone seemed to take it for granted. Whenever I won a contest, I could hear people whisper to each other: "Of course he won. He's the rabbi's son." Whenever I brought home a report card with all A's, inevitably friends visiting the house would say, "It doesn't surprise us. We expect that from Danny." This is often part of the price of being a rabbi's son or daughter. There are many wonderful benefits, but many congregational rabbi's children I know have struggled with this unfair expectation of near-perfection by members of the congregation, and the equally disillusioning reluctance to praise any accomplishment since it is part of what they would consider the norm. Such treatment made me furious, frustrated and resentful. There were moments when I felt as though I were being punished for being the rabbi's child, and though I loved Judaism and my father, there were also frequent occasions when I wished that I could just be like the other kids. It was a conflict that remained unresolved for many years.

The years on Glendale taught me lessons about life in general and Judaism in particular. Two stand out in my mind. The first was the day that I first experienced Orthodox intolerance. We lived across the street from two Orthodox families. They kept kosher homes, as did we. But they went to an Orthodox synagogue, and their children taunted me mercilessly. Many was the day when I came home from school in tears, my ears ringing from a relentless refrain: "Reform Judaism is nothing. You are not really Jewish. You practice phony Judaism." The words cut deeply. They hurt. Nothing in my life had caused me so much pain since a day in Butler when my entire class had accused me of killing Jesus. On such occasions I usually spoke with my mother, since she was always home when I returned after school. She listened carefully, then replied softly, "Danny, do you think that your father and I are phony Jews? Do you think that what your father does, the lives that he touches, the teaching that he undertakes has no value?" "Of course not," I replied. "You and Dad are two of the best Jews I know."

"Well, then," said my mother, "we are Reform Jews. You go tell your friends that you are a Reform Jew and proud of it."

I strode purposefully outside where my friends were playing baseball in the street. Approaching my chief tormentor I declared "I am a Reform Jew and I'm proud of it", whereupon he replied "You're a phony Jew, and your father is a phony rabbi." That was one of the few times in my life that I totally lost my temper. I don't remember all the details of what transpired next. I do remember, however, that two adults had to drag me away from my neighbor. Later, my mother told me that I had jumped on top of the older, stronger boy and begun to bang his head into the sidewalk. She instructed me sternly that I was never to do that again, that violence solved nothing. She turned and walked away, but as she did a small smile crossed her lips. Averse as she was to physical violence, I think she also felt pride that I had defended the honor of my father and family.

I learned from that encounter and from subsequent experiences with my neighbors that there can be tremendous divisiveness and denigration among Jews. My father took pains to point out that these boys were only repeating what they had heard in their homes. He urged me to remember that and one day to try to make my home a center of respect for every Jew and every human being. In time, the tensions between me and the boys across the street eased and we began to play together once again. They never again made derogatory remarks about Reform Judaism, and I must confess that I derived pleasure from inviting them to our house on Saturday to watch television, particularly when the Detroit Tigers were playing a televised game. Being Orthodox, they were not allowed to turn on the television in their own homes on Shabbat, but readily accepted my invitation. When my father saw this, he merely chuckled and shook his head. He would often say to me, "You see, Danny, they call themselves Orthodox, but they do not practice it. You have every bit of Jewish knowledge that they possess, and probably more. But at least you do not pretend to be something you are not."

The second experience on Glendale brought me to a first awareness of the existence of racism. For my eleventh birthday, I decided to have a party at my parents' home. I invited fifteen of my school friends to the party, one of whom was black. I didn't really think of him as black; he was just my friend. My mother didn't know whom I had invited. She had the names but never asked if any of my friends were Christian or black or Jewish. They were just my friends.

On the night before the party, the doorbell rang and my mother greeted a black woman at the door. Mom asked her to come in and told me to go to my room and study. Naturally, I snuck out and sat at the top of the stairs so that I could eavesdrop on their conversation. It turned out that this woman was the mother of my friend, Billy. She had come to the house to find out if her son was welcome in our home and to be assured that he would not be hurt or embarrassed. I couldn't hear everything, but my mother's voice was loud and clear as she said "Your son is Danny's friend. He is always welcome in this house. I know that Danny would be terribly hurt if Billy did not come to the party. Please don't be afraid at all. As a matter of fact, Rabbi Syme and I would very much like to have you and your husband as our guests as well." My mother never spoke to me of that conversation. Perhaps she was afraid I might begin to think that black people were somehow different from us. In fact, only when she reads these words will she know that I was on the staircase that night. As Billy's mother left, I felt mixed emotions. For the first time I began to understand that being a different color was somehow significant in America. Somehow, being black was less acceptable than being white. That thought mystified me. At the same time, however, I felt a deep sense of pride in my Mom. She had represented me well.

Perhaps it was the encounter with Billy's mother that in some measure led Mom to understand that stronger bridges had to be created between the Jewish and non-Jewish communities of Detroit. She began to seek out individuals within the Christian community who might be interested in establishing a program designed to foster interreligious understanding. After only eighteen months in Detroit, she built a sufficient network to hold Temple Israel's first small Interfaith Institute. Mom trained the members of the Temple

Sisterhood to explain each of the Jewish holidays, every Jewish ritual observance, every Jewish custom that might be of interest to Christians. The program, though modest, was a great success and deemed worthy of annual status. Mom, too, had begun to touch the world in a program that made a difference in Detroit's religious community.

By 1957 my father's position at Temple Israel was secure. The congregation loved him. He had revolutionized the religious school, the Hebrew school and much of the congregation's program in just three short years. In addition, his speaking ability attracted new members from far and wide. Most importantly, his caring and compassion earned him a growing reputation as one of Detroit's leading religious figures. The congregation thus approached him with the request that he remain in Detroit for an extended period and informed him that a new home had been found for us in the new Jewish neighborhood of Detroit.

CHAPTER X

A First Awareness of God

*N*ow that the congregation had decided that my father would remain with them for many years, they moved quickly to assure our family a home in what was then the most desirable Jewish area of Detroit. The Dexter-Davison section was changing rapidly, and northwest Detroit had emerged as the new Jewish enclave.

Unlike most major cities, Detroit had no central racial or religious ghettos during the 1950s. Instead, religions, races and ethnic groups spread throughout the city in layers. Detroit is laid out primarily in terms of mile roads. In 1957, when we moved "uptown," the northwest neighborhood of 5 to 6 Mile Road was essentially middle-class blacks, including many members of the Detroit Tigers baseball team, interspersed with a heavy concentration of Catholics near the University of Detroit, a large Catholic parish and parochial school. The block between 6 and 7 Mile Road was heavily populated by Jews, with a significant number of Catholic families near the southern border, again drawn by the university and the church. Then came the section from 7 to 8 Mile Road, almost exclusively Jewish.

Our home was located at the midpoint of the 6 to 7 Mile Road section, set in a neighborhood populated by affluent Jews, in a house which at the time I thought was the most beautiful I had ever seen. The congregation purchased the house as a parsonage, a home for the rabbi.

There were Jewish children everywhere, the majority of them Reform and Conservative. We went to elementary school together, many of us to Sunday school together, and forged friendships that exist to this day. A very few children in the area attended private schools, one of whom was the late, extremely talented Gilda Radner of "Saturday Night Live" fame, but the public school system was so remarkable in its quality that there was really no need for private education. Our school, Hampton Elementary, extended to eighth grade and had a superb faculty, virtually unlimited resources for extracurricular activities, programs for the arts, woodworking and music and ample sport facilities. We had the benefit of the best available teachers. The highly competitive environment made it almost inevitable that those of us who had the good fortune to attend Hampton would do well in high school and thereafter. Of course, there were many other excellent elementary schools in the area we considered 'the Jewish neighborhood,' but Hampton was 'my' school, and the memories of the years I spent there are among my fondest recollections.

We moved to our home on a street called Birchcrest in 1957. I was eleven years old, still teaching Hebrew lessons, but now just beginning to reach an awareness of the social dimension of life. The temple was our chief social center. Of particular importance to us were the dancing classes held each week, a sort of basic training course for the countless bar and bat mitzvah and confirmation parties on the horizon just a few years away.

As I grew older, I also became much more fully aware of my father as a rabbi. Until then, I had seen Dad primarily in terms of his role as a leader of services, a teacher and a speaker. Gradually, I began to notice a more significant aspect of his rabbinate, his counseling, one of the strengths that set him apart from other rabbis and made him an object of virtual adoration among those members of the congregation whose lives he touched.

Dad maintained an office in the house, and there were days when it seemed as though the parade of individuals and couples, young and old, never ceased. He ushered them into his study, closed the door, then reappeared with them an hour or so later. He never spoke of the substance of any meeting, since the confidences of those men and women were sacred to him. But from time to time there were subtle signals that even I at the age of eleven picked up. There were some who left our home with tears in their eyes. Others

61

embraced my father as though he had saved their lives. Still others departed with sullen expressions on their faces. I never knew the cause of any of these outward manifestations of emotion, at least not from Dad, but most of these grownups had children my age or about my age, and they often shared the story of what took place in that locked study. One of my friends told me that her parents were seriously considering divorce, but Dad helped them understand that they really loved each other and suggested ways for them to remain together. Another friend told me that his parents had been unduly strict with him, causing great tension in their home. Dad had shown them how to maintain their standards while respecting their child's dignity. And on occasion one of those adults would stop on the way out of our house and say to me "Your father is a great man. You should be very proud to be his son."

I was very proud. Even then I could see that my father had the capacity to heal, to alleviate pain, to ease bitterness, to calm troubled souls. Perhaps it was at that time that I also began to consider seriously the possibility of becoming a rabbi. If I could do what my father did, I thought—what a wonderful way to spend my life!

There was one realm, however, where I felt myself totally deficient, and that was my personal faith in God. I really didn't know if I believed in some supernatural being. In fact, I rarely thought of God at all. By comparison, my father spoke of God freely and without embarrassment virtually all of the time. When David, Michael or I narrowly escaped an injury of some sort, Dad instructed us to thank God. When bills weighed heavily upon him, especially those that came at critical and unanticipated times, he often remarked that God would take care of it. His faith, so pure, so primitive in a way, so totally without doubt, made me feel somewhat inadequate. When I raised this issue with him, he would just smile and say "Look, Danny, your belief in God is something that grows as you grow. Give yourself time." Then he would add, "I think that you would make a great rabbi, far better than I will ever be." That was his custom, always minimizing his own accomplishments, never boasting, and always encouraging me.

I finally began to resolve the question of my faith in December of 1957. One night as we sat at dinner, Dad received an urgent call from the hospital. A friend of mine, riding his bike in the snow, had been hit by a truck. An ambulance rushed him to the hospital, but the doctors expected him to live only a few hours. A member of the family called to ask that my father come at once. I asked if I might accompany him, since I knew the family so well and felt so badly about what had happened. My father hesitated, but then agreed as we both rushed to the car.

We arrived at the hospital to find a grim death watch underway. Dad spoke briefly with the family, then asked to see the doctor, a member of the congregation. I stood a few steps away, but clearly heard the prognosis. Death was imminent. The doctor hoped that my father would prepare the family accordingly. There was nothing to be done. My father asked if he might go into the intensive care unit and say a prayer for my friend. The doctor agreed, but pointed out to my father that I could not accompany him. I felt a sense of relief; there was no way I wanted to enter that forbidding room. I remained with the family until Dad returned about fifteen minutes later. I will never forget the glow that seemed to surround him and the broad smile on his face, totally inappropriate given the situation. He walked directly to the parents and said in a voice loud enough for everyone in the waiting room to hear, "I don't want you to worry about a thing. Your son is going to be fine."

His pronouncement was of such volume that the doctor outside in the hall heard it as well. He came racing into the waiting room, his face contorted in an angry, furious expression. Taking my father firmly by the arm, he said "Rabbi, I want to speak with you." They walked into the doctors' room, a small office with a door and a window. I could not hear what was being said, but the doctor, gesticulating wildly, was clearly berating my father. Dad stood quietly and impassively, waited until the physician had completed his harangue, then said something quietly to him. The doctor stalked out of the office, slammed the door and strode off down the hall. When Dad finally emerged, I asked him what had gone on. He replied softly "Danny, he just doesn't understand. Your friend is going to be fine."

We were awakened the next morning before 7 A.M. by a phone call from my friend's parents. They wanted my father to know their son had miraculously emerged from his coma and had now been pronounced on the road to recovery. My father thanked them for the call, repeated again what he had told them the previous night and assured them he would be by the hospital to visit later in the day. I was stunned. How had he known? How could he have spoken as he did in light of the doctor's instructions? For perhaps the first time in my life, I confronted Dad. I sat him down and demanded an answer to my question. He spoke slowly, choosing his words with great care. "I said a prayer, Danny, and I got an answer. There was no mystery here. There was no question. I knew." I pressed him for further clarification, but he simply shrugged his shoulders. "I can't explain it any better than that, Danny. One day perhaps you will understand. I just knew."

I had never seen a miracle before. The biblical stories of miracles never impressed me much. I always assumed that they were fairy tales. But in that hospital, I sensed that a miracle had taken place. I had seen at least part of an act of God first-hand, an intervention in the physical world by a supreme being, with my father somehow a conduit for interpreting it to others.

For the first time, I genuinely believed that there could be a God, and now I also knew that I could at least seriously consider the possibility of becoming a rabbi. About a month later, just after my twelfth birthday in February of 1958, my English teacher assigned a paper on the subject "What I Want to Be When I Grow Up." I titled my paper "How to Become a Rabbi." It read as follows:

Becoming a rabbi is a long and tedious work. Training to be a rabbi takes up practically all of your child and young adult life. You must start preparing when you are about 5 years old. Although many boys do not decide to be rabbis until they are in college, you are at a great advantage if you make your decision when you are younger. At 5, you enter school, not only public school, but also Sunday School. This course lasts 12 years like regular school. When you have reached the age of 7, you start Hebrew School. This course lasts up to your Bar Mitzvah. After that, you are free to continue or stop. Regular attendance at religious services is also required.

At the age of 13 you have your Bar Mitzvah. The following year you graduate from the first nine years of Sunday School. This is called Confirmation. By the time you are 17, you graduate from

Sunday School. Then, if you are going to be a rabbi, the real work begins.

You must go to college for 4 years, of course. After the first 4 years, you enter Rabbinical School at Hebrew Union College in Cincinnati. Here, you are drilled thoroughly in the various books of the Bible, famous Jewish documents, and many other things. It is really impossible to describe the things that a boy must go through before he is ordained a rabbi. Since many people come to clergymen with personal problems, a rabbi who hopes to be of service to his community also must take a course on psychology.

The course at the college is from 4 to 7 years. Even after all this work, which comes to about 23 years, a man is not assured of a job. His name is put on a list at the school, and if he is lucky enough to be chosen, he is set. The salary of a rabbi cannot be approximated. This item depends on the size of the congregation and the people of the congregation.

In this short space, I have taken you through the life of a boy who wishes to be a rabbi. I have shown you the work and the results. Some day I want to be a rabbi. I handle my hopes with care, for anything can happen at any time. I will be in my 8th year of Sunday School next year. I will be in my 7th year of Hebrew School. Next February, I will have my Bar Mitzvah. After that, who knows? I must keep on working and improving my knowledge of Hebrew life. It is my sincere hope that some day I will be the reality of my dreams. If God grants my parents years, I will be able to look my father in the eye and say to him: "Dad, I made you a promise a long time ago, and I intend to keep it. I made it, Dad. I am a rabbi."

From that day on, though I realize it only in retrospect, an irreversible process was set into motion that would result in my embracing the rabbinate. But at that moment in my life I know that I wanted to become a rabbi, a Reform rabbi, to serve Jews in as many different ways as I possibly could. I wanted to be like my father. I wanted to touch people's lives, to soothe their hurts, to help them realize their fondest aspirations. And deep down, I also wanted to know what it meant to get an answer to a prayer. I wanted to be part of a miracle.

Just after my twelfth birthday, I began preparations for my bar mitzvah. By then, Dad had also introduced bat mitzvah, so that girls as well as boys could experience its profound emotional impact. I did well in school and enjoyed a growing social life in the new neighborhood. Neither I nor my friends were really aware of circumstances in society as a whole that would shortly turn our world upside down and begin a period of great upheaval in the United States.

CHAPTER XI

My Bar Mitzvah Year—and the World Changes

*I*n 1959, I celebrated my bar mitzvah. The whole process of studying for the occasion, that moment in the life of a Jewish boy when he is at least nominally considered a man, was very strange indeed for me. After several years of teaching others, I suddenly became the student, entrusted to the care of a wonderful woman named Helen Gilbert, one of a growing corps of bar and bat mitzvah tutors trained by my father since his arrival in Detroit. Our families were very close, and thus we both realized the potential humor in this instructional setting. Still, Helen treated me as though I was just another pupil, patient but tough and extremely helpful in terms of moderating any overconfidence I might have felt.

During the preparatory period of instruction, which began in 1958, I felt more pressure than I wished to admit. Since I was the rabbi's son, my bar mitzvah would be more carefully scrutinized than those of my classmates. During my childhood and teenage years, I was expected to excel, this time in the context of a game that we played among ourselves as twelve year olds.

There were an increasing number of bar and bat mitzvahs at Temple Israel now, and most of us were invited to them. Therefore, virtually all of us sat together at the service, meticulously counting the number of mistakes our friends made in the course of pronouncing the blessings, reading from the Torah and the Haftorah, then scoring the bar or bat mitzvah in terms of errors. We gave weight to clarity of diction, presence, poise and a number of other intangibles, which when added together yielded the final rating.

The best score recorded thusfar was a plus–2, achieved by a brilliant member of our Hebrew school class. Actually, he made four mistakes, but two were excused as a consequence of strength in other areas. I participated in this exercise, which helped to pass the time in what seemed an endless service. From time to time, a friend remarked in jest that I would be judged much more carefully and critically than others, since I was the rabbi's son. These constant reminders, however motivated by friendship and goodwill, galled me. Then, as in my younger years, I genuinely resented the expectation of perfection. While I enjoyed the status of being the rabbi's son, on some level I still wanted to be just 'one of the guys.' That, however, was not an option for me. I needed to be perfect just to be okay.

During those years, Temple Israel also had a junior congregation. It was one of the means which Dad and Rabbi Fram used to guarantee a larger attendance at Saturday morning services. We gathered in the social hall as the adult service began and conducted our own Shabbat worship up to the beginning of the Torah service, at which time we joined the adult congregation for the Torah reading, the sermon and the conclusion of the service in the sanctuary.

As one of the "rabbis" of the junior congregation, I further honed my liturgical skills in preparation for my bar mitzvah. I grew to love standing before my peers as the leader of the service. The position of surrogate rabbi was considered high status, reserved for those who had demonstrated competency in their Hebrew studies. Dad was careful not to allow me to occupy that position too frequently. On the one hand, I know that he must have derived great pleasure from seeing me in a role he hoped I would adopt as an adult. On the other hand, I am now aware of how anxious he was to avoid imposing that decision upon me. Here, too, I felt that I had to be careful. Friends who ignored the mistakes of others snickered when I stumbled or mispronounced a word. I showed no outward sign of embarrassment, but inside it hurt.

Then there were the annual recitation contests. Religious-school students at Temple Israel had an opportunity each year to participate in a competition in which they wrote a speech, then delivered it in front of the entire religious school. Judges scored each recitation and awarded a prize to the best entry. Even as Rabbi

Freehof had worked with my father in Butler, Dad spent a great deal of time with me, teaching me how to deliver an address. By the time I was eight I had a firm grasp of sentence structure, the use of strong, illustrative language and a sense of how to build a presentation. Since I attended services each week, I also learned first-hand from my father's delivery. As a result of my training, I easily won the first recitation contest at age ten, and the following year as well.

This year, at twelve, I truly believed that my presentation was again clearly superior to any of the others, but the judges declared one of my classmates the winner. Bitterly disappointed, I rode home with my mother in silence. She, too, was bewildered by the decision, but did not make a big deal out of it in order to avoid stirring up any more feelings on my part. Later that day, when my father arrived home from teaching and a number of weddings, he sat me down and explained what had happened. Yes, he said, the judges had considered my speech the best, but in view of the fact that I had won for the two previous years, they felt that it was inappropriate to give me the prize once again, especially since I was the rabbi's son. It wouldn't look good.

There it was again. With all of the privileges that I enjoyed as the rabbi's son, there were also cruel penalties. I could not expect to be judged solely on my own merits. There would always be that emotional baggage attached to anything I did. My father asked me to understand, but I did not understand. It seemed totally unfair. I was hurt and angry, but it only made me more determined than ever to succeed.

While I prepared for my bar mitzvah, the Jewish world around me was changing in many ways. The Reform movement now grew rapidly. The Hebrew Union College-Jewish Institute of Religion reached westward in 1954 and initiated a satellite campus in Los Angeles, with a two-year academic program for aspiring rabbis who then finished their studies either in New York or Cincinnati. Also in 1954, Dr. Nelson Glueck secured a piece of land in Jerusalem for a branch of HUC-JIR in Israel.

Glueck's negotiations with the Israeli government went very well. A piece of property, considered one of the choicest sections of real estate in all of Jerusalem, was leased to the college-institute at a rate of one Israeli pound a year, renewable forever. Given inflation rates since 1955, the property rental for this priceless acreage now amounts to less than one cent annually. Arguably, this arrangement constituted one the most astute real estate negotiations since the purchase of Manhattan for twenty-four dollars.

Glueck's plans called for a chapel or synagogue on campus, a library, classrooms and a small number of suites for resident staff and visiting professors. The contemplated chapel occasioned the most impassioned response, both in the United States and in Israel. Orthodox leaders within Israel cried out in protest. Then as now, many of them denied the legitimacy of Reform Judaism. They were not about to stand idly by while an American Reform rabbi, however well-known, attempted to bring what they felt was the scourge of Reform Judaism to the holy soil of Israel. Nelson Glueck understood the actual and symbolic importance of the synagogue. He believed that it was his duty to bring religious pluralism to Israel and to establish Reform Judaism there. He advised the HUC-JIR Board of threats by the Orthodox against HUC-JIR in Israel, but indicated that he was prepared to meet any eventuality. He declared: "It is our determination to realize for ourselves the right which is guaranteed for all people in Israel, to preach and practice and pray to the God of our fathers in accordance with our own understanding."

In January of 1957, the first site of the proposed California school was formally acquired. Nelson Glueck tapped a new graduate of the Cincinnati school, asking him to go west and to build the new arm of the college-institute. The young rabbi, Alfred Gottschalk, would one day succeed Glueck as president. In the spring of 1957, the California campus of the HUC-JIR opened its doors and began its work. A year later, Alfred Gottschalk was named its dean.

In New York at the same time, Maurice Eisendrath and the Union of Hebrew Congregations also engaged in building and expansion. New congregations were formed, new programs added, with much of the emphasis placed upon a burgeoning program of social justice. In 1951, the UAHC created a Commission on Social Action, a joint instrumentality of the Central Conference of American Rabbis and the UAHC, supplementing the historic efforts of the CCAR Committee on Justice and Peace, which had long been a voice of Jewish social concern and social action. In 1953, the UAHC Biennial Assembly urged the establishment of a committee on social action in every UAHC congregation. The timing of these initiatives was no coincidence. The civil rights movement was emerging as a powerful factor in American life.

Blacks still did not enjoy equal rights in many parts of the United States. The right to vote was denied them in many locales. Discrimination in jobs and housing, in education and medical care was the norm rather than the exception throughout America. Eisendrath was determined to make the civil rights movement a priority. The Commission on Social Action became in large measure an instrument of his will.

In 1955, the UAHC publicly endorsed the United States Supreme Court's *Brown* vs. *Board of Education* decision, rejecting school segregation. The resolution declared: "We regard this decision as a major chapter in the history of the growth of true equality under the law . . . We, therefore, urge our congregants and congregations in all sections of the country to join with forward-looking racial, religious and civic groups in the community in using their influence to secure acceptance and implementation of the desegregation decisions in every community in our land."

Throughout the 1950s, the Commission on Social Action and the UAHC as a national body spoke out on many matters, including First Amendment freedoms, peace in the Middle East and many other issues of social concern. But growing numbers of Reform Jews made the civil rights struggle their own, joining together as a family of congregations to speak with a united voice.

In 1959, Maurice Eisendrath began a process of preparing the movement for a proposed Religious Action Center in Washington, D.C., devoted exclusively to the fostering of Jewish social justice as well as the voicing of Jewish concerns in the administration and the Congress. After two years of discussion and a tumultuous debate on the floor of the 1961 biennial convention, Eisendrath prevailed, whereupon the UAHC reaffirmed its prior acceptance of a large grant from a remarkable Jew named Kivie Kaplan, who served at the time as the white Jewish president of the NAACP. I must confess that I was unaware of these historic developments as I prepared for my bar mitzvah. I remember the television news reports of these beginning steps toward equal rights, but in 1959 I was much more concerned with acquitting myself honorably at my bar mitzvah.

A few months prior to the ceremony, our family made our annual trip to Winnipeg, Canada to visit my mother's parents, and my aunts and uncles there. Since none of the family could come to Detroit in February, we went to celebrate informally in advance. It was the last time I ever saw my grandfather, whom I truly loved. He was a tall, handsome man with a mustache silver with age. He and I had a special chemistry. Within minutes after our arrival in Winnipeg, he always excused himself, took me by the hand, then walked me down the street to the local grocery to buy me an ice cream. I miss him, and I only wish that he had lived longer. There are so many questions I have today that I would ask him about his life and his dreams. As we left Winnipeg on that trip, I remember that my mother had tears in her eyes. As we pulled out onto the highway for the beginning of our three-day journey home, she said to my father "I don't think that I will ever see him again." Sadly, she was right.

As my bar mitzvah day approached, I grew more and more excited, in spite of attempts by my father and Helen Gilbert to keep me a bit off-balance. Deciding that I had "peaked" too early, Dad and Helen changed my Haftorah portion two months before the service. That way, they knew I would have to concentrate on my studies and not become overconfident and careless. Then came the terrible news. Cantor Tulman had suffered a severe stroke.

Since the day when I first entered Temple Israel, Cantor Tulman was my friend. He frequently winked at me from the bimah at services and often sat with me just to talk. He was a marvelous teacher, and though the years had eroded his voice, members of the congregation adored him and found his singing as moving as when he was a younger man. Those of us preparing for bar and bat mitzvah had a special expectation regarding the service. It was Cantor Tulman who intoned the traditional three-fold benediction in Hebrew as part of the blessing ceremony. Following that, he chanted the kiddush, the blessing over the wine, gave the bar or bat mitzvah a sip and then a little tug on the ear. For some reason, that moment, reserved only for bar and bat mitzvah, was a highlight to which each of us looked forward with great anticipation. When I heard of Cantor Tulman's hospitalization, it cast a dark shadow over my impending celebration. I asked my father if Cantor Tulman would be well enough to come to the service. He shook his head sadly. In the days to come, the severity of the stroke became known. While the stroke was not fatal, Cantor Tulman was paralyzed. He had lost his speech. He would never sing again. I was devastated.

My bar mitzvah took place on Friday, February 13, 1959. I deliberately chose that 'unlucky' day as a means of demonstrating my capacity to triumph over any obstacle. On Thursday afternoon, I completed my 'dress rehearsal,' then asked my father if he would take me to Cantor Tulman's house. Even though I understood the nature of his illness, I still wanted to be with him, if only for a brief time.

On Friday, I came home directly from school. I dressed, we ate an early dinner, then Dad informed me that we would stop at Cantor Tulman's home before going to the synagogue. We drove to Cantor Tulman's home. I had not seen him since his stroke, and his appearance shocked me. Here was this man, my friend, sitting in a wheelchair, seemingly helpless. Without prompting from my father, I approached him and said "Cantor Tulman, tonight is my bar mitzvah. I came to receive your blessing." My father started to interrupt me for fear of embarrassing Mrs. Tulman. Both of them realized that there was no way for him even to respond. But then, on that February night in 1959, I witnessed the second miracle of my life. Cantor Tulman sat up in his wheelchair pushed his palms against its armrests and stood up. He placed his hands upon my head and sang the benediction in full voice. Then he bent over, kissed me, and tugged my ear, after which he eased himself back into the wheelchair. There were tears in his eyes and in mine. I kissed him on the cheek, thanked him for his blessing and turned to leave. The look on the faces of my father and Mrs. Tulman will always remain indelibly etched on my memory. Cantor Tulman had decided that he had to bless me and he did. He never spoke again. On the way to the temple that night, I again realized that there must be a God. I told my father so. He didn't respond. He was crying.

My bar mitzvah service began. The synagogue was filled with over fifteen hundred people, three hundred of them in chairs set up in the back of the sanctuary. Filled with the inspiration of Cantor

Tulman's blessing, and totally unafraid, I read my Torah portion without error. I recited my new Haftorah virtually from memory, the story of how Nathan the prophet condemned the mighty King David. Then came the moment of my blessing. I had specifically requested that my father sit with me and the family in the congregation that night, as my father instead of as the rabbi. Therefore, Rabbi Fram called me to the ark and charged me to be a link in the chain of Jewish tradition. In the presence of the entire congregation, he predicted that I would become a rabbi, fighting on behalf of Jews and Judaism, taking on tasks that others felt impossible, repeating as his motif for my life those words spoken by the prophet Isaiah centuries before: "Here am I, send me."

The night of my bar mitzvah will remain with me as a night of miracles, a moment when forces from without and within combined in ways that I did not comprehend, moving me a step further toward my destiny as a rabbi and a proud Reform Jew.

CHAPTER XII

Lonely in a Crowd

*M*y bar mitzvah was perfect. I knew it, and I'm sure my friends knew it as well. Therefore, I expected a flurry of congratulations on my errorless performance. Instead, there was only silence. Such a bar mitzvah had been expected. My friend's reluctance to recognize the results of my hard work stung a great deal. It only served to confirm what I had long felt, namely that I was destined to be a loner, the odd man out. No matter how significant my achievements might have been, I was still the rabbi's son, even to my closest friends.

My bar mitzvah party two days later further underscored my unique and often difficult position. Most of my friends had bar or bat mitzvah parties with just their classmates and close family friends. My parents, however, were the first family of the congregation, and did not wish to offend any of its members. My bar mitzvah invitation list, therefore, included every religious-school student in the seventh and eighth grade of Temple Israel. I would be willing to bet that my bar mitzvah party was the only one in history to have twelve adults—and three hundred seventy-five kids! Many of them were total strangers. I didn't even know their names. I milled about at my own celebration, feeling a little lost and awkward, lonely in a crowd of many dozens of children my age. To be sure, the party was fabulous. The food was wonderful, the band terrific, the music nonstop for almost five hours. But I felt strange, somehow.

I felt awkward physically too. Up until the age of twelve, I was a little fat kid. Unless you have been fat yourself as a child, and suffered the endless, merciless taunts of your peers, you have no way of understanding the pain that words can cause. At the age of twelve, I was five foot seven, but weighed 180 pounds. Day after day, I heard the same words over and over again. "Hi, fat boy." "Syme, do you think you could get any more food in your mouth?" There were nights when I cried myself to sleep. But the summer of 1958 changed everything. I was away at camp, and as the summer wore on, it seemed as though my pants were shrinking, becoming progressively shorter and shorter. Only after I returned home and saw the look of amazement on my mother's face, did it dawn on me that I had grown significantly. I still weighed 180 pounds, but now I was six feet tall, much leaner and by far the tallest boy in my class. Though the days of being a chubby little kid were behind me, however, every time I looked in the mirror, I still saw Danny the fat kid. At my bar mitzvah party, therefore, in spite of the fact that I had by now become one of the better dancers in my class, I still felt tremendous self-consciousness as a result of that residual self-image.

The party ended, and the family returned home to a mountain of presents. I sat down and opened them one by one, carefully recording the gift and the name and address of the person who sent it in a special notebook purchased for just this purpose. There were savings bonds, records, clothes, books and contributions to charitable causes made in my name, over six hundred in all, the great majority from total strangers. I asked my parents who these people were, and it was then that I learned another lesson about being a rabbi's child.

My father explained to me that there are certain things a rabbi does for which no payment is possible. How do you set a fee for saving a marriage? How do you establish a fair price for drawing a child out from the depths of depression? How do you issue a bill for bringing hope and faith at a time of crisis? You can't. Therefore, every congregation blessed with a caring rabbi also has many members who would do anything to repay the rabbi's kindness. One of the ways in which they express their thanks is by doing nice things for the rabbi's children. My bar mitzvah provided a perfect occasion for a tangible expression of this gratitude. On the one hand, I was delighted to receive so many extravagant gifts. On the other hand, I felt very odd writing personal letters of thanks to people whose faces I had never seen. The certainty I had felt less than forty-eight hours earlier about wanting to be a rabbi diminished a bit during those intervening days. I was more conscious than ever that I was not just Danny Syme. For better or for worse, as long as I lived in Detroit, I would always be identified as Danny Syme, Rabbi Syme's son.

In 1959, my mother emerged in her own right as a leading figure in the Detroit Jewish community. For several years, she worked conscientiously to build her interfaith program, and finally convinced the nuns at a major Catholic college to join in a co-sponsored Institute on Judaism. Many face-to-face meetings between Mom and the sisters who ran the college built a relationship of trust. After three full years of such meetings, a decision was reached that the first institute would take place. I still remember that day at Temple Israel, when literally hundreds of Jews and Catholics joined together in studying the symbols, rituals and values of the Jewish year. All of the Detroit newspapers sent reporters. Television and radio crews came out in force. This was a unique event in the Detroit area, and Mom had clearly come into her own. I was proud to see her picture in the local press, smiling, surrounded by those devoted Jewish women who shared her dream and the Catholic sisters who had come to call her their friend. The institute probably brought the various religious communities closer together than all of the national brotherhood weeks of that decade combined. Just as I had watched my father touch people in certain ways, so I witnessed my mother's impact in a totally different sphere. It was about then I began to wonder if I ever would find a niche of my own.

For a time, I thought I would make my mark in music, perhaps by becoming a great pianist. Like most Jewish kids, I took piano lessons. Mom possessed a musical gift, and had often accompanied my father on the piano at services and temple events in both Sharon and Butler. My aunt Estelle, my father's sister, had made a living playing the piano in Winnipeg's silent movie theatres. My brother, David, three years younger, used to fool around on the piano after I finished practicing. He often picked out melodies, some of them quite complex, but none of us paid too much attention. He was far too young to study piano, at least so we thought, so I viewed his child's play with some disdain. After all, he was playing nursery rhymes. I was studying Beethoven!

A few months after my bar mitzvah, I played my first major recital, showcasing that obligatory piano piece for all aspiring pianists, Beethoven's "Für Elise." I performed it flawlessly, receiving a loud ovation, and came home quite pleased with myself. David told me how much he enjoyed my playing. As a typical older brother would, I thanked him somewhat smugly for his kind words and began to walk away. Before I reached the kitchen, however, I heard the strains of "Für Elise" coming from the room where the piano sat. I couldn't believe my ears. I raced back into the living room to find David playing the piece I had struggled to learn for six months, totally by ear and without a single mistake! Mom and Dad also heard the music, and assumed I was playing an encore for their benefit. As they strolled into the living room, they must have seen the pained expression on my face before they realized exactly what had transpired. David, only ten years old, was demonstrating musical genius, without realizing the extent of his own remarkable talent. David finished playing, my parents applauded, and, without the slightest arrogance or smugness, he asked me how he had done. I turned and went to my room. I never played the piano again.

Mom came in a few minutes later and sat with me. She understood how I felt, and unsuccessfully tried to comfort me. Later, our live-in 'cleaning woman, a gentle, beautiful soul named Pauline, came to talk to me. I loved Pauline. I considered her one of my best friends. She was one of the kindest people I ever knew, and lived with us for close to five years. Pauline always was in the house when we returned home from school. Pauline babysat with us when Mom and Dad had to go out to fulfill their social obligations. Pauline comforted me when nightmares caused me to call out in my sleep. And now Pauline sat face-to-face with me to share her views on a number of subjects.

"I know that this has been a tough year for you, Danny," she began. "I know how you felt at your bar mitzvah party. I know how you felt today. You feel loneliness a lot of times. I can see that. But you are not the only one in the world who is lonely. How do you think I felt at your bar mitzvah party? Danny, I was the only Negro in that whole big crowd of white people. Do you have any idea how that feels? I don't expect you do. I was there because I love you, but it sure was a very strange experience for me. So you just remember. There's lots of kinds of loneliness in this world of ours. You have yours. I have mine. But at least we have each other. And we're friends. And don't you ever forget that." Pauline gave me a big hug, then retired to her own room. I felt better.

The next day I went to school and was surprised to find that my history teacher's lesson plan included a discourse on the problems of the Negro in American society. Coming on the heels of my talk with Pauline, it was perfect timing. My teacher spun out the history of Negroes in America, how they came to this country as slaves, bought and sold as property, and transported to these shores to work the plantations of the deep South. She told us the story of Abraham Lincoln, of the Emancipation Proclamation, of the Underground Railroad which brought the Negro slaves to freedom in the North. She emphasized, however, that even then, in 1959, Negroes did not enjoy equal opportunity in America. Negroes could still not eat in the same restaurants as whites. In spite of the fact that many thousands of Negroes had fought to defeat America's enemies in World War II, many still were not allowed to vote or to attend certain universities. In spite of the fact that a Negro named Ralph Bunche, won the Nobel Peace Prize for his mediation efforts in the Middle East, Negroes still were barred from many employment positions. In spite of the fact that the Supreme Court had outlawed segregation in public schools in 1954, many cities and states still maintained two separate school systems, one for white people, one for Negroes.

During that riveting hour, I heard the story of Emmett Till, a fourteen-year-old boy lynched in Mississippi after being accused of propositioning a white woman. For the first time I heard the name of Rosa Parks, who refused to give up her seat on a segregated bus in Montgomery, Alabama, and whose arrest set off a year-long Negro boycott of the Montgomery bus system. On that day, I first heard the name of Martin Luther King, Jr., a young minister who had dedicated his life to winning equal rights for Negroes in America.

My teacher described in the most graphic terms the activities of the Ku Klux Klan, of the White Citizens Council, of the hangings and beatings and night-riding vigilantism of hooded white mobs. She summarized the Civil Rights Act of 1957 and showed us pictures of the September 1957, confrontation between Governor Orval Faubus of Arkansas and President Dwight D. Eisenhower, which resulted in nine Negro students being escorted by one thousand United States paratroopers into a formerly all-white school.

No one in that room on that day budged for the entire class period. No one coughed. No one spoke. That night during dinner, I described the lesson to my parents and asked what Jews were doing in the struggle for civil rights. After all, I had been taught from the time I was a child that Jews had a responsibility to help the oppressed, for we had been strangers in the land of Egypt. Mother and Dad sat and listened without comment, then began to tell me a little bit about what the Union of American Hebrew Congregations had done.

The Reform movement's philosophy was based in large measure upon prophetic values. During the early days of the movement, only the rabbis as a group took an active interest in what was called 'social action.' Members of most congregations simply did not wish to engage personally in the logical consequences of resolutions, namely concrete actions. During the early 1950s, however, under the leadership of Maurice Eisendrath, the tide began to turn. In 1953, the Commission on Social Action began to function aggressively, after Rabbi Richard G. Hirsch, Rabbi Eugene Lipman and Albert Vorspan joined the UAHC staff. They were determined to give substance to the resolutions adopted by the UAHC's biennial conventions. Their first priority was the organization of individual social action committees in every temple.

The burning moral cause of the time was equal rights for blacks in America. The UAHC took stronger and stronger positions advocating desegregation, resolutions which not all member congregations welcomed. Reform Jews in the South were particularly frightened by the implications of these resolutions for their safety. They demanded that the UAHC not presume to speak for them. Synagogues were bombed, and Jews were accused of being 'nigger lovers' by southern neighbors who had been their closest friends only months earlier. The members of these temples asked the UAHC to adopt a less aggressive stance and to allow Christian groups to take the lead in demanding civil rights.

At the UAHC Biennial Convention in May 1957, a young rabbi named Roland Gittelsohn rose to speak to the issue of whether or not Reform Jews should be in the forefront of the civil rights struggle. Gittelsohn was already a rabbi of some renown, having delivered a famous eulogy for the fallen Allied soldiers on Iwo Jima during World War II. That one speech won him international recognition and kindled a spark within him that was to have an impact on Reform and world Judaism for the balance of his career. Gittelsohn was a fighter, a fiery champion of social justice. At that convention, he rose to speak, and said in part:

> 'Some of my friends in the South have pleaded in my presence that pronouncements on desegregation by bodies like our union will expose them to anguish and pain. I do not and cannot take their protestations lightly. I would not willfully and unnecessarily bring pain upon any human being. But I know that no battle has ever been won, no major social change has ever been accomplished without casualties. Jews who live in the South find themselves in the front lines in this war for human dignity. The only thing which gives me the moral right to speak to them as I do now is the fact that I myself have been in the front lines of war. I did not choose to be there. I do not pretend for an instant that I would have had courage enough to volunteer for such duty, but once it was thrust upon me I had to accept, whatever the possible cost to me or those I love.
>
> I presume to believe that exactly such is the situation of those Christians and Jews living in the South who know that desegregation is morally right. They, too, are in the front lines through no fault of their own. It is too late to shift the scene of battle; the war already rages. Their only choice is to do what they know is right, or surrender and then try to live with themselves. I do not envy their dilemma. I have profound pity for their pain. I pray that God may give them the strength to do what they must and the privilege of seeing the fruits of their triumph.'

Gittelsohn's words stirred the convention and moved the UAHC to strengthen its commitment in the fight for civil rights. By

June of 1959 there were 274 UAHC congregational social action committees.

That day, first in school and then at home, I felt part of a great cause beckoning my generation. In America at least the members of the Reform movement would not stand by idly. I began to understand much more clearly the loneliness that Pauline had described. I loved her so much. I could not conceive of fighting for the rights of an entire people, but I was determined to fight for Pauline. That night, I told her so. Tears rolled down her cheeks as she embraced me. She understood how much I cared for her, that I knew about the pain and degradation which she and so many of her friends had suffered. Even though I was just thirteen, 1959 was a year in which I became a man in many ways.

CHAPTER XIII

High School—A Jewish Anchor

I attended Detroit's Mumford High School, made famous by Eddie Murphy in the movie *Beverly Hills Cop*. There I participated fully in school activities, particularly in dramatics, but my Jewish involvements provided the most significant adolescent social contacts, growth opportunities and signposts for the future.

During freshman year, Temple Israel ninth graders prepared for confirmation. The seemingly endless classes moved slowly toward the day in June of 1960 on the holiday of Shavuot, when we would stand before the congregation to affirm our Jewish commitment.

Halfway through the confirmation year, representatives of the temple youth group met with us, giving us an opportunity to work on the annual Temple Israel Purim carnival. This impressive annual youth group fundraising event, overseen by a professional carnival firm, enabled the high schoolers both to sustain their programs and to make a significant financial contribution to the temple. During the spring, for one day, the temple became an indoor Jewish equivalent of a New York City street fair, with booths of all kinds, prizes, food and lots of fun.

This experience introduced the confirmation class to many older students at Temple Israel. I loved the excitement of the meetings, the endless hours of discussion and planning, the social interaction that took place as we slowly built the carnival concept into reality. As the year progressed, I looked forward to my formal youth group membership beginning in tenth grade.

I did not know it at the time, but the Temple Israel youth group, or TYG, was a constituent of a regional entity called Michigan State Temple Youth. MSTY, in turn, was part of the National Federation of Temple Youth, the youth arm of the Union of American Hebrew Congregations. NFTY (pronounced 'nifty') came into being in 1939 as a way of bringing together Jewish young adults from throughout North America for Jewish cultural, social and educational activities. Its founder, Rabbi Arthur Lelyveld, was succeeded a short time later by the man generally considered the father of NFTY, Rabbi Sam Cook. Cook had a dream of a national organization that would provide Reform Jewish young people with rich common Jewish memories and experiences. He built NFTY carefully and gradually, recruiting adult volunteers into service as local youth group advisors, forming chapters in as many congregations as possible, urging the development of UAHC camps in different areas of the country and offering national leadership training institutes for boys and girls, who then returned to their communities as leaders and advocates of the national agenda.

After the Purim carnival, our class of 120 began preparations in earnest for the impending confirmation service. Unlike today, confirmation in 1959 had all the characteristics of a pageant. The choreography alone was as complicated as that for any Broadway show. We were divided into a number of groups, almost like an army being deployed for a major invasion. We practiced entering the sanctuary properly, learned where the girls were to place their flowers, where and when to sit, when to come up to the bimah, the emphasis with which to recite the memorized parts, and the order in which each of us would be blessed individually by the rabbis.

My part, a dramatic moment in the Torah service, was to stand alone on the upper level of the bimah, remove the Torah from the ark, recite a Hebrew prayer and its English translation, then present the scroll to Rabbi Fram, symbolically affirming Jewish continuity from generation to generation.

After school on the day of confirmation, I dressed in a new suit, purchased for the occasion. With my confirmation robe carefully hung in the back seat of the car, the family departed for temple, where an hour before the service we took the class picture. Everyone looked so handsome and beautiful, the boys perfectly groomed with new haircuts and shined shoes, the girls resplendent with new hairdos and dresses, the boys in blue robes, the girls in white and holding bouquets of gorgeous red roses. We gathered in a special room above the sanctuary and listened to the sounds of hundreds of congregants making their way into the temple, mothers, fathers, siblings, grandparents, uncles, aunts and family friends.

The organ sounded the opening anthem, and we began our processional into the sanctuary. Now the many hours of preparation seemed worthwhile. Everything ran like clockwork. Murmurs of approval from the congregation echoed in our ears as we walked with military precision to our seats, then ascended the bimah for the singing of "Father See Thy Suppliant Children."

Just two days before, during dress rehearsal, we almost sent Rabbi Fram into a state of apoplexy. By prearrangement, the entire class sang, not "Father See Thy Suppliant Children," but rather "Father See Thy *Succulent* Children." Rabbi Fram was furious until he realized that he had been had. Then we all had a good laugh and went back to work.

Tonight, however, there were no practical jokes. We were aware of the occasion and touched by its spiritual significance. The song rang out with power and beauty. One by one, my classmates recited their parts loudly, clearly, leading up to that dramatic moment when the Torah would be taken from the ark. I felt a rising sense of excitement. Slowly, confidently, I ascended the steps to the ark, removed the Torah and turned to face the congregation. The class completed its song, the organist ended with a flourish, and I stood before the congregation, twelve hundred strong. I glanced down to the bimah, where my father bowed his head in pride, awaiting my declaration.

There is no way to predict when disaster will strike in life. It comes without warning. Such was the case on my confirmation night. I opened my mouth to say the familiar words, only to discover that I had gone totally blank. I stood there, dumbstruck, unable to utter a single word. The congregation first took my silence as a dramatic pause. My father looked up at me with a quizzical expression, then, realizing what had happened, he began to mouth the words. Our eyes met for a moment and I whispered to him, "Dad, I forgot my part." He came to my rescue, and pronounced the first few words aloud. My mind kicked into gear, and at last I recited the declaration like a machine, albeit an embarrassed and humiliated one. After handing over the Torah, I returned to my seat. No one said a word. I felt totally alone. The service went on, through the blessing, through the presentation of gifts to each class member on behalf of the Temple, through the final prayers and the concluding hymn. Even as we had entered the sanctuary dramatically, so did the recessional proceed with total dignity. We climbed the stairs to our private room to remove our robes before joining the postservice reception in the social hall. I just wanted to hide.

Suddenly, a few friends in my class came up and congratulated me for making a mistake! They shook my hand, patted me on the back, and expressed their delight that I was capable of being human. One of my closest friends told me how happy he was for me to learn at last that you didn't have to be perfect all the time, that no one could live without making errors. This I could never have anticipated. My friends were actually praising me for messing up my part! Only with the perspective of many years did I understand that on that night I finally became 'one of the gang.' On confirmation night, I shed a burden I had carried since elementary school years. I was me, just me, and I was grateful.

A few months later, in late August, at a camp in Northern Michigan, I attended my first MSTY conclave. Having indicated my desire to become more deeply involved in Temple Israel's youth group, I was approached by one of the senior members who asked if I'd like to attend a week-long event under the auspices of Michigan State Temple Youth. I accepted immediately. On the day when I boarded the bus, I knew very few of the people. Many of those on my bus came from other temples and high schools, Reform Jewish boys and girls I had never met. Many of them, veterans of conclaves past, seemed to enjoy a special bond, something akin to a secret society. They sang songs I had never heard, joked about rabbis I'd never met, but went out of their way to welcome us newcomers. During the ride, which lasted a good five to six hours, a bonding took place among us as fellow travelers. There was a clique, no doubt about it; but the clique consisted of those who were involved, and the circle remained open to those who chose to be part of it.

Once we arrived at camp and were directed to our cabins, a

kindly senior took me under his wing and showed me the ropes. As we unpacked, he provided a detailed description of the week to come, with special emphasis on the possibility of meeting cute girls. With total sincerity, I told my new friend that I was at conclave for the study, religious services and workshops. He looked at me to make sure that I was serious, laughed, shrugged his shoulders, put his arm around me and led me from the boys' side of camp to the dining hall.

There were over two hundred teenagers at the conclave, from cities throughout Michigan and Indiana. Members from Detroit formed the largest contingent, but there were others from smaller cities; Muskegon, Kalamazoo, Battle Creek, East Lansing and Benton Harbor. For these small-city teens, this was the largest group of Jewish kids they had ever seen and one of the few opportunities each year they had to be with a significant Jewish peer group. That is what NFTY was and is all about. Whether in Michigan, Arizona or Mississippi, NFTY reinforces Jewish commitment through positive Jewish contacts. NFTY makes Jews, Reform Jews, with regional camp conclaves a primary tool to that end.

Beginning that evening, and throughout the week, we became a sort of family. Each day began with classes taught by rabbis from temples in the region, my father among them. Though all of my cabinmates knew that I was the rabbi's son, Dad was sensitive enough to stay away and let me participate on my own.

As the week progressed, I began to love the experience. After lunch each day we attended workshops, building a religious committee in the youth group, for example, or developing leadership skills. Each evening after dinner we had a song session, where we learned new melodies and built our common MSTY musical repertoire, followed by services, an evening program and then a midnight curfew. Just prior to lights-out, one of the rabbis came into our cabin and led us in 'cabin prayers.' He shared a few observations about the day, and sometimes even a story or two, after which anyone in the cabin who wished to share an observation or a prayer was free to do so. Some of these spontaneous expressions were quite moving. Others, seemingly profound and serious, actually had the aim of mocking the process and sometimes dissolved all of us into hysterical laughter. More than one rabbi beat a hasty retreat from the cabin in embarrassment at the graphic language of a story shared in the guise of a 'meditation.'

A highlight of conclave was the faculty-camper baseball game, played on Saturday afternoon. This was really the only time I had contact with my father at that first conclave, and I was genuinely proud of him. He pitched for the faculty, got three hits and scored two runs. A superb athlete, he could easily have struck out every player on our team, but instead lobbed the ball so that we could hit it. When it came time for me to bat, however I found myself facing another pitcher. Dad deliberately arranged a shifting of positions by the faculty so that I would never have to hit against him.

Dad never competed with me in athletics of any kind. I never understood why until I was much older. It was then that he told me that as a boy he used to arm-wrestle with his father, a powerful man who never lost. Though my father tried and tried, he could never defeat this bull of a man. But one day, when Dad was in his late teens, young and strong, he won. His feelings of exhilaration, however, were quickly dashed as he looked into his father's eyes, for at that moment he realized that his father was growing old. That was the only reason Dad had been able to win. He told me that day was one of the saddest of his life, and that he would never allow such a moment to occur in his relationship with his children. I got a hit, scored a run and the game ended in a tie. It always seemed to end in a tie.

By the last night of conclave, individuals who had arrived just a few days earlier, gathered as a unified group. After a festive closing 'banquet' and loud, enthusiastic singing, we participated in the traditional Havdalah service, formally ending the Sabbath, then moved to the social hall for a dance and the presentation of the conclave skit. The joy of this Reform Jewish experience was something special, something that could be shared with large numbers of kids my own age from every walk of life. I knew that every NFTY region had conclaves, but wondered if teenagers in other movements in Judaism had such experiences. If not, I thought, they were really missing something.

The bus ride home was much quieter than the ride to camp, with most of us totally exhausted from seven days of little sleep. Now we had new friends and promised to see each other soon, whether in school, at our individual temple youth group functions or at future conclaves, which took place in winter as well as summer. We said goodbye with tears, handshakes and hugs, reassured by the knowledge that a reunion was only a phone call or a car ride away.

The summer of 1960 was over, along with freshman year. Through confirmation and youth group, many new Jewish doors had been revealed in my life—some of which were yet to be opened.

CHAPTER XIV

Sophomore Year—Self-insight and NFTY

*T*he fall of 1960 brought with it many exciting events, two of which had special Jewish significance to me. That was the year in which the film *Exodus* made its debut, taking the moviegoing community by storm, even as the novel by Leon Uris had captivated millions of Americans, Jew and non-Jew alike. In addition, the mass murderer of the Third Reich, Adolph Eichmann, had been spirited from Argentina to Israel to stand trial for his heinous crimes.

Though I had seen many films and newsreels relating to the Holocaust in Sunday school, the fact that there was a real person, a name and a face associated with those terrible scenes, brought the Holocaust home to me in an entirely new way. I felt a consuming hatred for this plain-looking man, who I knew was responsible for the deaths of countless Jews.

While Eichmann stirred anger within me, the novel *Exodus* aroused a genuine Zionist impulse. I loved that book and must have read it twenty times. It still sits on my family's library shelf, worn and tattered. When the movie opened, I insisted that my father take me to see it. We watched, we laughed, we cried and left the theater somehow closer as father and son and as Jews. It nudged me yet another step along the road to engaging the Jewish world in a more activist manner. Jewishness—as opposed to Judaism—took a more central position in the constellation of my interests.

The most accessible vehicles for the expression of that interest were the Temple Israel youth group and MSTY. It was literally possible to attend a meeting at our advisor's home every afternoon and every evening with teenagers from the various Detroit temples, socializing, planning, having a great time. As a new youth grouper, I tagged along to as many meetings as possible, gradually joining others in my class in full involvement in every aspect of the program's fundraising and religious activities.

Nor was youth group activity confined to meetings. Large numbers of MSTY members went to Mumford High School, and we often met between classes or in study hall to discuss an upcoming conclave or social event. In 1960, most synagogues had no concern about security, and youth group members had keys to the temples. Therefore, we often decided on Thursday to have a joint youth group dance on Saturday night at one of our congregations. Many members played musical instruments, and thus we could easily put together a pickup band. Our rabbis and parents were open to our impulse programming—indeed, they welcomed it.

There were those at Mumford, however, who could not fathom this omnipresence of Jews and Jewish activity. One was a Christian boy whose family relocated to Detroit from the deep South. He had never met a Jew before, and did not even know that Judaism was a religion. Since Mumford was overwhelmingly Jewish, the school virtually emptied on Rosh Hashanah, with films shown in the auditorium for those few students who came to class. The student, puzzled by this mass disappearance, said nothing. A week later on Yom Kippur, the same thing happened. Our new classmate could stand it no longer. The day after Yom Kippur, he raised his hand and asked: "I would like to know how long you have to live here before you become Jewish and can skip school?"

Another event that captured my generation's imagination was John Kennedy's election victory. Here was a man who seemed to understand what it meant to be young, what it meant to want to change the world. When he spoke of 'the New Frontier,' we heard him and felt his passion. When he spoke of putting a man on the moon within a decade, we somehow believed that it would be accomplished in spite of all obstacles. His victory opened a door for millions of teenagers like ourselves to envision real involvement on the American political scene and a real chance to change things for the better as citizens and as Jews.

Between school, youth group and Kennedy-watching, my Jewish involvement and political maturation moved into high gear. Still, something was missing. Mom and Dad were rapidly becoming the first Jewish family of Detroit. My brother David, having discovered his unique talent, moved to nurture it, and even Michael began to display musical and artistic ability. I wanted something uniquely my own. As so often is the case, the conscious search led nowhere, but serendipity opened my eyes to a new possibility. The Mumford drama department presented two major productions in the school auditorium each year. The director, a fine actor in college, turned to teaching rather than a performing career. He was a pro and treated each of his productions as though they were opening on Broadway.

I had performed in a number of religious school and youth group skits but never considered the possibility of active involvement in theatre. Not until I noticed an announcement for the Mumford production of a play entitled *Dino*. This drama about a teenage rebel had particular contemporary interest, especially in light of the impending release of the film *West Side Story*. On a whim, I bought a ticket and went alone to the opening night performance. In the sweltering auditorium, a packed audience sat, captivated by this moving play performed by fellow students. At the play's conclusion, the audience rose as one, offering a standing, cheering ovation. I knew one or two cast members, and went backstage to offer congratulations. One of them introduced me to the director, who graciously accepted my compliments, then encouraged me to enroll in drama class come fall and to consider reading for the next semester's play. I left Mumford that night musing about how terrific it must feel to stand before a large audience, do your best and have the audience respond in a positive manner. I filed the idea away for further consideration.

A week or so later, I received a call from our youth group advisor, asking if I might be interested in attending a July leadership institute for teenagers in Great Barrington, Massachusetts, under the auspices of the National Federation of Temple Youth. The leadership institute, she told me, was limited to a small number of youth groupers from across the country, sent to acquire programming and leadership skills with which to build their local chapters. Over a period of twelve days, we would interact with some of the best and brightest teenagers from all of North America. She concluded the conversation by expressing her hope that I would be one of two representatives from Temple Israel.

I had no plans for the summer as yet, but I liked the idea of going to Massachusetts for the first time. The notion of meeting Reform Jewish teenagers from all over the United States in a sort of 'superconclave' also intrigued me. Perhaps there would be students there from southern Jewish congregations. I wanted to talk to them and get their reactions to the 1961 influx of Freedom Riders into their communities, and to the mob that attacked protesters in Montgomery, Alabama. I wanted to know if any of them had ever met Martin Luther King, Jr., about whom I had heard so much. I wanted to talk politics with others who might have been as excited as I by John Kennedy's election or Alan Shepard's first American flight into space. I wondered if there might be others who loved the book and the movie *Exodus,* who shared my intense fury toward Adolph Eichmann, and who perhaps might have had already been to that strange, exotic place, the state of Israel. Encouraged by my parents, I decided to go to Great Barrington.

Those of us representing the various area temples traveled by train from Detroit to Boston. The ride through the various states, through the beautiful countryside of America, was a treat. We saw a part of rural America, the America by the tracks, the farms and barns, the sleepy little towns and what so many today who grow up in big cities and travel only by air never even glimpse. Detraining in Boston, we transferred to a bus to Great Barrington, another two hours or so away. The bus deposited us in the downtown area, a tiny little business section that might easily have served as a Hollywood set. Seeing the waiting camp truck, we tossed our bags into the back and joined about a dozen other new arrivals, kids from Illinois, Texas, Georgia and Colorado. Our positive feelings were further reinforced by our first sight of the camp itself, formally called the UAHC Joseph Eisner Camp–Institute for Living Judaism.

The camp had once been an estate owned by an affluent family who spared no expense in developing the property. Formal gardens, statues, spectacular shrubbery and stately trees of every sort dotted the landscape. The centerpiece of the estate, a building known as the Manor House, served as a faculty dorm and dining hall, but had once housed a single family! We gasped when we saw its interior; the wood-paneled library and music room, countless bedrooms, exquisite in every way. Alas, this would not be the place where we would sleep! Instead, we were escorted to our quarters, boys on one side of the camp, girls on the other, with a bold white-painted line marking the division between the two sections, a barrier over which neither could cross after midnight on pain of some horrible fate, never articulated but always implied. The cabins reminded me of army or prison barracks I had seen in television or in films, but no one really cared that much. Eager to meet the other institute members, we dumped our clothes and hurried to orientation and the first meal.

My youth group advisor did not mislead me. After just one evening, it was evident that we were in the midst of an elite group. In retrospect, that Institute produced five Reform rabbis, countless congregational presidents and numerous Reform Jewish organizational leaders. The faculty, made up of some of the movement's finest rabbis, was headed by Rabbi Bob Schur from Fort Worth, Texas. He was a gentle man, a kind man, the sort of individual who brought honor to the title of Rabbi. Setting the tone for the Institute, he told us that the following twelve days would approximate a full year. Each day would consist of religious services, songs, programs and special events, a full month's program in 'real life,' which we could take home and use in our own youth groups.

I can't remember ever working harder than I did over the next week and a half, or enjoying it more. The days began at 6:00 A.M. and concluded after midnight. The intensity of the planning and execution of programs was such that a fierce competitiveness grew between the groups assigned to prepare presentations for separate days. We constantly struggled to do better than the day before, than the morning of the same day. Excellence was the aim, and those present had the creativity to attain it.

At this leadership institute, in contrast to MSTY events, we learned many Hebrew songs in addition to the folk melodies we sang in English at MSTY summer conclave. That was a departure, one I enjoyed very much, especially since these new melodies came out of Israel and were taught by people who had learned them there! I questioned those lucky enough to have visited Israel. They were celebrities of a sort within camp, and sat for hours with many of us whose closest contact with Israel had been buying trees to be planted there by the Jewish National Fund. And then there were the surprises, one of which I remember in particular.

Just prior to our leaving Detroit, banner headlines in the local press announced the conviction of Adolph Eichmann for "crimes against humanity." The question now arose as to the appropriate punishment for these crimes. Israel had, and still has, no death penalty. Therefore, the maximum potential sentence was life imprisonment. The prospect of this mass murderer being allowed to live set off waves of angry protests by many survivors of the Holocaust in Israel and throughout the world, counterbalanced by pleas for mercy and compassion by other survivors who felt that Jews had to be different, more compassionate. A similar debate raged within the institute.

One night, at 2:00 A.M., I was awakened from a dead sleep by one of the counselors, who asked me to follow him to the Manor House. I thought this was some sort of joke, but arrived to find a group of approximately a dozen fellow campers, grim-faced, sitting in the library. The leader of the discussion told us that we had been selected as a representative group of members of NFTY to take a position on behalf of the national youth movement with respect to an appropriate sentence for Eichmann. Rabbi Sam Cook, we were informed, was currently in England, and wished to issue a statement on behalf of American Reform Jewish youth. He had just cabled, the counselor advised us, and asked for a directive from a cross-section of the membership. We were to be that representative sample.

Deadly earnest about our responsibility, we debated far into the night, raising and dissecting issue after issue until almost 4:00 A.M. Finally we reached consensus on a statement advocating life imprisonment without possibility of parole. We took great pride in our decision and the maturity with which we reached it. We did not know at that time that the whole situation was manufactured. This was a socio-drama, a popular group dynamics device during the 1960s designed to teach through simulations, evoking creative thinking on difficult issues as if they were occurring at the time. The problem was that no one told us that we had anguished for hours over a nonexistent crisis. Only several months later did we learn that we had taken part in a socio-drama. To this day, many of those present still speak with bitterness about being "had," but there is no question but that we learned from the exercise.

As Institute moved toward its conclusion, the realization set in that we were about to leave a group of people about whom we cared deeply and whom we might never see again. Accordingly, the last seventy-two hours of Institute took on an intensity of emotion and spirit possible only among teenagers. The last night's program was a cabaret-style evening, with the camp barn transformed into a gorgeous night club, complete with posters of new and old feature films, blinking neon lights and an interior almost as glamorous as the old Copacabana. A talent show ensued, where Institute participants, many of them extraordinarily talented, sang and danced into the night. Finally, when sanity dictated that we must rest before our parents arrived, we gathered in a large friendship circle, each of us holding a lighted candle and expressing the feelings felt deep in our hearts. Many of us then walked arm-in-arm back to our cabins. Institute was over.

Those of us from MSTY boarded the bus the next morning for the ride back to Boston and then the train to Detroit. It seemed almost as though we had been part of a dream, so perfect, so special, so out of the ordinary. We all knew that Temple Youth Group, MSTY and NFTY would continue to be an important part of our lives. In the weeks that followed, prior to the beginning of school, I was gripped by a profound sadness, feeling the loss of the community in Great Barrington. Then one day the mail arrived with a letter from Rabbi Schur. He wanted me to know how much he enjoyed getting to know me at camp, and closed by expressing his hope that I would consider becoming a rabbi. There it was again, the destiny I was not yet ready to acknowledge. But I knew that I was proud to be a Reform Jew. NFTY had helped to make me so.

CHAPTER XV

The Detour

*T*he flyer on the Mumford student bulletin board read, "This week! Auditions for the Fall School Play. Pick up script from Drama Office." It was the first day of school, the first day of my junior year in the fall of 1961. After a restful, productive and exciting vacation, I was ready for a new challenge. The memory of the spring play of the past semester and the sense of excitement I felt in watching it led me directly to the drama office even before I had registered for class. A pleasant young woman greeted me, then explained the audition process.

This semester's play, entitled, *My Three Angels,* was a comedy about three convicts escaping from a prison island. If I wished to try out, she suggested that I read the script several times, then come to the school auditorium on Thursday afternoon at 3:00. I inquired as to whether or not those who had never been in a play before had any chance of being cast. She assured me that the director, Earl Matthews, was always on the lookout for new talent, whether or not the individual had any prior experience. I signed my name, took a script, stuffed it in my book bag, then went to get my class schedule.

Over the next few days, I reviewed the play. It was funny, and I envisioned myself in a number of roles. Telling no one of the auditions, not even my parents, I walked into the auditorium that Thursday, determined to give it a try. The auditions themselves were a fascinating exercise, and after almost three hours of readings, no one had the slightest idea as to whether or not he or she had made it. We were told that the cast list would be posted the following day, turned in our scripts and were excused with thanks.

That night, as I did my homework, I realized that I *wanted* to be in this play, more than I would ever have admitted to anyone. I hardly slept, and arrived at school a full half hour before my first class. I ran down the hall to the drama department bulletin board, and was overjoyed to see my name listed as one of the three leading characters in the play, one of the convicts! I went to the phone, called my parents and conveyed the news, totally forgetting that they had no idea of what I was talking about. They were thrilled.

For the next six years, theater was a major focus of my life. I loved the rehearsals, the agony of memorizing lines, the frustration of missed cues and scenes cut short by a change here, an alteration there. I relished the gradual evolution of a smooth production, the appearance of sets, the tailor-made costumes and finally the dress rehearsal itself. In the process, the members of the cast grew closer, despite petty squabbles. Mr. Matthews, always the perfectionist, prodded us along, tolerating almost anything short of lack of preparation and concentration. Then came the final dress rehearsal, the final set of notes on our performance, and final instructions for the play's opening.

The night before *My Three Angels* debuted at Mumford, I didn't sleep a wink. I had memorized not only my part, but the entire play, and recited it to myself, word by word, far into the night. I left school early that day, took a nap, then arrived at the auditorium fully two hours before curtain time. The cast arrived, the makeup people went to work and we donned our costumes. This was the real thing. The auditorium filled with fellow students and parents, the curtain opened and the play began. The energy of that interaction between actor and audience was almost magical. I felt my heart pounding as I made my first entrance, but the initial nervousness disappeared as the flow of the production began. The lines and blocking flowed effortlessly. Then came my best moment in the play, a scene in which I moved center stage to deliver three successive humorous lines, each one of which, Mr. Matthews assured me, would be greeted with laughter. I was to deliver the first line, wait for the laugh, deliver the second line with greater intensity, wait for the laugh, then deliver the third line and stand motionless.

My director was right. The laughter built and built until the third line, which was followed by an enormous outburst of both laughter and sustained applause. I stood motionless, the waves of applause washing over me, feeling an indescribable euphoria. I was hooked on theatre!

The next day, I entered my first class to the applause of my classmates. Suddenly, everybody at Mumford High School knew my name. They congratulated me in the halls, teachers as well as students. Overnight, I became a personality in my high school's culture. At last I had found my niche.

The next semester's play was Arthur Miller's *All My Sons,* the story of Joe Keller, a World War II manufacturer who cuts corners in the production of airplane engines. Keller blames his partner when the engines prove defective and result in the deaths of many pilots, remains silent as his partner goes to jail, then becomes rich while the innocent partner languishes in prison. Ultimately, it is revealed that Keller's own son, Larry, committed suicide by crashing his own plane after learning that his father bore responsibility for the deaths of his fellow pilots. My role in this powerful drama was that of the surviving son, Chris Keller. Near the end of the play, Chris discovers the terrible truth about his father, beats him in uncontrolled fury, then finds his father's body after he commits suicide in shame and remorse. After this second play, I privately began to reassess my career plans. Perhaps I would go into theatre and give up the idea of becoming a rabbi. In less than nine months my involvement in dramatics had given me new self-confidence and an activity in addition to youth group, to which I was still attached with a passion.

By junior year, I had been elected vice-president of Temple Israel Youth Group. That spring, I also became the vice-president of MSTY, and went to summer conclave as a regional officer. Between theatre and youth group, the pieces of my life came together, and as my senior year began in September of 1962, I believed that I had come into my own. As one of the officers of MSTY, the other officers and I traveled the length and breadth of the region on what we called 'caravans.' We drove from city to city, visiting each youth group in turn, celebrities in our own way, with the added bonus of being excused from Sunday school!

At Mumford, I had the lead in both of the year's plays, played a part on a local television series and took first place in a citywide acting competition. I was accepted into the University of Michigan, and chosen as one of the two Mumford graduation speakers.

Finally, I entered a speech contest sponsored by Detroit's Jewish Community Center. The contest had as its first prize a summer in Israel as a U.S. representative at a World Jewish Youth Conference in Jerusalem. In 1963, virtually no one I knew, save for a few teens at Great Barrington, had ever been to Israel. My father urged me to enter to see how I would do. Out of several hundred preliminary participants, I was selected as one of eight finalists. Three nights later, I sat before a panel of judges for a personal interview, and two weeks later received word that I had won!

At high school graduation, I stood before my classmates and spoke about civil rights. Starting with Robert Frost's poem, "Mending Wall," I presented a message of hope in the future, a dream of one American people blind to color, rejecting bigotry, united in common purpose. As I left Mumford as a graduate on that June day of 1963, I did so with a sense of closure and anticipation. Israel lay ahead, and then the great new horizon of college. But at least now I knew where I was going. I told my father that my future lay in show business, not in the rabbinate. He said very little, simply urging me to take my time in deciding what to do with my life. But there was no doubt, in the summer of 1963, that I was headed for Broadway, or perhaps Hollywood. Little did I know that this was to be just a detour.

CHAPTER XVI

Israel—1963

*A*s the date for departure to Israel drew near, I considered just how fortunate I had been. Out of hundreds of contestants in the speech contest, I had emerged as the winner. Only a number of years later did I discover the reason why.

During the final interviews, each of the eight finalists faced a committee, drawn from every religious stream in the Detroit Jewish community, whose task was to ascertain which of us would best represent American Jewry. As my interview drew to a close, one of the judges, an Orthodox rabbi who knew I was Reform, asked me a loaded question: "If you fell in love with a non-Jewish girl, would you marry her?" Attempting to buy a little time to compose my thoughts, I began my response with the words "Well, Rabbi, love does many strange things!" Before I could utter another word, the judges began laughing, complimented me on the diplomacy and tact they assumed I had shown, then moved on to the next question. The Orthodox rabbi later told my father that my response to that question guaranteed me his vote, in spite of the fact that I was the son of a Reform rabbi. On such strange twists does the course of our lives depend, for despite my personal fantasy of a career in the theatre, that journey to Israel during the summer of 1963 moved me a step closer to a deeper commitment to Reform and the rabbinate.

Four of us from Detroit traveled to Israel on the trip, which was sponsored by the National Federation of Temple Youth. I would leave the group for the conference later in the tour, but for some eight weeks, forty high school students from Reform congregations around the country toured Eretz Yisrael together, student pioneers, some of the first teenagers to visit Israel in those days.

My friends and I had never been to New York City before, and certainly none of us was prepared for the enormity of what was then Idlewild—now Kennedy—Airport. There we met our group leaders, a young rabbi, Leon Jick, and an HUC-JIR rabbinic student, William Cutter. Jick later became a distinguished professor at Brandeis University, Cutter the founder of HUC-JIR's School of Education in Los Angeles and a professor of modern Hebrew literature. That summer, however, they were our friends and our leaders. We could have done no better.

The flight, over twelve hours on El Al, was a genuine party. We sang songs, got to know each other and slept very little, the excitement building as the airplane brought us closer and closer to Lod Airport near Tel Aviv. At last, the 'Fasten Seat Belt' sign came on for the descent. I remember vividly everyone singing "Hatikvah," the Israeli national anthem, as we made our final approach. This was it, the place we had heard of for so long, the homeland for all Jews, the place where the passengers of the *Exodus* had so desperately sought a haven. Now we were here. The wheels touched down, and we erupted in cheers. Some of the older people aboard wept openly. Today, many Jews have been to Israel numerous times. But this was 1963 and a first visit for each and every one of us.

We gathered our belongings and moved toward the plane's open door. There it was. Israel! Just an airport for now, but Israel nonetheless. The July heat beat down mercilessly upon us, but no one cared. We were here. After clearing customs, we boarded the waiting bus for the ride to Jerusalem. In 1963, there was no super-highway connecting Tel Aviv and Jerusalem. We traveled on a narrow road, the same road where combat claimed so many Jewish lives during the 1948 War of Independence. Along the way, our guide pointed out one memorial after another, sculptures, burnt-out trucks left as a permanent reminder of the sacrifice so many had made to assure Israel's existence in the face of all-out attacks by Arab legions. From time to time, we saw soldiers standing on the side of the road hitchhiking or 'tramping,' as it was called. Invariably, the bus stopped to pick them up. They were then the unquestioned heroes of the nation and accorded every honor. We applauded every time one of the soldiers joined us. Here were fellow Jews, teenagers like us, brothers and sisters to whom we were related in some mystical fashion.

As we approached Jerusalem, we passed that now-familiar floral greeting with Hebrew words translating into "Welcome to Jerusalem," then continued on down Jaffa Road, past the King David Hotel and the YMCA, then up a hill to a modest youth hostel called the Goldstein Youth Village, our home base. We settled into our cabins, gathered in the dining room for our first meal together with the Israeli residents of the village, then went to bed in preparation for the beginning of the greatest adventure of our young lives.

The next eight weeks brought one new experience after another. As a group of Reform Jewish youth, we traveled Israel's length and breadth within the limits of the pre–1967 borders. We explored the Galilee, went scuba-diving in Eilat, then a sort of frontier town. We surfed in the Mediterranean at places like Ashdod and Ashkelon, which our guides assured us would one day be bustling cities. We explored the Negev, climbed Masada before there was a cable car, swam in the Dead Sea, bathed in desert oases and worked for ten days picking fruit on a southern kibbutz. In the process we immersed ourselves in Jewish history, not through books but through real life, and uniquely as Reform Jews.

My kibbutz experience differed somewhat from that of my friends. At the time, I was six foot three inches and weighed 200 pounds. The kibbutzniks took one look at me and decided not to waste me on fruit-picking. They gave me 'the honor' of a work assignment alongside regular kibbutz members. My task was to move irrigation pipe, since Israel at the time had no underground sprinklers. Long sections of aluminum pipe were transferred from one field to another and water pumped through them to keep the fields from parching in the summer heat. Inasmuch as there is *no* rain in Israel during summer months—not a drop—this was a significant responsibility. Unfortunately, it was one full day before someone instructed me to tilt and empty the sections of aluminum before moving them! Without water inside, a child can lift them. Full, however, they are impossible for five people to budge, let alone carry. After this inauspicious start, I became quite proficient in my task, working alone in the fields from 4:00 A.M. until breakfast, and then for a few more hours before the midday heat.

Our group also visited Reform institutions in Israel. We spent a weekend at the Leo Baeck School in Haifa, under the tutelage of Rabbi Robert Samuels, who had come to Israel to build a dream. We held our own services each Shabbat. But there was one place to which we all looked forward to returning, and that was Jerusalem. Jerusalem embraced us with an emotional tug that few of us understood and none of us could fully articulate. We combed its environs block by block, gazing in sadness at the military installations manned by Jordanian soldiers that in 1963 prevented us from reaching the Old City and the Western Wall. Still, we could see the city at least, and dream of a day when we might be able to return to Israel and an open Jerusalem, and perhaps experience the thrill of standing at the Wall of which our grandparents prayed and dreamed.

The closest we came to the Old City was attending the dedication of the Jerusalem campus of the Hebrew Union College-Jewish Institute of Religion, the school for which Nelson Glueck fought for so long, the chapel for which he struggled so courageously. Our group was present on the day when it officially opened its doors, and we attended the historic ceremonies in its outdoor garden. One Israeli dignitary after another spoke, in spite of threats by the Orthodox to disrupt the proceedings. To my surprise, my parents arrived as part of a delegation of rabbis and their spouses who had journeyed to Israel to partake of this significant moment in Reform Jewish history. Near the end of the ceremony, Nelson Glueck rose and addressed us, his eyes flashing in the summer sun. Whenever I think of Nelson Glueck, I remember his eyes—piercing eyes, eyes that seemed as old as the Bible itself, eyes through which one could seemingly look back in time. In retrospect, I never saw him happier than he was on that day.

Because Temple Israel had made a significant financial contribution to the building of the school, I was invited to join my parents in a personal tour of the campus. At one point, Dr. Glueck asked me if I was going to be a rabbi, and, without waiting for an answer, urged me to do so. I had never met a rabbi without a congregation. Rabbi Glueck served the whole of the Reform movement and the Jewish people. He was so proud of his Reform Judaism and made all of us proud as well, speaking candidly but determinedly of the resistance that Reform Judaism would have to overcome in order to take its place in Israeli society.

After concluding my brief reunion with my parents in their hotel, where I took a hot bath and shower, my three Detroit friends and I walked up Jerusalem's Ben Yehudah Street, then turned off onto a smaller thoroughfare to have dinner at our favorite restaurant, Cafe Italiano. We had come across it during our first free afternoon in Jerusalem. It hardly seemed possible! Having eaten fruit soup, chicken and vegetables day after day, the thought of a good Italian meal delighted us. We walked in and were seated by the owner, a man named Mr. Levy, who asked for our order. I ordered spaghetti, but he indicated that was not available. My friend asked for lasagna. Again Mr. Levy shook his head. Finally, we asked what kind of Italian food was on the menu. He chuckled and told us that there was only one main dish: salami and eggs! Why, then, we asked, was the restaurant called Cafe Italiano? He smiled, then told us the story of his family, who had come to Israel from Italy. That was the origin of the name, but the cuisine consisted solely of salami and eggs.

We all had a good laugh, then dug in to this unexpected meal, still a welcome change from our usual fare. Over the ensuing weeks, Mr. Levy became our friend, advisor and confidante. We sometimes ate at his restaurant two or three times a day, always salami and eggs. He helped us to understand Israel through the eyes of an Israeli. One day, he took us out on Ben Yehudah Street and gestured expansively at all the teenage girls walking up and down the road. "Did it ever occur to you, my young friends, that all these girls are Jewish? If you lived here, you could go out with any one of them!" For the four of us, that was probably the first time that we understood in our terms what it meant to live in a totally Jewish state.

Everybody on the street was Jewish! It was an insight whose impact remains with me today more than twenty-five years later, even though Jerusalem is no longer 'all Jewish,' Cafe Italiano is now a felafel stand, and Mr. Levy is gone.

Two weeks before the end of the tour, I left the group in the Negev for the World Jewish Youth Conference in Jerusalem, where I and others represented the United States. Hundreds of teenagers from countries throughout the world came together in a United Nations-type setting, complete with earphones and simultaneous translation of all speeches. David Ben Gurion was the first keynote speaker, followed by Golda Meir, Moshe Dayan and many of Israel's leaders. Each in turn spoke of the importance of Israel as a homeland for every Jew, and of the centrality they attached to *aliyah*, Jewish immigration to Israel. They urged us to come. They urged us to convince our families to come. For several days, we listened to speeches, met in workshops, then retired to special housing reserved for delegates.

I became friends with a group of boys and girls from South America, Argentina, Australia, France and England—a microcosm of world Jewry. On the last night of the conference, our private 'United Nations' sat around a campfire, singing Hebrew songs, telling stories, vowing to see each other some time in the future in our own countries or back in Jerusalem. As the embers of the fire slowly died, all of us—Reform, Conservative and Orthodox Jews—promised one another that we would also work together to build the Jewish state regardless of our ideological differences and in spite of any barriers. For Israel's sake, for the sake of the Jewish people as a whole, we would not let walls of prejudice separate us. Sadly, the sincere commitments of our youth were not able to prevent the erection of those walls we sought to avoid. It was a promise we have yet to fulfill, but fulfill it we must, as a sacred responsibility.

On the day the conference concluded, the rest of the NFTY group returned to Jerusalem from the kibbutz for the last leg of our tour. On our last night in Israel, we sat on a hillside of the youth village, gazing out at the fiery orange hills of Judea at sunset. There were skits and songs, speeches and prayers, then a night without sleep, a night of reminiscing, a night of holding on to an experience and feeling we knew could not be recaptured.

To this day, some of us who were on that trip remain in touch. A few live in Israel, most in the United States. For me, at least, that summer forged a bond between me and the Jewish state that never can be broken.

CHAPTER XVII

The University of Michigan—
Freshman Year

*A*nn Arbor, Michigan, is a small town. The University of Michigan is the city's largest employer, and has long been known as one of America's foremost academic institutions. When I entered the University of Michigan in fall of 1963, its campus activity reflected the turmoil of American society. Earlier that year, in Birmingham, Alabama, Sheriff Bull Connor turned tear gas and dogs against peaceful black demonstrators led by Martin Luther King, Jr. King went to jail, and the violence would have continued had not President John Kennedy dispatched three thousand federal troops to restore order.

During this time, King composed his famous "Letter from Birmingham Jail." Two hundred thousand men, women and children, including my father, descended upon Washington, D.C., in the great Freedom March of that year, when Dr. King delivered his famous "I Have a Dream" speech. In June of 1963, Governor George Wallace tried to prevent black students from registering at the University of Alabama by standing in the doorway of the university. Confronted by then-Deputy Attorney General Nicholas Katzenbach, Wallace withdrew and the students registered. That same month, President Kennedy appeared on national television and within days asked Congress to enact the broadest set of civil rights laws in United States history. Medgar Evers, a leader of the Mississippi NAACP, was shot in the back and killed. And days after registration, four black girls died in the brutal, cowardly bombing of one of Birmingham's black churches.

At the same time, the divisive nature of the 'police action' in Vietnam became increasingly apparent. Until then, the news coverage given that area of the world was so muted that the American public in general did not react to any significant degree. Many of those drafted into the armed forces and sent to Southeast Asia to fight Communism genuinely believed that they were going as advisors, not combatants. By fall of 1963, however, this assumption had been exposed as false. Though most of America's citizens still supported the United States presence in Vietnam, concern and protest were growing, particularly on college campuses, including the University of Michigan.

Even the popular melodies of the day reflected the transition going on in society. Rock and roll, with its simple, innocent lyrics of adolescent infatuation and romance, gave way to other forms of music, most notably in a revival of interest in folk music. Bob Dylan, Joan Baez and Peter, Paul and Mary leaped onto the pop charts with songs you couldn't dance to, political in nature, sharp in their message, anthems of justice and peace. Since music reflects society, just by turning on the radio, any sensitive listener could know that change was in the air.

Just such a sensitivity to that change permeated the deliberations of the Union of American Hebrew Congregations at its early November 1963 convention. The delegates endorsed one resolution on racial justice, a second urging a speed-up in the process of school desegregation in America. In addition, foreshadowing what would ultimately become an out-and-out condemnation of U.S. involvement in Vietnam, the convention delegates adopted a sweeping resolution on peace, calling for support of the United Nations, peace through negotiations and an implied withholding of the use of military force.

As I settled into my dorm room in South Quad, one of the dormitories near the center of campus in Ann Arbor, I looked forward to engaging these and other issues free of my parents' immediate influence. The initial strangeness of this totally new setting was eased by the presence of half a floor of Mumford High School classmates. The four of us who were active in MSTY went to the local Hillel House for the preschool mixer. Hillel, founded by B'nai B'rith as a system of Jewish centers on major campuses throughout the country, provided a place where Jewish students could congregate, hold religious services and obtain kosher food. At Michigan, a reception on the night before registration was intended both to help us establish a network of Jewish friends and build Hillel membership. On the way to the party, we were joined by other former youth groupers, and decided to suggest that Hillel create a sort of college extension of MSTY and NFTY.

That evening marked the end of my college student Jewish activity at Michigan. As we entered the Hillel office, one of the professionals greeted us, then asked us what we had in mind. I briefly outlined our notion, namely occasional Reform services at Hillel, possibly some activities in the realm of social justice, one or two social events, and publication of a roster of those who had been part of MSTY and other NFTY regions. We watched, expecting his immediate and enthusiastic support. Instead, he frowned, shook his head and declared that "This is not a place for Reform things. We don't do Reform here." Furious and disillusioned, we walked out of the office and out of the University of Michigan Hillel House, never to return. We got the message. As Reform Jews, we were welcome at Hillel only insofar as we were prepared to accommodate ourselves to the more traditional norms of the institution.

I wonder how many other hundreds or thousands of Reform Jewish college students dropped away from Jewish involvement as a result of similar experiences during that period. Hillel has changed its policies over the years and now actively recruits Reform rabbis as campus directors. Furthermore, discrimination against any segment of the Jewish student body today receives swift attention from national headquarters. But that's today. In 1963, a group of Reform Jews was turned away, no credit to Hillel, and a shame for us as well. Two days later, classes began.

Two other events during freshman year had an impact on my life, both as a U.S. citizen and as a Reform Jew.

The first episode took place during Homecoming Weekend, always a big party in Ann Arbor. The weekend festivities began with a Friday afternoon parade. Floats and bands moved past the student union, one more beautiful than the next. Then, even from a distance, a rumbling in the crowd could be heard, growing in intensity and anger as more and more of the thousands lining the route realized the theme of the parade's last, unauthorized entry. An anti-Vietnam campus political group had constructed a replica of a concentration camp. Inside the camp and surrounded by barbed wire were group members in prison garb, designated with signs as Vietnamese civilians. Outside the barbed wire stood other members, dressed as American soldiers. The crowd went wild and quickly became a mob. The protesters were pelted with rocks, their creation ripped apart, and a number beaten and left bleeding in the street. It was the first time I realized the depth of feeling aroused by the Vietnam War. Within a very few months, however, the prowar convictions that led to this horrifying violence would begin to shift dramatically.

Then there was November 22, 1963. As do all American citizens old enough to remember that day, I recall precisely what I was doing at the moment that President John Kennedy was assassinated in Dallas. It was a Friday afternoon, and a group of us sat playing cards in anticipation of a terrific weekend. Suddenly, a friend burst in to say that Kennedy had been shot. We berated him at first for indulging in such inappropriate humor. Seeing that he was serious, however, we raced to the student lounge and TV room. There we watched as Walter Cronkite followed the story, sharing the facts as they emerged. A co-worker handed him a bulletin. He looked directly into the camera and read it aloud. President John F. Kennedy was dead. Some students screamed, others cried. We watched a little while longer, then returned to our rooms.

Almost by instinct, those of us from Detroit packed our bags and called our parents, to say we would be home for the weekend. We wanted to go to the synagogue that night. On the bus ride from Ann Arbor to Detroit, no one spoke. Every person on that bus was lost in thought, mourning in some way.

That night, my father gave one of the finest sermons of his life. He reminded the congregation of the hope that John Kennedy had instilled in the American people. He taught them and me that the Reform movement in particular had a special relationship with Kennedy. He related how Dr. Nelson Glueck, president of the Hebrew Union College-Jewish Institute of Religion, delivered a prayer in Hebrew at Kennedy's inaugural, and how Rabbi Maurice Eisendrath, president of the Union of American Hebrew Congregations, presented a Torah to the Kennedy family not long before the tragedy at the dedication of the UAHC Religious Action Center in Washington. Then he spoke of John Kennedy's mother, Rose, and how she must have suffered at the news of a child's death, her second such loss. I listened to my father, marveling at his capacity to say exactly the right thing in such circumstances, to remember the human dimension of this tragedy, not just the political and histori- cal ramifications.

I looked around and suddenly became aware that the syna- gogue was filled as though it were Rosh Hashanah or Yom Kippur. The Jewish community had come to the synagogue to share its pain. I reminded myself on that evening never to forget that phenome- non. The fact is that Jews always gather in synagogues at such times, Jews always need to be with other Jews in this particular setting at such moments. The synagogue is the center of Jewish life. Every- thing else, all our Jewish institutions, all our Jewish clubs, all our Jewish societies, are by-products of the binding power of the temple to make Jews and forge them into a community. There was, I mused, a great deal to be said for organized religion. You could joke about it, but at times of crisis, you could always depend on it.

The service ended with the Kaddish, the prayer recited in memory of the dead, and the congregation filed out to hurry home for the late news. There was a new president of the United States, Lyndon B. Johnson. He was not cut out of the same cloth as Ken- nedy, but he was our president now, and all of America wished him well.

For many young Americans, the assassination of John Kennedy brought an age of innocence to a close. The following day, as Jack Ruby shot Lee Harvey Oswald, we were brutalized for the second time in seventy-two hours. Something was different, and not just in a cosmetic sense, not just in a political sense. Our whole world had changed, and we wondered what the ultimate consequences would be.

CHAPTER XVIII

1964–1966—The World Explodes and Reform Jews Respond

*I*continued my studies at Michigan, as well as my involvement in dramatics, still weighing a career in theatre. After a small part in Molière's *Thieves' Carnival*, I was cast in the starring role in a campus production of the Broadway musical *Fiorello*. Fiorello LaGuardia was a bit over five feet tall when he was mayor of New York, hence his nickname, 'the Little Flower.' At six-foot-four, I was arguably the tallest person ever to play the role, and received much playful ribbing from my friends.

Meanwhile, in the aftermath of the Kennedy assassination, campus life in general took on a more somber cast, with skepticism replacing hope as the primary motif of day-to-day life. The United States became a study in stark contrasts. On the one hand, the play *Fiddler on the Roof* warmed the hearts of men and women of every faith with respect to Jewish tradition. On the other hand, a little known figure by the name of Yasir Arafat became head of a new, radical Arab organization named Al Fatah, devoted to the destruction of the state of Israel and the modern expression of that self-same Jewish way of life. On the one hand, 1964 saw Martin Luther King, Jr. win the Nobel Peace Prize. On the other hand, racial violence continued to grow in cities of America such as St. Augustine, Florida, with intimations of more to come. In 1965, radical black leader Malcolm X was shot and killed by one of his own followers. The Watts neighborhood of Los Angeles erupted, with riots leaving 35 dead, 4,000 arrested, and $40 million in damage, this at the same time that King led a peaceful march from Selma to Montgomery, Alabama.

Protest against the Vietnam War continued to grow, as increasing numbers of Americans began to question the morality of the conflict. America was a nation divided against itself, with many adults screaming "America—love it or leave it!" and many youth yelling "Hell no, we won't go!" On the one hand, Congress passed, and President Lyndon B. Johnson signed, the 1964 Civil Rights Act banning racial discrimination in public accommodations, declaring new voting rights and specifying provisions against discrimination in employment and education. On the other hand, three civil rights workers, James Chaney, Michael Schwerner and Andrew Goodman were kidnapped and murdered in Philadelphia, Mississippi. The sheer weight of events and a sense of resignation about our ability to make an ultimate difference often led to a turning inward and a sense of hopelessness. The world was too much with us, and the question was how we as individuals could hope to have any impact.

It was just about this time in my life that I again began to hear the name of Albert Vorspan. Born in St. Paul, Minnesota, in 1924, Al Vorspan had attained the reputation of 'the conscience of the UAHC.' Coming from a vulnerable, precarious, lower-middle-class family, Al knew the meaning of financial hardship from the time he was a young boy. His father, a traveling salesman, could not pay the mortgage during the Depression, resulting in the repossession of their home. With the outbreak of World War II, Al rushed to enlist in the armed forces, and wound up in the U.S. Navy as a gunnery officer. He was at Iwo Jima, Okinawa and many other naval battles in the Pacific. He believed in the rightness of the war and the value of defending America, and his idol was Franklin Delano Roosevelt. Vorspan believed that even in the very worst of times, Roosevelt would pull the country through. This was typical of the Jewish community during the war, and when Roosevelt died on April 10, 1945, the Jewish community mourned his loss as if he had been a family member.

Once the war ended, with America the clear victor, Vorspan had to decide what to do with his life. His own leanings as a young man had been radical, socialist. His great passion, however, was Zionism. His two heroes were Theodore Herzl and Abraham Lin-

Isaac Mayer Wise

Rabbi Stephen S. Wise

Dr. Jacob Rader Marcus

Dr. Nelson Gleuck

Rabbi Maurice N. Eisendrath

Dr. Alfred Gottschalk

Rabbi Alexander M. Schindler

Albert Vorspan

Rabbi Solomon B. Freehof

Max Syme

Anna Syme

Edith Hendin

Abraham Hendin

Daniel Syme (left) and David Syme

Confirmation Class, 1960, Detroit Temple Israel.
Author is on far left, second row from top.

NFTY's 14th Annual National Leadership Institute, Great Barrington, Massachusetts, summer, 1961. *(courtesy Tassone Studio)*

Rabbi M. Robert Syme and son, Rabbi Daniel B. Syme, at the author's ordination, June, 1972. *(courtesy Jack Warner)*

Rabbi Sally Priesand, at her ordination as Judaism's first woman rabbi, June, 1972.

Author teaching at Kutz Camp-Institute, summer, 1973.

Rabbi Priesand, on the pulpit at Monmouth Reform Temple, Tinton Falls, New Jersey. *(courtesy Ken Kerbs)*

Rabbi M. Robert Syme (left) and Dr. Nelson Glueck. *(courtesy S. Lavie)*

From left, David Syme, Rabbi M. Robert Syme, Sonia Syme, the author, Joshua Syme, and Deborah Shayne Syme. *(courtesy Leo Knight)*

Deborah Shayne Syme and Daniel B. Syme.

Joshua Syme, age 9, and friend.

coln, with whom he shared a birthday. Up until the age of thirteen, he was certain that his destiny was to become a professional baseball player. But that year he received a bar mitzvah gift, a typewriter. His first sentence on the new machine read: "When I grow up, I want to serve the Jewish people." Deeply influenced by his brother Max, now a Conservative rabbi, Al organized a Zionist youth organization called the Young Judean Trail Blazers. Within one year after its formation, it became the most creative, dynamic Zionist youth organization in the country. The sixteen members, who were inseparable, had a great impact on other Zionist groups, especially since they came from one of the most anti-Semitic cities in the United States. They had two stated goals: securing a Jewish state and asserting a Jewish will for justice. The war intensified those feelings, embellished by Roosevelt's New Deal, and by the time Vorspan graduated from college, he was ready to launch the career in Jewish life he had envisioned as a teenager.

His first job was with the National Community Relations Advisory Council, which worked to combat anti-Semitism and to create interreligious harmony. His reputation as an organizer and orator attracted the attention of the leadership of the Union of American Hebrew Congregations and led to his appointment in 1953 as director of its Commission on Social Action. Al was unique at the Union, inasmuch as he was a layman on a staff consisting almost exclusively of rabbis. In some ways, that status was beneficial, since it gave him credibility with both the lay and rabbinic members of the movement.

Fired by his own passionate outrage against bigotry, and supported wholeheartedly by UAHC President Maurice Eisendrath, Vorspan plunged into the civil rights struggle. In Vorspan's mind, there were evils here so palpable that there was no way you couldn't feel them and call yourself alive. Something had to be done, and he was on the front line of that effort. The moral clarity of the issue demanded nothing less than total commitment. Vorspan crisscrossed the United States, spending much of his time in the deep South, calling the Jewish community to action on behalf of equality. In June of 1964, he joined a group of sixteen rabbis marching with Dr. Martin Luther King, Jr. in St. Augustine, Florida. Together with his colleagues, Al was arrested for sitting and eating with blacks in a segregated restaurant. They were jailed and subjected to cattle prods, simply for having lunch with people who were black. Ironically, the sheriff who put them in their cell was himself the head of the local chapter of the Ku Klux Klan!

While in jail, a member of the group, Rabbi Eugene Borowitz, then Director of the UHAC Department of Education, and now a professor at the Hebrew Union College-Jewish Institute of Religion in New York, penned a statement entitled "Why We Came," which Al Vorspan joined in signing. Published in Jewish newspapers all over the United States, it touched the very souls of Jewish students like myself, who at last felt a sense that some members of the Jewish community were taking action. The statement read in part:

> 'We went to St. Augustine in response to the appeal of Martin Luther King, addressed to the CCAR Conference, in which he asked us to join with him in a creative witness to our joint convictions of equality and racial justice.
>
> 'We came because we realized that injustice in St. Augustine, as anywhere else, diminishes the humanity of each of us. If St. Augustine is to be not only an ancient city but also a great-hearted city, it will not happen until the raw hate, the ignorant prejudices, the unrecognized fears which now grip so many of its citizens are exorcised from its soul. We came then, not as tourists, but as ones who, perhaps quixotically, thought we could add a bit to the healing process of America . . .
>
> 'We came because we could not stand silently by our brothers' blood. We had done that too many times before. We have been vocal in our exhortation of others but the idleness of our hands too often revealed an inner silence; silence at a time when silence has become the unburdened sin of our time . . .
>
> 'We came as Jews who remember the millions of faceless people who stood quietly, watching the smoke rise from Hitler's crematories. We came because we know that, second only to silence, the greatest danger to man is loss of faith in man's capacity to act . . .
>
> 'We do not underestimate what yet remains to be done, in the north as well as the south. In the battle against racism, we have participated here in only a skirmish. But the total effect of all such demonstrations has created a revolution; and the conscience of the nation has been aroused as never before. The Civil Rights Bill will

become law and much more progress will be attained because this national conscience has been touched in this and other places in the struggle . . .'

When my parents sent me the full text of the article, I read it several times. I was both moved at its message and exceptionally proud that it emerged from a group of Reform Jews: sixteen rabbis and a man named Albert Vorspan. Who was this man, I wondered, so fearless in the face of enormous power? I knew he had fought against the hysteria of the McCarthy era. I knew that he was one of the earliest Jewish critics of the war in Vietnam, speaking against American involvement there from the very beginning. Now I realized that Al Vorspan was willing to put his life on the line in behalf of his personal values. I had never met Al Vorspan, but I determined in 1964 that I would one day have an opportunity to tell him face-to-face how profoundly he had touched my life. Both he and the rabbis jailed in St. Augustine gave me a sense that individuals could still make a difference. Whether or not you were a rabbi, there was a job to be done, and no one was exempt.

By the fall of 1965, as I began my junior year of college, it seemed more and more likely to me that I would make my contribution on a lay level. But life is strange and often brings terrible surprises at the most unexpected moments. I was about to learn that lesson first-hand.

CHAPTER XIX

The Vow

I first felt the lump in my groin in January of 1966, while taking a shower in the fraternity house. I didn't think much of it at the time, since I assumed it was the result of a bruise from the regular hockey games we played on the homemade ice skating rink in our enormous backyard. Besides, there was far too much going on in the world at that time to permit even the thought of a dangerous medical situation.

Campus politics now centered increasingly on the Vietnam War, and the number and intensity of protest meetings and rallies grew from day to day. Time and time again, I heard the speeches of Al Vorspan in response to the war and took great interest in the clear and unequivocal stance adopted by the Union of American Hebrew Congregations calling upon the United States to declare a cease-fire, to negotiate directly with the enemy and bring an end to the conflict. No longer were the hawks in the majority. The country was divided now, and the Jewish community had begun to emerge from its cocoon to assess the war critically and carefully.

To be sure, many sincere individuals supported the war on the merits. Many in the Jewish community, however, were cowed into silence by an overt threat by Lyndon Johnson to cut off aid to Israel if American Jews opposed his policies in Vietnam. As a result, most Jewish organizations simply stayed away from the issue. Not the UAHC. The courage of Maurice Eisendrath and the unbending idealism of Al Vorspan stood as profiles in courage at a time when opposition to the war had many costs. The UAHC Religious Action

Center in Washington, directed by Rabbi Richard G. Hirsch, began to serve as a center for Jewish demonstrators during protests. Vorspan and another outspoken critic of the war, Rabbi Balfour Brickner, were tear-gassed at one demonstration, and the center at times became an infirmary, filled with people stretched out on cots receiving medical treatment. Eisendrath, Vorspan, Brickner and many other Americans, Jews and non-Jews alike, were vilified for their opposition, and a UAHC 1965 anti-Vietnam biennial resolution occasioned an avalanche of protest within the organization itself. One of the UAHC's largest constituent members, New York's Congregation Emanu-El, resigned from the UAHC as an expression of outrage against the UAHC's position. But Eisendrath and Vorspan held fast. One particular situation led them to an increasingly certain belief that the people themselves were far ahead of Jewish leadership in terms of understanding the war's essential immorality. One large temple on the East Coast, issued a board statement denouncing the Union. In response, the UAHC leadership challenged the temple board to poll the entire membership in a democratic process, even as the UAHC had taken its position to the full biennial plenary. The board of the temple agreed, the membership in its entirety voted and the result sustained the UAHC position by a ten-to-one margin.

As January and February of 1966 passed, the lump remained and my concern grew. In spite of countless hot baths with epsom salts, I could not wish it away. By the time mid-March arrived, I was in a state of terror, afraid to go to a doctor and just as afraid not to. Speaking to no one about my condition, I lay awake nights, fearing the worst and hoping for the best. I guess that this is typical of many individuals. Indeed, I have learned exactly that over time. An objective observer would say that my avoidance of the inevitable was foolish, even stupid, and in retrospect I would have to agree. But at the age of twenty, the fear of not acting had to reach a sufficient level of intensity before I could bring myself to move decisively.

On March 27, 1966, I could stand it no longer. As I sat in the university library, going through the mechanics of completing a homework assignment, I suddenly put down my pen, walked to the bank of telephones and called my parents' home in Detroit. My hands trembled as I dialed. My mother answered and I spilled out the details of the now all-consuming fear that gripped me. As always, my mother was very calm. She asked me detailed questions about my symptoms, drawing from her own medical background. Mom was unfailingly cool and collected in a crisis situation. From the time I was a little boy, I remember how her absolutely composed manner brought me a measure of calm when I was most frightened, whether it was rushing to the hospital after pouring an entire pot of scalding hot coffee over my hand, or racing to the doctor after falling through a glass window. When the crisis passed, Mom would react. But now her voice had no emotion; it was detached and professional. After listening carefully, she assured me that this was probably nothing, but that she would call the doctor at once for an appointment the following day in Detroit. She instructed me to go back to the fraternity house, pack my things and await her call.

Only in later years did my mother confide her own alarm during that telephone call. She knew at once that something terrible had occurred and how frightened I was. Without realizing it, I called her "Mommy," a total regression to early childhood born of my own hysteria. She swung into action immediately. By eight o'clock the next morning, I was on my way to Detroit. Ann Arbor is just forty-five minutes from the city, and my father picked me up for a two o'clock appointment with Dr. Raphael Altman, then one of Detroit's most prominent surgeons, a temple member and a close family friend. On the way to Dr. Altman's office, Dad tried to reassure me. He was really of little help, inasmuch as I was well aware of his total lack of medical expertise. Unlike my mother, Dad never asked doctors any questions. His feeling was that they knew what to do, and there was no point in having a procedure or a medication explained, since he wouldn't know what it meant in any case. He trusted doctors and he believed in God. That was sufficient for him.

We stopped at the house in Detroit, where Mom was waiting. In a sense, I was relieved to see that Dad leave for a series of appointments rather than coming to the doctor with me and Mom. I remember reflecting that it couldn't be that critical if my father felt free to complete his daily schedule. I never stopped to consider that Dr. Altman was one of the busiest surgeons in all of Detroit, and that if he was seeing me on less than twenty-four-hours' notice, he had to be concerned.

We arrived at his office, packed with patients waiting for their appointments, and were ushered directly into an examining room. Dr. Altman came in almost immediately to examine the lump. He was a remarkable man, a man who healed not only with his skill but with his very being, his manner, his words. Sizing up my mental state, he began a discussion of a variety of other matters even as he was proceeding with the probing and testing of the affected area. As the examination progressed, however, he became less talkative and more serious, then instructed me to get dressed and come into his office. As I took a seat next to my mother, he told us that he had ruled out the minor condition he had initially suspected, and wanted to get another opinion from a urologist, the best in Detroit, Dr. Sherwin Lutz. He called Dr. Lutz from another room, then returned and instructed us to go directly to New Grace Hospital a few miles away. I waited in vain for him to say that this was really nothing, that it would be fine. I understood that the stakes had been upped.

My mother did not speak on the way to the hospital. I, too, remained silent, trying to keep my emotions in check, successful outwardly, but failing miserably in my gut. We pulled into the parking lot of the hospital and walked into the emergency room, where a nurse was already waiting for us. We were told that Dr. Lutz would be with us in just a few minutes and sat down in a bare room with a wooden bench and a storage closet.

I cannot remember a moment in my life when I felt more alone. In spite of my mother's presence, I realized that I was facing a moment of truth, and I had a very bad sense of what the truth would entail. Mustering every bit of composure that I could out of concern for her, I awaited the doctor's arrival. The door opened, and Dr. Lutz appeared, followed closely by two student interns, I had never met Dr. Lutz, but was struck at once by his appearance. He was a tall, handsome man with cold, gray-blue eyes. He was obviously a no-nonsense doctor. I was going to get the news, good or bad, with no punches pulled.

Dr. Lutz apologized for the unavailability of a formal examining room, then ushered me into the storage closet to examine the lump with the aid of a flashlight. It was a horrible moment for me, a feeling of total helplessness and impotence, having such a critical diagnosis made in such a dirty environment, with the doctor and his two interns all gazing intently at this thing that had erupted on my body. The examination lasted only a minute or two, but seemed like an eternity. We emerged from the closet, and my mother moved to my side, whereupon Dr. Lutz gave it to me straight. There was no doubt in his mind. This was a tumor. He told me that I could return to school and finish the semester before having it removed but said "If you were my little guy, I would take it out tomorrow." To which I replied, "Let's do it, then." Dr. Lutz told my mother that he would call with details as to when we should be at the hospital, apologized for having to convey such difficult news at a first meeting, assured me that "Ninety percent of these sorts of tumors turn out to be benign," shook my hand and left.

In total shock now, overwhelmed by the rapid sequence of events of the previous twenty-four hours, I sat in the car, dazed and speechless during the ride home. Once we reached the house, however, I began to cry uncontrollably. The pent up fear of the preceding months came pouring out. In spite of Dr. Lutz's odds, I felt that I was going to die, and the intensity of emotions understandable in a twenty-year-old could no longer be stemmed. I went to my room and closed the door, then proceeded to call my girlfriend Martha in Ann Arbor to give her the story. I broke down again. In the interim, my mother called Dr. Altman on the other line, and he asked to speak to me. He was very tough, and told me in no uncertain terms that I was to keep calm for my parents' sake. It was great psychology. I quieted immediately. At eight o'clock that evening, the hospital called. I was to check in the following day.

March 29, 1966 was a blur of activity. What I do remember is that as we left for the hospital, the last thing I decided to bring with me was the Bible I received at confirmation. I wanted it there with me in the hospital, whatever lay ahead.

Once settled in my room, a constant procession of nurses came to draw blood and do other tests. Numerous interns took my medical history time and time again. I couldn't understand why I had to repeat this procedure until my mother explained that this was the way young doctors learned. I begged her to make them go away and leave me alone, and she promised to see what could be done. I didn't sleep that night. I shared a room with a friendly man who was going home in a day or two. He could sense my fear, and a member of his family loaned me a transistor radio so that I might listen to that evening's heavyweight bout between Muhammed Ali and some un-known opponent. Just before the fight began, a black man with a cart came into my room and introduced himself as Jake the Shaver. It was his job to prepare patients having surgery in the groin area by removing all hair to prevent any infection. I asked him to be very careful!

As he worked, we began to talk. He was the first person on the hospital staff who treated me as a human being rather than just an object of medical interest. We discussed the upcoming fight, his own family and world events in general. As he finished, he looked me straight in the eye, and offered me more comfort than had anyone thus far, albeit in a funny sort of way. He said: "Danny, I ain't no doctor, but I looked at your chart, and I want you to know that I've been in this hospital for a long time, and nobody died from what you have yet." Jake, in his simple manner, gave me what no one else had been able to provide as yet—a sense of hope.

My father arrived at the hospital early the next morning to bless me before the doctors took me up for the biopsy. The surgery was a relatively simple procedure, performed under a general anes-thetic. As my father intoned a Misheberach blessing with his hand on my head, I silently repeated over and over again the words of the Shema as an affirmation of my personal faith in God, alternating that with a 'replay' of Dr. Lutz's assurance that ninety percent of the tumors that I had turned out to be benign. My mother kissed me, told me not to worry, then stepped aside as an intern gave me a shot to sedate me. I stepped out of my bed onto a gurney and was wheeled off down the hall to an unknown future.

The events of the next forty-eight hours became known to me only years after they occurred. The biopsy was performed and a frozen section of the tumor sent to the lab. Dr. Altman examined the results. After stitching up the incision and moving me to the recovery room, he grimly shared the news with my parents. He chose his words carefully, avoiding explicit mention of cancer, but conveyed his message clearly nonetheless: "We think that the tumor is not benign. We won't know for sure until the lab report is in, but we have to prepare for major exploratory surgery."

My mother asked that I be heavily sedated so that I would not have to deal with the psychological trauma of my cancer until after the exploratory surgery. There would be plenty of time to explain later. Dr. Altman agreed. He promised to schedule the surgery as soon as possible, certainly no longer than two days thereafter.

Unbeknownst to me or my mother, Dr. Lutz asked to see my father privately. He bluntly told my father that I had a rare form of cancer, very fast-spreading, and that there was little chance that I would survive. He wanted him to know the whole truth so that Dad could prepare my mother. My father asked Lutz not to tell Mom yet. If he was right, there would be plenty of time to cry.

When I returned to the room after the biopsy, the doctors loaded me up with sedatives, and I drifted in and out of consciousness for forty-eight hours. I recall only snatches of reality, but somewhere along the line my mother told me explicitly that another surgery was imminent. She began to cry, but promised me that I would have the best treatment available, regardless of where in the world she had to take me. Though I could not react, I then realized the gravity of the situation. I had cancer. The only questions were what kind, and if it had spread beyond control.

My exploratory surgery was scheduled for April 1, 1966. As various interns prepared me for the grueling eight-hour ordeal, my father entered the room with a smile on his face. He proclaimed loudly "Danny, you're going to be fine. I got an answer to my prayer. You don't have to worry."

I looked at Dad and, drugged as I was, saw the same look on his face that I had witnessed in the emergency room the night doctors said my friend was about to die. My father had defied their diagnosis. I asked my father not to joke with me and insisted that he tell me if he was serious or just trying to make me feel better. He never hesitated, and repeated his assurance. He had prayed the whole night and at first thought that what he perceived as an answer to his prayer was merely wishful thinking. Now, however, he was certain. I was going to be okay. Though I appreciated the words of hope, I didn't believe him.

Again the nurses came to wheel me off down the hall to the

operating room. My father walked alongside the gurney with his right hand on my forehead, repeating the blessing over and over again until we reached the elevator. I saw tears in his eyes as the door closed between us. We reached the waiting room for surgical patients and Dr. Altman came out to see me and to tell me that he would be working with Dr. Lutz during the surgery. At that moment, I looked him directly in the eye and made a vow. "Dr. Altman," I said, "I want you to get me through this. If I survive, I am going to become a rabbi and dedicate the rest of my life to God." He smiled. I guess he was used to 'deals' of this kind on the part of his patients. He took my hand and simply said, "We'll do the best we possibly can."

The scheduled exploratory surgery normally lasted five hours. If the tumor had resulted in a metastasized cancer it would show up in the lymph nodes on one or both sides of the aorta. Therefore, the surgical procedure involved removing the nodes, two by two, beginning with those at the very top of the chest cavity. If frozen sections of these glands showed cancer cells, it would indicate that the cancer had spread beyond control and the doctors would simply sew me up and return me to the recovery room. If these were clean, they would proceed to the next set, and so on. In other words, the longer the surgery, the better the chances of treatment and survival. My parents, therefore, hoped that neither Dr. Altman nor Dr. Lutz would appear in the waiting room for a long period of time.

My parents looked at their watches and began the vigil. One hour passed, then two, then four. Finally, five and a half hours after the surgery had commenced, Dr. Altman appeared with a smile on his face to tell my parents that he and Dr. Lutz had found no evidence whatsoever of any metastasis. He confessed that he had expected to find something, then embraced my sobbing parents. In later years, I reflected upon the fact that the reversal of the initial prognosis came on April Fool's Day. Life has its little ironies.

I was returned to the room, still heavily sedated and in great pain. Through the haze of the anesthetic, I remember hearing my parents repeat over and over again the news that I was all right, that I would live, that everything was clean. Even then, I did not believe them. I did not believe anyone. In my own mind, I had determined the condition was terminal, hopeless. On the third day after surgery, following a visit from a well-meaning friend who melodramatically took my hand and assured me of a complete recovery, my extremely sensitive inner antennae set off an alarm and I started screaming that I was going to die. Dr. Altman, in the hospital visiting patients, strode into the room with a clipboard in his hand and smacked it down on my still raw incision, causing tremendous pain. Affecting a mood of anger, he stormed, "If you don't believe me, read this. This is the pathology report. Read it!" I could not even focus my eyes at that point, let alone read a medical report whose contents were as incomprehensible to me as a foreign language. I understood, however, that if he was showing me the report, he must be telling the truth. Perhaps I was going to live after all. Perhaps I would be okay. I lay back on the bed and drifted off again into a heavily sedated sleep.

That evening, Dr. Lutz came to visit me. Just the two of us were in the room at that time, and he uttered the words that irrevocably changed my life.

"Danny," he began, "you know that I have been absolutely honest with you from the beginning of this process. Now there is something I have to tell you. There is no medical explanation for this. I expected to find something and I did not. In my opinion, this was a miracle. You were saved for a reason, and you should become a rabbi. There are things that you have to do." Coming from this tough, hard-bitten doctor, the words had enormous impact. He put his hand on my shoulder. In halting, choked words of gratitude, I managed to articulate a thank you. He left, and my parents came in. I repeated my discussion with Dr. Lutz, then asked my father if he would make arrangements for me to attend classes at Hebrew Union College in Cincinnati that summer. Though it was only my junior year, I felt a need to begin at once. I had made a sacred promise, a vow. It could not be broken. Any thought of a career in show business disappeared from my mind. I now had a destiny to serve the Jewish people as a rabbi—a Reform rabbi.

CHAPTER XX

Summer 1966—A Visit
to Cincinnati

*F*or the sixteen days in the hospital following surgery, I fought to get back to complete health. With the doctor's promise that I was out of danger, and with the added reassurance of no follow-up radiation or chemotherapy, I devoted every ounce of energy to my recuperation. As news spread of the surgical results, there was an outburst of caring for our family that overwhelmed us. A constant stream of visitors arrived at the hospital, including rabbis from local congregations; family and friends; members of my college fraternity and classmates; even nuns from Marygrove College, who worked with my mother in her interfaith programs, and who led prayers for my recovery at a retreat attended by three hundred sisters. I received hundreds of letters, each one precious, each one a little prayer. I acknowledged each of them in time. They remain to this day in a suitcase in my parents' basement. Occasionally, I take them out and read them. Every time, I am just as moved.

The day I was released from the hospital, there was one person to whom I had to say a special goodbye, Margaret McKee, my Irish private nurse, my constant companion since the second surgery. Tough, feisty and encouraging, she more than any other person rallied my spirits and gave me back a sense of balance. As my parents and I bade her farewell, I wept in sadness and in gratitude for the great gift that she extended to me. The attending nurse eased me into a wheelchair for the ride to the elevator, but acceded to my request that we make one more stop. I wanted to say goodbye to a fellow patient, a girl my own age stricken with leukemia, who visited me every day of my convalescence, who painted little pill containers in beautiful colors and brought them to cheer me. I can no longer remember her name, but she, too, gave me a gift of hope. Three weeks later she died, a gentle soul who was not so lucky as I.

When we reached our house, I stepped out of the car into the bright sunshine of a gorgeous spring day. As I looked around, I truly saw many things for the first time in my life; the tree in front of my home, flowers in the garden, the blue sky. It's a shame we often must be touched by pain before we realize the many blessings we so often take for granted. I uttered a silent prayer of thanks to God for this third miracle in my life, and that night slept in my own bed, soundly for the first time in many weeks.

The balance of April, May and June were filled with activity. While I could not go out except for weekly visits to the doctor, I had to complete my college classwork. Fortunately, I hadn't missed too much, since the University of Michigan was on a trimester system and school had already adjourned for the summer. Each of my professors sent me material and promised to arrange for oral final examinations as soon as I returned to campus.

One evening, I received a call from the chairman of a committee charged with the selection of the head of Michigan's next Winter Weekend, an all-campus program celebrating the university's 150th anniversary. The committee wished to offer me the chairmanship but wanted to know if my health permitted me to head up the effort. I promised to call back, then walked into my parents' bedroom, posing a question that must have been exceedingly difficult for them to answer. Speaking softly but directly, I related the substance of the invitation and told Mom and Dad that I wanted to take this on only if I was really out of danger. There was a long silence; then my mother spoke. More than my father, she understood the nature of the cancer that had been excised from my body. Even the most sophisticated medical tests were no absolute guarantee against a recurrence. She was fully aware that at that time only twelve percent of patients with my form of malignancy survived a year beyond surgery, and that a recurrence within six months was highly probable. Moreover, she knew that the decision to forego radiation and chemotherapy was as much an effort to preserve the possibility of my fathering children as it was an expression of total confidence in my recovery. Still, with a smile on her face and no outward sign of ambivalence, she told me to do it. My father, of course, echoed her encouragement, but with no qualms whatsoever. He was absolutely certain I was fine, with or without any medical statistics to encumber his enthusiasm. I breathed a sigh of relief and, aware that I had just consciously tested my parents, called Ann Arbor to accept the chairmanship.

Four weeks later, my incision sufficiently healed to permit me to resume an almost normal schedule of activities, I returned to Ann Arbor to take my final exams. When I entered the hospital, my grades shaped up as two A's and two B's, and I was gearing up for an all-out push on the two weaker subjects to bring them up. It is interesting, however, to see what can happen if you are stricken with cancer. My professors, themselves unsure of my prognosis, gave me only the most perfunctory of tests, serving up questions that I probably could have answered without studying. When my transcript arrived, it contained all A's, their gift of kindness and concern.

In the meantime, my father made contact with the Hebrew Union College in Cincinnati and arranged for me to attend a summer program intended for entering first-year rabbinic students. The program, dubbed Towanda, was so named because it originally took place at a camp by that name in Pennsylvania. Now situated at HUC in Cincinnati, the intensive academic schedule was designed to bring entering students up to a level of proficiency in Bible, grammar and textual study sufficient to help assure success in the first year of the five-year rabbinic program. I received special dispensation to participate and set off for Cincinnati and a new world.

As the taxi sped along the expressway from the Cincinnati airport, which is actually in Kentucky, I tried to envision what this historic institution for rabbis might look like. In my mind's eye, I saw a sprawling campus, filled with students and faculty, certainly smaller than the University of Michigan, but imposing nonetheless. As the cab turned up Clifton Avenue, I looked to my left and was not disappointed, for there were large buildings, spacious grounds, everything I had expected. The driver, however, did not turn left, but rather right, into a small parking lot. Sure enough, the sign at the entrance read "Hebrew Union College-Jewish Institute of Religion," but the grounds were small and I could see only three buildings. Surely this could not be the famous institution that had trained so many of the great leaders of the American Jewish community.

I got out of the cab, retrieved my luggage from the trunk, paid the driver and entered what turned out to be the student dormitory. A gracious woman greeted me in the lobby, gave me a number of forms to sign and a key to my room for the summer. I was among the first arrivals, she indicated, but dinner began at six o'clock that evening, followed by orientation. I went to the room, unpacked my suitcase and, still certain that this small enclave could not be the entirety of the Hebrew Union College, set off to explore.

Sure enough, this was it. In addition to the dormitory, there was a classroom building, a gymnasium, a library and a building called the American Jewish Archives. I strolled through each of the buildings in turn, arriving at the archives last. There in the lobby, I encountered a gray-haired gentleman who introduced himself as Dr. Jacob Marcus. He asked me my name, and upon hearing my response said, "Oh, you are Monte's boy. I want you to come to my house for dinner this Friday night."

Suddenly I realized the significance of the man to whom I was speaking. This was *the* Dr. Jacob Rader Marcus, the founder of the American Jewish Archives, the closest friend of Dr. Nelson Glueck, the foremost historian of American Jewry. He knew my father, and now he was inviting me to have dinner at his home! Thus began a relationship that extended over the course of my rabbinic studies and beyond. Dr. Marcus became my mentor and friend and ultimately my thesis advisor as well.

I returned to the dormitory, which now bustled with activity as more and more students arrived. We introduced ourselves to one another, joined in a shared sense of anticipation and anxiety about what lay ahead. I felt a bit like an outsider, inasmuch as this was just an exploratory trip for me. These guys were here for the long haul.

That night at dinner, the dean of Towanda, Dr. Julius Kravetz, a professor at the New York campus of HUC-JIR, introduced himself and the faculty for the summer, then explained the procedures to be followed. We would be grouped into classes on six levels, based upon Hebrew competence, to be determined by oral interviews that evening. The following morning we would begin classes, three hours each day, six days a week, with examinations in each class on Friday and an assessment of our progress at the conclusion of each week. I was certain that given my background and experience at Temple Israel, I would be in the highest class. To my amazement, however, I wound up in the second *lowest* class. It was a humbling but truly educational experience. My classmates came from every possible background. Some possessed extensive Hebrew ability, having majored in Jewish studies in college. Others grew up in Orthodox or Conservative homes, and were educated in Jewish day schools. Therefore, even though I had gleaned a significant amount of practical rabbinic experience because of my father's instruction and my involvement in temple and youth group, I had nowhere near the Hebrew proficiency of most of the entering students.

This experience opened my eyes to the richness of Reform Judaism. Here was an institution that could welcome and accept a group of young men as potential rabbis whose personal religious practices and academic backgrounds were so varied. There were no value judgments made, only an injunction to study hard and succeed at the level of your particular class placement. HUC existed to make rabbis, not merely teach them. Those with a minimal Hebrew background would be prepared, those with a maximal level of ability challenged further. By the end of five years, the college aimed at producing rabbis well-equipped to serve Reform congregations across North America and throughout the world.

Towanda was not all academics. We found time to socialize, to get to know one another well, to go out and explore Cincinnati and the surrounding area. A sense of camaraderie grew, along with bonds of friendship that exist between many of us to this day. We helped each other with our homework. We quizzed each other in preparation for exams. We rooted for each other when we were low, and celebrated each others' birthdays and anniversaries.

Then, on one Shabbat morning, we had a surprise visitor. By the fifth week of the program, we knew one another well enough to engage in harmless practical jokes. Very few of the faculty members were on campus, and therefore we were a closed community, with no outside observers. That gave us a great deal of latitude in terms of our behavior outside of class hours. As part of our summer experience, each of us led services from time to time, read from the Torah or lead the blessing after the evening dinner meal. Dr. Kravetz spared no one from detailed criticism of any errors, but most of us dealt with this pressure in a balanced manner. One of our classmates, however, was extremely nervous about leading services. His academic performance had been less than glittering thus far, and he knew that there was always a possibility that the decision to admit him to the college could be reversed. He therefore spent an inordinate amount of time in preparation. We knew that he was in no serious trouble, and therefore decided to prepare a surprise for him.

Hanging in the lounge of the HUC-JIR student dorm was and is a picture of the wife of Isaac Mayer Wise, founder of the Hebrew Union College. On the Friday night before our classmate was to conduct services, a group of us hit upon an idea that we thought would be a hilarious prank. We went to work early Saturday morning, carefully removed the portrait from the wall, and inserted it inside the ark, the repository of the Torah to be read by our classmate in a few hours' time. Dr. Kravetz was out of town for the weekend, so we knew that only students and perhaps a few upper classmen would be present. The idea was that when our nervous friend opened the ark to remove the Torah, he would look directly into the face of Mrs. Wise. This, we knew, would shock him beyond belief. We arrived at chapel in anxious anticipation and awaited the beginning of services.

Our smug attitude was violently shattered by a fellow student racing into the chapel to inform us that Dr. Nelson Glueck, president of the Hebrew Union College, had just arrived from Israel, would be joining us for services, and was just emerging from his car in the parking lot. Those of us who planned the joke suddenly saw our entire careers passing before our eyes. We had to get that portrait out of the ark before services began! A group of us ran down the aisle up to the ark past our astonished classmate, who was about to begin the service by announcing the opening hymn. With five of us forming a human shield, a sixth opened the ark, removed the painting and disappeared quickly down the stairs into a storage room just behind the pulpit. At that exact moment, Dr. Glueck entered the chapel. As calmly as possible, those of us still on the bimah descended the stairs and returned to our seats in ceremonial fashion. Dr. Glueck said nothing, but looked at us quizzically before assuming his seat. The service began and went on as scheduled. Our careers were saved, and to this day, our intended victim has no idea of what transpired during that ninety-second period.

After services, Dr. Glueck welcomed us formally to the Hebrew Union College. There was something about the man that commanded respect. Though I had met him in Israel three years earlier, I looked at him through new eyes in this setting. He spoke of the tremendous challenge and opportunity now open to us. He spoke of the need for more rabbis in the Reform movement. He emphasized the impact that we would have on the growth and vitality of American Judaism. He urged us to study, to learn, to prepare ourselves for the great tasks that lay ahead. We all left the chapel on that morning imbued with a sense of importance, a sense that we somehow would make a difference in the world.

During the final weeks of Towanda, I felt totally at home at HUC-JIR. As the summer ended, I joined Dr. Marcus for dinner one last time, said goodbye to my classmates who were already preparing for the fall semester, thanked Dr. Kravetz and my teachers and returned home to begin my senior year at Michigan. There was now no doubt in my mind that the Reform rabbinate was where I would make my contribution to Jewish life. I only wondered if I could be as effective a congregational rabbi as my father. Perhaps something other than a congregational setting would be best for me, but that was a decision that could wait at least five years.

When I related my experiences to my parents after returning home, my mother was pleased, my father ecstatic. I realized then just how much my decision to become a rabbi meant to him. Still, he took me aside one day and assured me that I was not to feel obligated to become a rabbi just because I had made a promise in an extreme situation. If ever I had doubts, if ever I felt this was not the way for me, he would release me from the vow that I had made to God. I was grateful for that, and will never forget the integrity of that statement. As anxious as my father clearly was for me to follow in his footsteps, he wanted the decision to be mine and mine alone.

The summer of 1966 drew to a close. It was a fateful year in my life, the year of my vow.

CHAPTER XXI

Senior Year—Two Tastes
of the Rabbinate

*A*s I began my senior year in Ann Arbor, the battle for civil rights and against the Vietnam War intensified. James Meredith had been shot, violence had broken out in Chicago, a new face on the civil rights scene, Stokely Carmichael, had coined the phrase "Black Power," and Martin Luther King, Jr. had been stoned by whites as he led a march through Chicago's Southwest side. By October, Huey Newton and Bobby Seale would establish the Black Panther Party. Clearly, we faced turbulent times ahead.

Regarding Vietnam, a sizable majority on campus opposed the war ever more emphatically and passionately. Students in Ann Arbor began to flee to Canada rather than be drafted into the armed forces. As the casualty toll mounted and Lyndon Johnson continued to defend the war in words that sounded increasingly hollow, the American public as a whole took heed of student concerns and began to embrace them as their own.

In the midst of this turmoil, members of Michigan's class of 1967 tried to sort out their personal futures. While my classmates studied for placement exams and applied to law schools or medical schools, I already knew where I would be. I could hardly wait to return to Cincinnati.

My fraternity brothers were wonderful that senior year. Cognizant of my anxiety following my surgery, they provided a true support group for which I will always be grateful. Once they had satisfied themselves that the prognosis was excellent, and that I was not really in danger of dying, they even engaged in merciless kidding to help me lighten up a bit.

My girlfriend Martha Schlesinger and I decided to get married the following September. We had grown up together at Temple Israel, shared many MSTY events and dated for four years. We were young and in love, and had shared a trauma that tested both of us in the crucible of crisis. Our logic was irrefutable, at least in theory. What challenge could life hold that we could not surmount? We set the date.

Early in the fall, I received an invitation from a newly formed temple in Ann Arbor to teach in the religious school and to serve as the "rabbi." Members of the congregation learned of my presence on campus and decided to approach me. I was delighted. Though the congregation had no building as yet, its temporary home was conveniently located only a few blocks from my fraternity house. Furthermore, now that I had decided to enter the rabbinate, this would be one way in which to launch my career. The members could not have been more gracious, and some of them remain friends to this day. They showed enormous understanding, tolerating my occasional disheveled appearance on Sunday morning at religious school after a late-night party, or one Friday night when I read the Torah on crutches, having broken my leg in an intramural football game that afternoon. In retrospect, that year's experience served to confirm my resolve and conviction that I could be an effective rabbi.

The new year dawned, and I expressed a prayer of thanks to God that I was still alive. More than six months had passed since my surgery, and my doctors began to relax. But as I became less preoccupied with myself, the world came rushing in with a vengeance. I saw hate breeding hate, as George Lincoln Rockwell, the head of the American Nazi Party, was shot by one of his own members in Arlington, Virginia. Then came the spring mobilization to end the Vietnam War, when fifty thousand people marched on Washington, D.C. In Ann Arbor, following a similar event at the University of California at Berkeley, thousands of students gathered for a Vietnam War 'teach-in' designed to inform students of the atrocities currently taking place in Southeast Asia. Then, amazingly, the university announced that President Johnson would be our graduation speaker. A new wave of protests began, culminating in a partial boycott of the April graduation. It was a bittersweet way to conclude college, but soon I would be back in Cincinnati again for another summer of Towanda, this time for real, followed by my wedding and then five years of preparation for the rabbinate.

I remained in Ann Arbor for two months following the conclusion of classes, working to save extra money for the summer. Then, just before my departure, on the morning of June 5, 1967, I was awakened at the fraternity house by a call from my father. Excitedly, he instructed me to turn on the television. War had broken out in the Middle East, and Israel had invaded Egypt. The Six-Day War had begun, with Israel launching a preemptive strike against Arab forces that were themselves poised for an invasion. For six days and nights, I remained glued to the television screen as little Israel, outnumbered by a substantial margin, knocked out the Egyptian air force, liberated East Jerusalem, reclaimed the Western Wall of the Temple and established more secure borders. Egyptian President Nasser offered to resign, but massive demonstrations encouraged him to remain in office. General Moshe Dayan became a household name overnight, and America proved again that it loves a winner. Every magazine, every newspaper, every television broadcast, hailed the victory. It was suddenly 'in' to be Jewish. Jews everywhere in America and throughout the world walked a bit taller as a result of the Six-Day War, and never more so than when Israel returned 4,500 Arab prisoners of war in exchange for 9 Israelis. A few days later, I left Ann Arbor as a student for the last time, even prouder to be a Jew and an aspiring rabbi.

The summer in Cincinnati passed quickly. This time I was placed in the highest class of the Towanda program. The studies were a breeze, and I spent a great deal of time with Dr. Marcus. On July 23, however, my calm summer was shattered by the news that rioting by blacks had broken out in Detroit. I hurried to a friend's room to watch the seven o'clock news as a cold shiver of fear ran up and down my spine. There on the screen before me was a picture of tanks rolling down Livernois Avenue in Detroit, just three blocks from my parents' home. The entire neighborhood was aflame, devastation everywhere, and part of my childhood lay in ruins, destroyed by Molotov cocktails, bricks and guns.

I tried to reach my parents, but there was no answer. I waited five minutes and tried again, but still no answer. In that searing moment, I felt the ugly impulse of racism and hate swell up inside me as terror gripped me for the safety of my family. A few hours later, I learned that my parents and brothers had gone to a friend's home in the Detroit suburbs and were safe. Relieved but still shaking, I went back to my dorm room. How ironic, I thought. Here it was, less than six weeks after Thurgood Marshall became the first black United States Supreme Court Justice, and yet Detroit was in flames. Over the next week, forty-three people died in my neighborhood and surrounding areas. Similar violence occurred in Newark, New Jersey, and Cambridge, Maryland, all part of the 'Long, Hot Summer' of 1967, which led many Jews—including many Reform Jews who had fought fiercely for civil rights—and those of other faiths as well to withdraw from the civil rights arena. Disillusionment and a sense of betrayal are never conducive to full-hearted involvement in any cause.

A few weeks later, Towanda ended. Martha and I had rented an apartment in Cincinnati, and we looked forward to our wedding. Returning home to Detroit, we attended my brother David's Detroit Symphony Orchestra debut. In four short years, he had been transformed from a dabbler on the piano to an accomplished concert artist, receiving rave reviews from the Detroit press. Just a few weeks later, my father officiated at our wedding, and after a brief honeymoon, Martha and I set off for Cincinnati.

Once classes began in the fall, I understood more fully the enormous spectrum of observance, theology and Hebrew competence of the HUC-JIR student body and faculty. Every conceivable shade of Jewish orientation lived side by side on campus, reflecting the tremendous security inherent in Reform Judaism. My classmates and I often discussed the strength that a movement had to have not only to tolerate, but to encourage such diversity. We studied with professors some from Orthodox backgrounds who had come out of Eastern Europe after the Holocaust. Others, like Dr. Marcus, were native-born Americans, who themselves had been ordained at the college. The academic schedule was brutal at times, demanding hour upon hour of homework, papers and exams. Particularly in that first year, the curriculum weeded out those who would not be able to succeed in the full five-year program. You had to have a great deal of commitment to become a rabbi. The required studies tested that commitment every day.

Nor were our responsibilities confined to class hours. Students also served smaller congregations of the Reform movement on a monthly or biweekly basis, providing rabbinic leadership for many communities throughout the country who could not afford a full-time rabbi. Because placement was based upon seniority, first-year students were rarely called upon for these congregations. Martha and I therefore planned to return to Detroit for the holidays to be with our families at Temple Israel. In early September, however, I received a call from my father, asking if I would be interested in filling in for a rabbi in Detroit who was ill and could not lead services at a large congregation called the Downtown Synagogue.

The Downtown Synagogue was the unique creation of businessmen working in the inner city. A small group created this tiny temple so that those who wished to attend a daily service might do so without traveling all the way back to the Jewish suburbs of Detroit, many miles away. During Rosh Hashanah and Yom Kippur, this same group of businessmen determined to provide a setting where any Jew with no place to go for the holidays might find a home, regardless of whether or not he or she could afford membership. The service, a modified Conservative liturgy, was accessible to the largest number, and therefore the mode for the group. The temple rented a large hall next to Ford Auditorium in what is now Detroit's Renaissance Center. My father explained that there would be some two thousand people in attendance, and the board had voted to invite me to be their rabbi. Though I expressed great concern about my capacity to meet the group's expectations, particularly in terms of sermons, my father urged me to seize this opportunity and I finally assented.

Over the next three weeks, I worked day and night on my five required sermons. Dad assisted me, and by the time Rosh Hashanah arrived, I was fairly well prepared. Nothing, however, could have enabled me to gauge the extent of my initial anxiety as I looked out at the sea of men and women on the first night of the Jewish New Year. This congregation had more members than Temple Israel! I plunged ahead, grateful that the Conservative service depends much more heavily on the cantor than the rabbi, and by sermon time I had achieved a modicum of calm.

The congregation was most kind, obviously rooting for me, and greeted my talk with praise. From that point on, I simply enjoyed the experience. It was almost as if I had been cast in another play, except now I had to write my own lines and move the audience with no direction. Before Yom Kippur, a columnist from the Detroit *News* heard about my presence at the Downtown Synagogue and wrote a feature story about this 'open' congregation and its philosophy. The result was a standing-room-only crowd for the Day of Atonement. It was an incredible thrill. As the shofar sounded to announce the end of the holiday season, my eyes filled with tears of gratitude. Whatever life held, I had this moment to remember. I had led a real congregation and been welcomed as their rabbi. I moved them with my words and with my presence. Above all, in spite of the Conservative nature of the service itself, I brought them a message of Reform Judaism and its values, which they embraced as their own.

In November of 1967, the Union of American Hebrew Congregations held its biennial convention in Montreal, Canada. The plenum adopted many resolutions, one of which endorsed selective conscientious objection to the military draft as a valid option in the context of the Vietnam conflict. Nowhere was the Reform movement's position on this issue followed with greater interest than on the Cincinnati campus of the Hebrew Union College. A fellow rabbinic student decided that, for reasons of personal conscience, he would return his Selective Service card to his draft board. This was not an uncommon form of protest against the war in Vietnam, but no HUC-JIR student had ever done it. The student asked for and received permission to make the announcement of his intentions from the pulpit of the college chapel, immediately following daily services. In the crowded chapel he read an eloquent statement, expressing his opposition to the war. Dr. Nelson Glueck then stepped to the bimah to respond. Most of us were surprised. He had addressed us in the past on the plight of Soviet Jewry and on matters concerning Israel, but few of us anticipated that he would comment publicly on a purely political issue. It was not his style. He generally left political statements to the UAHC biennial and concentrated on running the college.

Dr. Glueck began by complimenting the student on his courage. Then, asserting the intellectual and spiritual freedom of the school and of Reform Judaism in general, he went on to declare that neither he nor the faculty would attempt to dissuade him. Though Dr. Glueck expressed his doubts about the efficacy of the act, he pledged that the college would defend the right of any student to follow the dictates of his conscience. He affirmed that ordination would be contingent only upon the successful completion of academic requirements, then closed with these words, "I praise and bless you for the spirit that has animated this gesture."

He sat down. The chapel was absolutely still. We had been present at the clearest possible affirmation of Reform Judaism's devotion to freedom of conscience. I wondered at the time if such a statement could have been made from the pulpit of other rabbinic institutions of North America. It did not matter. For me, Glueck's words enhanced my pride and belief in the Reform movement.

Later that same year, Dr. Glueck moved forward with proposals for a compulsory first year in Israel for all entering rabbinic students. In place of the Towanda program, the entire entering class would spend the first of its five years studying Hebrew and texts in Jerusalem at the new campus. In the light of Israel's victory in the Six-Day War, Glueck's timing could not have been better. While no final decision was taken, it was now clear that the act was simply a matter of time.

In spring of 1968, Nelson Glueck was called upon to respond to another political act of protest against the Vietnam War. A student scheduled an open public event protesting the war in Vietnam on college grounds and invited outside speakers known for their radical views. When Dr. Glueck heard of the plan, he summoned the student involved and instructed him to cancel the event. When the student refused, Glueck threatened to expel him. The student body, up in arms, met with Glueck, who made his position clear. He maintained that the students could say whatever they wished on college property, but only for the student body and faculty. Inviting outsiders made it appear as if the college-institute itself was a sponsor, and that he would not permit. The tension eased when it was agreed that the speakers appear only before the college family. Once again, we witnessed the freedom of Reform, this time in the context of responsibility to the larger community.

The balance of 1968 was a nightmare for America. On April 4, Dr. Martin Luther King, Jr. was shot and killed on the balcony of a motel in Memphis, Tennessee. In a classic instance of too little, too late, Congress passed the 1968 Civil Rights Act barring racial discrimination in housing, precisely one week after Dr. King's murder. A Poor People's March on Washington began shortly thereafter, culminating in a solidarity rally by fifty thousand men, women and children. America had lost one of its greatest voices for sanity and decency. The UAHC planned to organize in support of the Poor People's campaign. Instead, it joined in expressing condolences to Coretta Scott King and Dr. King's children.

As if this were not enough, America received another blow in June, when Robert Kennedy was struck down by an assassin's bullet in Los Angeles. Americans wondered what would happen next.

CHAPTER XXII

Winds of Change Touch
Reform Judaism and Me

*D*uring the fall of 1968, the seeds of protest against the war in Vietnam and racial violence yielded bitter fruit. During the summer, the Democratic Convention in Chicago was marred by what many called a police riot. Thousands of students and adults were gassed and beaten by Chicago police as they demonstrated, calling for an end to the conflict. Hubert Humphrey, one of the most decent and noble politicians America has ever produced, secured the presidential nomination in the aftermath of Lyndon Johnson's decision not to seek another term, and the Chicago Eight, an unlikely group of protesters including Abbie Hoffman, Bobby Seale and Jerry Rubin, were arrested and charged with conspiracy. Later in the summer, former Vice-President Richard Nixon, once thought politically moribund, rose phoenixlike to grab the Republican presidential standard, with a promise to end the war in Vietnam and a call to action to those whom he dubbed "the silent majority." The bitter, vicious campaign stretched into September and October, culminating in a landslide Nixon victory.

The general societal motif of significant change was mirrored in many developments within the Reform Jewish community as well, albeit in a much gentler and constructive direction. Our HUC class, for example, slowly came to an awareness that we would be part of Jewish history. Not since the early days of the college had a woman studied for the rabbinate—not until our class. Quiet, unassuming and hardworking, Sally Priesand of Cleveland, Ohio, blended into student life in a way that made her potential historic role in Judaism barely noticeable.

To be sure, Reform Judaism had long stood for the principle of the equality of women. Women had started to enter the senior ranks of congregational and UAHC leadership, as presidents and officers. And here was Sally Priesand, preparing to be a rabbi, the first woman ever to receive ordination from a major rabbinic institution.

Not until many years later did I fully understand the remarkable statement about Reform that Sally's presence symbolized. Here again was Reform Judaism at its finest, making room for change at the most basic level in response to a modern world. Here was Reform Judaism, first of all the movements to understand that women were entitled to full and equal participation in all areas of Jewish life, and ready at last as a consequence of the fulfillment of its values to live out that ideal through action.

We were very fond of Sally. She was kind and considerate, asked for no special favors, and abided our occasional good-natured kidding with a smile. She never sought the spotlight. Hers was a genuine commitment to the rabbinate, and we knew and respected that. If anything, the members of our class went out of our way to protect Sally, shielding her, often without her knowledge, from prying eyes and any potential prejudice. We knew the time would come when the whole world would know Sally's name, and we considered her a friend and companion on the long road to ordination.

The year also witnessed a breakthrough in Reform Jewish education, with the beginnings of a grass roots movement in support of Reform day schools. For close to a century, the Reform movement championed the public school and officially resisted any attempt to create a system of Reform Jewish private schools, the only one of the three major movements to do so. By early 1969, the Orthodox community claimed nearly five hundred day schools, the Conservative movement, fifty. Reform Judaism as yet had none.

To be sure, the Union of American Hebrew Congregations affirmed the right of other groups to establish private schools. At the same time, however, Reform as a community staunchly upheld support of the public school system as a debt to the past and a guarantor of equality for all in the future. Even the suggestion of deserting the public school system was generally considered heresy.

The one entity within Reform that continually discussed day schools was the UAHC-CCAR Joint Commission on Jewish Education. During the last years of his tenure as director of the commission, Dr. Emanuel Gamoran began to advocate Reform day schools, an appeal that essentially fell on deaf ears. His successor, Rabbi Eugene Borowitz, persisted in bringing this issue before the commission. When Borowitz left the UAHC to become a professor at the Hebrew Union College-Jewish Institute of Religion in New York, the cause of day schools was assumed by the new director, a young rabbi named Alexander Schindler, and by the UAHC's vice-president, Rabbi Jay Kaufman. In November of 1963, Schindler and Kaufman issued a public statement, which appeared in the New York *Times,* calling for the establishment of Reform day schools. Response from the movement was swift and sure, overwhelmingly negative. But the issue had been placed on the table in a preliminary way, a seed planted for cultivation and growth in years to come.

The Six-Day War of 1967 and a growing Jewish pride and assertiveness helped to move the option of full-time education in a Reform setting into the mainstream of the movement's debate and decision-making. Seemingly overnight, growing numbers of Jewish families realized the inadequacy of the Sunday school Jewish education of their own youth and moved to develop an alternative mode of Jewish study and experience that would engage their children daily, as opposed to four to six hours each week. They sensed a diminution in quality in the public school system that had served them so well during their childhoods. As importantly, they sought an alternative to Orthodox or Conservative day schools, now that they had made up their minds to provide their children with a full-time Jewish educational experience.

Opponents of Reform day schools were just as vocal and sincere in their arguments. Given the limited resources of the Reform movement, they foresaw a disproportionate amount of money and staff resources being diverted from other programs, which in their opinion held a much higher priority. They also affirmed that day schools insulated Jewish children from the mainstream of American culture. Had Jews not come to America to escape ghettoization, they questioned? How could we now abandon the public schools and withdraw into a model of education more typical of a time when

145

Jews could not participate freely in society? Would this not be a betrayal of all those principles for which Reform had stood?

During the spring of 1969, word spread that a resolution affirming the validity of the option of full-time Jewish education within Reform Judaism would be brought to the UAHC's fall biennial convention in Miami Beach, Florida. Students at the college had strong feelings on both sides of the issue, and many discussions lasted long into the night on the wisdom and appropriateness of this educational model within Reform. Nevertheless, even those who opposed day schools expressed grudging admiration for a movement that refused to shrink from the debate, refused to remain static in its ways and was ready to take on the tough issues and decide them in a national forum.

In May of 1969, I was elected president of the student council of the Cincinnati school. As a result, in early August, I received a letter from Dr. Glueck inviting me to attend the biennial as a representative of the HUC-JIR student body. I would have an opportunity to hear the debate on day schools and many other matters. Above all, I would have an opportunity to see first-hand the workings of the larger Reform Movement, a cross-section of that community that I would serve. I called the office at once and indicated my acceptance.

My life, too, entered a period of transition in the fall of 1969, when I took my first student pulpit in a small town some thirty miles from Pittsburgh, Pennsylvania called Steubenville, Ohio. Steubenville is one of those communities that helped to build the Union of America Hebrew Congregations. Some fifty percent of the UAHC's member temples have a membership of less than two hundred families and, like Temple Beth El of Steubenville, could not afford a full-time rabbi. For many years it served as a training ground for rabbinic students from the Hebrew Union College in Cincinnati. A fellow student and I traveled to Steubenville on alternate weekends, conducting services on Friday night, teaching bar mitzvah lessons on Saturday morning, then working with the religious-school students on Sunday before returning home.

During two years in Steubenville, I grew tremendously in terms of my appreciation of what the Reform movement meant to Jews in small, isolated areas. First of all, the UAHC as a family of congregations did for Temple Beth El and hundreds of congregations like it what no one of them could accomplish alone. Individual congregations could not possibly afford to train their own rabbis, but the movement as a whole sustained the campuses of the Hebrew Union College-Jewish Institute of Religion in Cincinnati, in New York and in Los Angeles, preparing rabbis, cantors and educators for service to the entire community.

No single congregation could afford to create its own textbooks and curriculum guides for Jewish education. But in Steubenville and elsewhere, we employed the UAHC's curriculum guidelines, UAHC textbooks and teacher materials, UAHC filmstrips and other audio-visual aides, available to us only because a UAHC existed.

No single congregation with one or two exceptions, could afford to operate its own camp. But many of Steubenville's high school students traveled to one of the nine camps supported by the movement each summer to meet other Jewish young people, to learn and to study, to be strengthened in terms of their own Jewish identity and commitment.

No single congregation could create its own prayer books. But we in Steubenville had the Reform movement's Shabbat and High Holiday prayer books, published by the Central Conference of American Rabbis.

Furthermore, the regional director of the UAHC was always available for consultation and assistance in areas ranging from synagogue management to creative programming suggestions. Here in Steubenville, then, in addition to all the other personal opportunities for growth afforded to me, I found a *raison d'etre* of the Reform movement as an institution. Steubenville was one of the building blocks of a vast and growing community of Jews pursuing Jewish identity in a modern world from a liberal perspective. After the holidays and an additional month in Steubenville, I settled into a routine. I knew that I had found a place in which I would continue to learn, mature and serve.

My responsibilities as president of the student council in Cincinnati added yet another dimension to my school experience, and never more so than on October 23, 1969 at the college board of governors meeting. An air of anticipation filled the room as Dr.

Nelson Glueck began an historic presidential report. He said in part:

> 'I am convinced that sooner or later the College-Institute will add a year of study in Israel to its rabbinic program. And I believe the time is now. We have thought and dreamt about this compulsory year in Jerusalem for all our rabbinic students for a long time now. It is our conviction that Jewish history is pushing us hard in this direction, and that we have no choice but to move forward accordingly. It requires courage and vision to put this first part of a radically new program of rabbinic studies at HUC-JIR into effect. I pray that the Board of Governors will approve it.'

Dr. Glueck took his seat. After a brief discussion, a vote was taken. It was unanimous. The dream which Dr. Glueck nurtured for many years had come to fruition. The next generation of Reform rabbis would have at least one year of training in Israel. As I sat in that meeting, I was struck again by this tangible evidence of the capacity of Reform Judaism to change and to grow. Less than two decades earlier, such a proposal would have been met by protest, if not outright derision and scorn. This was the same institution that one generation earlier had made Zionism almost a dirty word. Today, a new group of leadership reached out to the future with a totally different orientation to the Jewish State.

Within a few days after this session of the board, I packed my bags for the UAHC biennial. The convention, based at Miami Beach's Fontainbleu Hotel, attracted some two thousand Reform Jews from across the United States and Canada. These men, women and young people came from congregations large and small to join in a celebration of Reform Jewish identity. They packed the various workshops and plenary sessions, articulating their views and commitments in an open forum, a legislative body that constituted the ultimate policy-making authority for all of Reform Judaism. This was real participation, real decision-making, including vigorous discussions on the great issues of the day. I attended debates on the new course of interfaith activity, listening avidly as speaker after speaker spoke of the pros and cons of continuing UAHC involvement in this sphere. There were those who urged withdrawal from the arena, while others passionately advocated continued engagement, pointing out that ultimately the coalitions of decency, now weakened by diminished support for Israel in some quarters, could be renewed and strengthened only by an absolute refusal to allow any single issue, however painful, to drive us apart.

Discussions regarding Israel commanded a large chunk of plenary time, with a resolution calling upon the United States to maintain its level of military aid to Israel, urging assistance to Jews captive in Arab lands, expressing outrage at the United Nations' election of Syria to the Security Council, and affirming the need to encourage Progressive Judaism in Israel.

The biennial urged a continuing presence in the civil rights struggle in spite of the growing defection by many Jews from the cause of black self-determination, and reiterated its hope for an immediate cease-fire and a negotiated settlement in the Vietnam War. In addition, the movement as a whole joined in commitment to an intensified effort to enable Soviet Jews to leave Russia and the oppressive conditions there. By 1969, the Soviet Jewry movement was in full swing, as the North American Jewish community assumed responsibility for assisting this segment of imperiled Jews as it had done elsewhere so many times in the past. Three million Jews lived in Russia at the time, one of the largest Jewish communities in the world. Subjected to discrimination and forbidden to practice their religion freely, growing numbers of Soviet Jewish men and women heard of Israel's victory in the Six-Day War and fashioned their own dream of coming to live in the Jewish state. Those who expressed such sentiments publicly were often removed from their jobs, consigned to menial tasks in factories or warehouses and labeled "parasites" for living off the state and ungratefully criticizing it. The UAHC was among many national bodies who fought for the rights of these men and women to live as Jews or to leave as Jews.

Successive workshops and plenary sessions made clear that Reform Judaism was no simple parochial body concerned solely with its own needs, dues, fundraising, membership recruitment and the like. Here was a movement that reached out to encounter the world in a Jewish context. There were disagreements and debates, but when all was said and done, this was a movement joined in common purpose, proud, assertive, linked over time and space by a Jewish vision of a better world.

I took this all in with a growing sense of excitement. The gradual realization of what this Reform movement embodied reinforced my determination to be part of it. For the first time, though I did not meet them, I saw from afar people about whom I had only read; Rabbi Maurice Eisendrath, Al Vorspan, Rabbi Balfour Brickner, Rabbi Richard Hirsch. And then there was a new face, a man about whom I knew little at the time—Rabbi Alexander Schindler.

Alex Schindler was born in Munich, Germany, in 1925. His father, Eliezer, was a Yiddish poet, his mother, Sali, a businesswoman who formed what came to be the largest mail order house in Germany. As a boy, the young Alex was raised in a home that, while not Orthodox, was traditional in the sense that he was taught to love everything that was Jewish. He attended an Orthodox day school in Germany, but his father also brought him on many occasions to the great Reform congregation in Munich. His grandparents were Hasidim, and from them he also learned a love of that orientation within Judaism. He had distant relatives who were rabbis and Jewish leaders, and traced his lineage back to the scribe of the Baal Shem Tov, the founder of Hasidism, on one side, and to a classical Reform rabbi from Boston named Solomon Schindler on the other.

Fortunately for the family, Eliezer Schindler read Hitler's *Mein Kampf* in the 1920s and believed that Hitler would ultimately live out his monstrous agenda. He brought his family to the United States, saving them from the genocide of the Nazi Holocaust. Alex entered college at the age of fifteen, intending to study electrical engineering, but with the advent of World War II, he joined the army and served in the United States ski troops in Italy. When the war concluded, Schindler borrowed a jeep and drove into Germany to see if he could find the remnants of his family. The impact of witnessing what Hitler had done irrevocably changed his life.

Returning from the war, he left engineering school and began taking social studies courses focusing on Jewish history, driven by a will to understand how and why the Holocaust could have happened. In addition to studying at City College, he took courses at the Jewish Theological Seminary in New York, Manhattan's New School for Social Research and the Hebrew Union College. During his senior year, Schindler determined to enter the rabbinate, motivated by a desire to serve the Jewish people.

He enrolled at HUC-JIR in Cincinnati in 1950 and completed the normal five-year course of study in just three. Though cautioned by one professor that his German accent would preclude success in the American Jewish community, Alex disregarded the professor's advice that he see a speech therapist and instead set out for Worcester, Massachusetts, as an assistant rabbi of the Reform congregation there.

After five years in Worcester, Schindler joined the staff of the Union of American Hebrew Congregations as regional director for the Northeast, and helped to form close to a dozen congregations during his five-year tenure. Maurice Eisendrath took notice of the success of this young rabbi and brought him to New York to head the UAHC's Department and Commission on Jewish Education, elevating him five years thereafter to the vice-presidency of the movement. At the 1969 convention, Schindler held that post but maintained a relatively low profile. He did not deliver an address, but many of those present already spoke of him as the logical successor to Eisendrath. Schindler sat on the dais as the resolution on Reform day schools was introduced. The debate was spirited and well-reasoned on both sides, but the resolution failed. It was clear, however, that the issue would return to the plenum at some future time. Two communities, in Miami and New York, had already taken matters into their own hands and launched day schools in their respective temples. If their pioneering efforts were emulated elsewhere, the movement as a whole would have to respond.

The final evening of the Miami Beach convention produced one of those unplanned, spontaneous experiences that no program committee could ever structure. Earlier in the day, delegates to the convention marched up Miami's Collins Avenue in a display of support for Soviet Jews. That night at the plenary session, Elie Wiesel, not yet a Nobel Laureate and just reaching the heights of renown as a writer and speaker, addressed and moved the convention deeply. The program ended on a high, and the delegates drifted out of the hall, returning to their rooms to pack and prepare for the trip home. Just before midnight, however, I happened to be walking through the lobby precisely at the moment when Theodore

Bikel, the Jewish folk singer and Soviet Jewry activist, entered the hotel, fresh from an appearance at another convention. Bikel impulsively pulled up a chair, opened his guitar case, sat down and began to sing Hebrew and Yiddish songs. As if on cue, Elie Wiesel appeared. Almost always solemn in his demeanor, Wiesel nevertheless joined in the singing, laughing and dancing in the center of the Fontainbleau Hotel lobby. A crowd of several hundred people, teenagers and adults, gathered around, and for some two hours we sang and celebrated our Judaism. Those who were present that night will never forget it. At 2:00 in the morning, as we finally, reluctantly ended the song session, I went back to my room, inspired and more convinced than ever of Reform Judaism's enduring vitality and promise for the future of North American and even world Jewry.

CHAPTER XXIII

A New Direction

*A*fter the emotional high of the fall, school was almost a let-down for the balance of 1970. Work continued, classes met, but I was already thinking ahead to the future. My work in Steubenville now became the major focus of my attention. The people there, by now 'my' shared congregation, occupied my thoughts and energy. The programs of the congregation, enriched and strengthened by what I learned at the UAHC convention, provided me with great satisfaction and a sense of fulfillment. Still, I felt vaguely uneasy about a subtle change that I sensed in myself.

It has always been very important to me to have my own identity. I never wanted to be known by a title, a designation that labeled me as what I did rather than who I was. At the temple in Steubenville, in spite of all my efforts to the contrary, I fast became aware that the position of rabbi carried with it a certain emotional baggage. Since childhood, it troubled me that members of my father's congregation never referred to him by his first name. He was always "Rabbi Syme." When I came to Steubenville, therefore, I began my tenure by consciously encouraging the members to call me Danny. A few did, but the majority persisted in referring to me as Rabbi Syme. After my third attempt to get one of my closest friends in the congregation to use my first name, he finally said to me, "Look, Danny. You are my rabbi. I need to call you rabbi, and the rest of the members of this congregation need to call you rabbi. Please don't ask us to give that up."

I learned an important lesson that day. Jews need rabbis. They don't want their rabbi to be just another person. They want their rabbi to be something other than just another man or woman whose social acquaintance they might value. The rabbi is more than that. The title rabbi symbolizes something beyond the person who holds it. A rabbi is a symbol to a Jew at a time of joy, a bar or bat mitzvah, a wedding, the birth of a child or a baby-naming, an anniversary or other joyous occasions. The rabbi provides a sort of certification of the Jewish authenticity of the event in a manner that provides special meaning to that moment.

More importantly, however, the rabbi is a symbol at a time of tragedy. By his or her very presence, a rabbi can provide comfort and ease pain, as much a function of the title as of the human being. When I officiated at my first funeral in Steubenville, the reality of that status became crystal clear. A young father, just over forty years of age, died of a sudden, massive heart attack, leaving a wife and two young sons. The tragedy occurred during one of my weekends in the city, and I was summoned to the house. Realizing that I had absolutely no idea as to what was expected of me, I called my father and asked for advice. Dad spoke very softly and slowly, giving me various bits of advice, but above all emphasizing that my presence and listening were really all that were required. When I arrived at the family's home, I expressed my condolences, then sat for three hours in the living room as the family and friends talked to me about the man taken at such an early age. I cannot remember uttering more than four or five sentences during the entire period. Yet, as I was about to leave, members of the family individually thanked me for bringing them comfort. I returned to my hotel room and reflected for several hours on that experience. What a remarkable thing, I thought, to be able to help people in this way. If, in addition to that, there was a human dimension of caring and gentleness on the part of the individual rabbi, the salutary effect of a career in congregational life could be immeasurable.

But there was, I found, another side to the title of rabbi. Even as congregants accorded the rabbi respect and honor and the enormous gratification of a sense of importance in their lives, so they expected the rabbi to behave differently from them and their circle of friends. Members of Temple Beth El did not want to see me in jeans and a sweatshirt. They did not want to see me playing bridge or poker with them in their social settings. They wanted and needed a certain dignity and distance from their rabbi, and in order to please them, I found myself acceding to their expectations and needs. There were a very few families in whose homes I felt free to let down that rabbinic persona. In public, however, and in the pulpit, I began, however slightly, to take on mannerisms and a mode of speaking that made me feel almost bifurcated—one of me for public consumption, the other the real me. It was disconcerting, upsetting, and I wasn't quite sure how to resolve the conflict. My teachers at the college were of very little help. Their standard response was that eventually I would find a happy medium. Nor was my father of any great assistance, because he both accepted and embraced that difference between himself and the members of Temple Israel in Detroit. It was therefore up to me to find some way to deal with a potential dual identity.

As the year went on, society as a whole continued to boil over with the fallout of world events. Though the violence associated with the civil rights movement began to abate, the war in Vietnam still hung over America like a storm cloud. Richard Nixon initiated a withdrawal of United States soldiers from Southeast Asia, albeit only to the level of four hundred thousand troops. The pace was not satisfactory to a great segment of the American public, and protest marches continued throughout the country.

The ugliness of Vietnam in terms of its domestic impact was never felt more graphically than during the spring of 1970, when four students at Ohio's Kent State University were shot and killed by National Guard troops as the troops broke up a demonstration. The American public was stunned at this totally unnecessary and un-provoked slaughter of innocent young people. On campuses across the United States, students declared a day of mourning for their fellow students at Kent State and decided to travel to Washington for a massive expression of anger and outrage. At the college, in my capacity as president of the student council, I chaired a meeting at which a proposal was raised to close down the school so that students might go to Washington without being penalized for missing classes and their final exams. Many members of the faculty angrily rejected this proposal, threatening to fail any students who did not take exams at the prescribed time. Though Dr. Glueck personally appeared at a late-night prayer vigil on the lawn of the college in memory of the Kent State students, he was adamant in his insistence that classes and exams continue.

A large number of students, however, felt otherwise, and convened a meeting of the entire school. In a long and acrimonious debate in the college chapel, a majority of the students voted to close the school. Those who wished to remain on campus and attend classes would of course be free to do so, but the demand was made that final examinations be postponed until after the memorial march on Washington. Some faculty members were dispatched to try to reverse the decision, while others sat with us just to listen and respond to our concerns. Dr. Glueck took counsel with both groups, then decided not to issue an ultimatum. He directed that classes be held, that exams proceed as scheduled, but also instructed that those who chose to go to Washington be given an opportunity to make up their exams after they returned. In explaining his decision to the college board, many of whom reacted negatively to his decision, he spoke as follows: "We had no strikes or vandalism on our campus ... the tragic events exerted, however, and continue to exert a powerful impact on all of us. We could not, however, pursue our regular courses of study without taking more cognizance than ever before of the problems and disturbances of our society and our world." The crisis was averted. The collective wisdom of the faculty and Dr. Glueck avoided the sort of upheaval at HUC that occurred on so many other university campuses.

But Vietnam was not the only painful issue of 1970. It was also a time in which Arabs began to pursue their goal of destroying Israel through a new form of terrorism, the hijacking of international flights of travelers, holding them as hostages or executing them in order to gain the world's attention. This entirely new development caught the world by surprise and placed Arab demands on the front page of every newspaper throughout the world. President Nasser of Egypt died and was succeeded by one of his chief aides, Anwar El-Sadat, little known to the western world. According to press reports, Sadat sympathized with the Nazi cause during World War II, and that perception alone created anxiety in Israel and in the Jewish community as a whole. At least with Nasser, Israel knew what to expect. Sadat was an enigma.

As the summer of 1970 approached, therefore, it was with some ambivalence that my wife Martha and I applied to the National Federation of Temple Youth for consideration as tour leaders for one of that summer's series of high school trips to Israel. Dr. Glueck and Dr. Marcus wrote letters of reference, but we simply did not know if my prior trip to Israel, combined with my congregational experience and my work with one of the local youth groups in Cincinnati, constituted sufficient credentials. We were therefore pleasantly surprised when the UAHC director of overseas programs contacted us and asked if we would lead a trip of forty high school students on the NFTY Antiquities Tour. The trip began in London, followed by several weeks in Israel, thereafter moving to Italy, Istanbul and Amsterdam before returning to New York. The answer was an immediate 'yes'. Martha, who by now held a position with a local Jewish agency, negotiated a leave, and we were off.

Though I had travelled to Israel in 1963 as a teenager, leading a group was quite a different story, especially since this trip took place after the Six-Day War and Israel had undergone tremendous change. In a sense, then, though Martha and I and a young woman from London were the nominal leaders of the tour, we were seeing much of Israel for the first time ourselves. The Western Wall was now in Israeli hands, and our group went directly from the airport to the Wall to offer our personal prayers of thanks. We toured Israel from top to bottom, climbing mountains, working on a kibbutz, but also visiting the growing number of Reform Jews and institutions. The Leo Baeck School in Haifa had grown significantly in stature and size. The Jerusalem campus of the Hebrew Union College now had students in residence year-round, including the first-year rabbinic class, which in prior years would have been part of the Towanda program. We met new rabbis who had come to live in Israel to build progressive Judaism there. Though Reform Jews were small in number, it became patently obvious that the Reform movement had committed itself to a future in Israel.

In all honesty, the post-Israel portion of the trip paled by comparison. After traveling in Israel, with its history dating back thousands of years, the Colosseum in Rome, the Forum, the magnificent museums and art, Istanbul and Amsterdam, though impressive, were not quite as dramatic in their impact as they might have

been had we gone there first. In each country, however, we continued to meet Jews, young and old, who shared a vision of liberal
Judaism.

Returning to New York and then to Cincinnati, I reviewed the
summer's events. One in particular stood out, a reunion with an old
friend. One of our tour members was a sixteen-year-old girl from
Detroit named Julie Chafets. Her brother Bill, a former president of
both MSTY and NFTY, went to live in Israel following the Six-Day
War. In order to support himself, he secured a position translating
press releases from Hebrew into English for the leading opposition
party to the long-reigning Labour government. Labour was the
party of David Ben Gurion, Golda Meir, Moshe Dayan and virtually
every major political figure in Israel. Bill Chafets, now Ze'ev
Chafets, worked for the man known as Israel's most eloquent loyal
oppositionist, Menachem Begin. All of Israel 'knew' that Begin
would never ascend to any great heights in Israeli politics, but he
had given my friend a job. Ze'ev and I reestablished our friendship
that summer and promised one another that we would try to stay in
touch by mail, by phone and in person, in either the United States or
in Israel. Now I had a real friend in the Jewish state, at whose home
I would always be welcome. I never again had to feel like a tourist in
Israel.

CHAPTER XXIV

Sadness and Joy

*A*s our class began its fourth year of studies, rumors persisted that Dr. Nelson Glueck had been stricken with a serious illness. No one spoke about it openly, but many of Glueck's lifelong friends seemed deeply concerned. In spite of his affliction, Dr. Glueck was present at the dedication exercises at the Jerusalem school on October 13, 1970 to award an honorary degree to Prime Minister Golda Meir.

In his address, he uttered these words: "We shall labor quietly but determinedly for complete freedom of religious practice here in Israel in all the phases of life, and are confident that such freedom will eventually be established here for all Jews to exercise in accordance with their own tradition and judgment."

Many who knew Glueck well feel that this particular day was the highlight in his career. Aware of his illness, he nevertheless derived great comfort from the knowledge that his dream of a presence in Jerusalem had now at last been fulfilled.

A few weeks later at the HUC-JIR board of governors meeting in Cincinnati, Nelson Glueck was elected chancellor of the college, beginning July 1, 1972, with an additional proviso calling for him to become chancellor emeritus three years thereafter.

By now, Glueck was probably aware of the fact that he would not be able to realize one last dream, that of ordaining the first woman rabbi, our classmate, Sally Priesand. Every year he went to the annual convention of the Central Conference of American Rabbis and listened to the members arguing in long and learned debates over whether they could ordain a woman. At those moments, Glueck merely folded his hands in silence; he knew that he would do the ordaining. This last aspiration eluded him. Nelson Glueck died on February 12, 1971 at the age of seventy. People all over the world mourned his passing. National magazines and periodicals eulogized him. In Israel, men and women who did not even know him wept openly at services in his memory. An era had ended in the history of the Hebrew Union College-Jewish Institute of Religion, an era of tremendous growth. The man, the times, the people had meshed into a network that had accomplished remarkable things. But now it was time for the presidency to be passed to a new generation, a new Reform Jewish leader, the man who had built the California campus of the college, Dr. Alfred Gottschalk.

On February 24, 1972, Alfred Gottschalk was formally inaugurated as the fifth president of the Hebrew Union College-Jewish Institute of Religion. The following morning, at Plum Street Temple in Cincinnati, he stepped to the bimah to deliver his inaugural address. He paid tribute to his predecessors and recalled his own childhood. As a young boy in Germany, he had been taken by his grandfather to the synagogue the morning after the infamous *Kristallnacht* and shown devastated sanctuary and the Torahs, ripped to pieces, floating on the waters of the Rhine. For Gottschalk, the nightmare created a sense of mission:

> 'I will never forget that nightmare of Nazism. Yet out of it emerged a dream. That dream possesses me like an unbendable resolution: to piece together the scraps and bits and restore them to unfragmented unity. It has been with me since my early youth—as a source of encouragement and direction, as a norm, as a guide.'

The new president listed some of the problems that the coming generation of Jews would have to face: conversion, anti-Israel sentiment, the plight of Soviet Jewry, alienation from Judaism by youth and above all the need for Jewish unity. He pledged that the college would concern itself with wider world problems as well as specifically Jewish issues, and emphasized that one of the major priorities of the college would continue to encourage a sustaining relationship between Christian students in residence at the college and Jewish students, to keep the bond between the two communities alive.

During the fall of 1970, however, none of these events had as yet transpired. Those of us in the fourth-year class, deeply saddened by our growing awareness of Dr. Glueck's illness, pursued our studies with the realization that the man who had been the leader of our academic institution would probably not be present at our ordination.

By spring of 1971, after Dr. Glueck's death, most of us began to prepare our rabbinic theses, the last academic requirement of major consequence before ordination the following June. My sole desire was to work with Dr. Marcus. We had become extremely close over the years, and I went to him, unlike most of my classmates, not with a specific proposal, but rather with an offer to undertake whatever he felt would be a significant project in the area of American Jewish history. Inasmuch as the centennial of the college was three years away, and since many historians would undoubtedly require research materials, Dr. Marcus urged me to dig out and synthesize various sources germane to HUC-JIR history. On that basis, he said, he would be willing to work directly with me and to assist me in every way possible. I was delighted, and set to work at once.

In considering postordination job opportunities, I had come to realize that, despite my positive experiences in Steubenville, the congregational rabbinate was not for me, at least not as the first step in my career. Having grown up as the son of a rabbi in a large congregation, I knew both the pluses and minuses of that life. Having served a small congregation, I was cognizant of a personal need to express myself in a larger arena. Surely, I thought, there must be some other initial way in which to serve the Jewish people than in a temple. I shared my misgivings with one faculty member, who insisted that I would never be a "real" rabbi outside of congregational life. Deeply shaken by this encounter, I went to see Dr. Glueck in the last meeting I had with him before his death. After listening attentively to my concerns, he stood up and declared: "That is absolute nonsense! I am not a rabbi in a congregation. Am I any less of a real rabbi than those who serve temples throughout the movement?" He waited for my response. None was really necessary. He had made his point. I thanked him and left his office.

Now, several months later, still pondering my options I received a lunch invitation from Rabbi Steve Schafer, the director of NFTY, who came to Cincinnati to recruit camp rabbis and Israel tour leaders. At a nearby coffee shop, Schafer came right to the point. He wanted me to come to New York to join the staff of the Union of American Hebrew Congregations as one of the directors of the National Federation of Temple Youth. Furthermore, he wanted me to begin work in February of 1972, which meant that I would have to finish all my academic work during the first semester and write my rabbinic thesis while employed full time. He was sure, he said, that all the arrangements could be made, and indicated that he would also like me to come to the National NFTY Camp in Warwick, New York that summer to get acquainted with the other staff members. Finally, he asked for an answer within a week.

I could not help but laugh out loud. The whole thing was so bizarre! I had fantasized about coming to work for NFTY, but certainly a few years later in my career, and the prospects of trying to cram all of my courses and my dissertation into such a brief period was more than a little intimidating. Schafer did not laugh. I took a deep breath, thanked him and promised an answer within seven days.

That evening, I shared the news with my wife. Neither of us were prepared to make such an important decision so fast, but we both loved New York City and found the prospect of being there exciting. An hour later, I called Steve Schafer and accepted his offer.

In July of 1971, Martha and I traveled to Warwick, New York, the site of Kutz Camp-Institute. Though it is hardly an attractive place physically, beautiful things happen there. Kutz is the national youth camp of the Reform movement, with summer programs devoted exclusively to teens fifteen to eighteen years of age. Young men and women from across North America, Israel and other countries gather there to learn in a sort of Jewish mini-university. Daily courses are offered in Jewish studies, the arts, youth group programming and leadership skills. In addition, the camp environment itself becomes a twenty-four-hour program site, with singing, evening activities, heart-to-heart discussions and an informal but powerful process of Jewish identity-building. In the course of my few weeks at camp, I taught classes, led programs and spent countless hours with individual boys and girls who just wanted to talk.

I sought out the sons and daughters of rabbis and made myself available to help them work through their special concerns as others had helped me. This would be, I realized, a natural place to touch the future, a place in which I and my UAHC colleagues could help these youngsters shape themselves into a new Jewish leadership, more knowledgeable and more committed to Reform Judaism than those who preceded them. This was where I wanted to be. This was where I could make a difference. I returned to Cincinnati certain I had made the right choice.

As December passed and the year came to a close, only a month remained until our departure from Cincinnati. My classes concluded, and I wrapped up the basic research for my thesis. There was one more item of business before the move, an interview in New York with the vice-president of the Union of American Hebrew Congregations, Rabbi Alexander Schindler. Nervously, I entered Rabbi Schindler's office, and he immediately put me at ease. He told me to call him Alex, then proceeded to ask me questions about everything but my qualifications. He wanted to know who the professors were who had most affected me at HUC. He asked about my personal theology. He inquired as to the sort of career I envisioned in the rabbinate. Finally, he congratulated me on joining the UAHC staff and wished me well.

Two weeks later, Martha and I said goodbye to our friends in Cincinnati and set out for our new home in Stamford, Connecticut, a suburb of New York, and a new life.

CHAPTER XXV

Ordination—One Road Ends, Another Begins

*I*n 1972, the war in Vietnam wound down, culminating in the Paris peace talks. President Nixon opened channels to China as a potential partner of the United States in trade, commerce and the arts. The Supreme Court banned capital punishment, but shocking violence dominated the headlines—an attempt on the life of presidential candidate George Wallace, airplane hijackings, the brutal Arab terrorist kidnapping and murder of Israeli athletes at the Munich Olympics. Then, almost as a footnote to this turbulent twelve months, five burglars were apprehended while breaking into the offices of the Democratic Party in the Watergate office building in Washington. No one thought much of it at the time. The team of Nixon and Agnew seemed unbeatable, especially given the opposition of George McGovern and Sargent Shriver.

As I began my work at the Union during that same year, I felt a little bit like a kid in a candy store. In spite of the tiring experience of commuting from Connecticut to New York and back each day, life could not have been more fulfilling. All the leaders of Reform Judaism who had been so prominent in my life from afar were suddenly part of my day-to-day work. It took a little getting used to. Al Vorspan and Balfour Brickner sometimes stopped by the office to ask my opinion on a proposed youth program. Alex Schindler continued to insist that I call him by his first name rather than Rabbi Schindler, as I continued to do. Maurice Eisendrath was present at many meetings I attended, and though much more formal than the rest of the staff, was always gracious. Eisendrath now suffered from a series of medical complications arising from his successful battle against cancer a year or two prior, and though every member of the staff showed Eisendrath the utmost deference, to all intents and purposes Alex Schindler was running the Union and had been designated president-elect.

It was hard to believe that I was actually getting paid for work I enjoyed so much. Every day was an exercise in unfettered creativity. I generated programs, visited youth groups across the country and attended weekends at camps and synagogues. Rabbi Sam Cook, near retirement, now worked at developing programs for college youth. I came to understand the special genius of this man, whose imagination never ceased to formulate new dreams until the day he left the Union.

Martha also worked at a Jewish organization in Manhattan, and thus we commuted together by car each day. We were a real team, and we both loved our work. Every weekend, I locked myself in a room in the house in Connecticut, sat down at the typewriter and pounded out a chapter of my thesis. On Monday of each week, I mailed the draft to Dr. Marcus, and by the following Monday I had his notes. Therefore, in a space of just under two months, I completed my dissertation long distance. Now only my actual ordination remained to mark closure on one stage of my life and open the door to the next. Each of my classmates in turn secured a position, with three choosing to enter the military chaplaincy. By the time June arrived, every member of our class of thirty-six knew exactly where we would begin our careers.

The weekend of ordination in June of 1972 was not only special for our class but also a unique moment in the life of Jewish people, for on that Shabbat Sally Priesand became the first woman rabbi in four thousand years of Judaism. Accordingly, family and friends of the ordinees arrived in Cincinnati to find the Jewish and general media there as well. My NFTY colleagues gave me a beautiful set of books as an ordination present. I received another surprise when, at the awards ceremony prior to the ordination, I learned that I had graduated first in my class and in addition had been awarded a special prize for the best sermon of the year. That in itself would have made the weekend, but there was more to come.

There was and is a custom at the campuses of HUC-JIR that

when the son or daughter of a rabbi becomes a rabbi, the parent blesses the child at the moment of ordination. I knew that just after Dr. Gottschalk formally pronounced me a rabbi, I would stand before the ark of the Torah to receive my father's blessing as well. That would be my finest moment.

On the Friday night before ordination, our entire class gathered in the chapel of the college for the last time as students. Dr. Gottschalk spoke to us for a few moments while we stood on the bimah. Then, removing one of the Torahs from the ark, he passed it to each of us in turn, giving us an opportunity to say what was in our hearts. I honestly don't remember what I said on that night, though I recall vividly that some members of the class wept unabashedly. We had walked a long road together. Now, together, we shared the satisfaction of journey's end.

Saturday morning dawned on the day for which we had waited for five long years. Plum Street Temple was filled as our class of thirty-six marched down the center aisle to our seats. The service was a long one, but to us it seemed to hurry along. At last, the time arrived when we would ascend the steps of the bimah in that magnificent temple and receive the blessing of ordination. We walked in alphabetical order, and Sally Priesand's turn came before mine. There was utter silence as her name was called and she walked to face Dr. Gottschalk. He placed his hands on her head and pronounced a blessing, whereupon cameras appeared all over the synagogue, recording for all time this deeply significant occasion in Jewish history. Then, with total spontaneity, the members of our class rose to applaud our classmate Sally, now Rabbi Priesand.

A few moments later, my turn arrived. I climbed the stairs to Dr. Gottschalk, who asked me quietly if I was prepared to be a rabbi and serve the Jewish people. I nodded my head in assent. He placed his hands on my shoulders and then on my head, offering a blessing and proclaiming me a rabbi. He then turned me to face the ark, where my father waited. I walked to him, and in those few steps the memories of a lifetime flooded my consciousness. I had already seen my mother, my brothers David and Michael and many friends in the congregation. But this was an existential moment, a moment when time stood still: a moment where I was the little boy of five waiting to go see fifty cartoons; when I was the seven-year-old walking to synagogue with my Dad every Shabbat; when I was the teenager in youth group; when I was the twenty-year-old lying in my hospital bed and hoping that my father's assurance of my recovery was not just wishful thinking. Now I approached him as his son and as a rabbi, having fulfilled the vow I had made to God. I wondered what he would say, how he would express what was in his heart. He always had a gift for saying exactly the right thing at the right time.

This time, however, there were no words. He placed his hands on my head and we both began to cry. It was the ultimate blessing, the blessing that comes from one's most innermost being. We embraced and my father kissed me. Then, like Abraham and Isaac descended Mount Moriah, after God's commanded sacrifice was revealed to be no sacrifice at all, we walked down from the bimah together, father and son, rabbi and rabbi.

At the reception following ordination, a small luncheon my parents hosted in my honor, I reread the essay on becoming a rabbi that I had written at the age of twelve, predicting that one day I would follow in my father's footsteps. After all these years, that little paper turned out to be prophetic.

There was not much time to savor ordination, inasmuch as the camp season began in about three weeks. Martha and I packed up and headed for Warwick. She continued to commute to the city each day, but returned to camp each evening and for the weekend.

As the camping season moved into full swing, I began to reflect upon how I had become a Reform rabbi. Certainly part of it was an accident of birth, attributable to the series of chance encounters my father had experienced, which had brought him to the Jewish Institute of Religion, then under the tutelage of Rabbi Freehof, and then to Detroit. I was a Reform Jew, then, in large measure because of circumstances over which I had no control. Now, however, I had to begin to answer another question. If I were to devote my life to a particular branch of Judaism, I had to assure myself that this was the right place for me. During the summer of 1972, then, I began to consider the question: "Why *remain* a Reform Jew? Why be a *Reform* rabbi?" As the ensuing sixteen years unfolded, the answers became increasingly clear.

CHAPTER XXVI

A Commitment to Youth

Certainly one of the major sources of pride for all Reform Jews is the Reform movement's youth program. The National Federation of Temple Youth, born officially in 1939, today encompasses hundreds of local youth groups, twenty-one regions and a national umbrella serving high school youngsters across North America. It is estimated that nearly twenty thousand teenagers currently participate in youth groups affiliated with NFTY, which in 1988 was renamed the North American Federation of Temple Youth in recognition of its growing Canadian presence.

Foremost among the programs sponsored by the UAHC in the youth realm is a system of nine camps, extending from California to Mississippi, from New York to Texas. Each year, some forty thousand young people of high school and college age—and a significant number of adults—journey to UAHC camps for experiences in Jewish living and learning. Out of these camps have come literally hundreds of the current leaders of the UAHC, including rabbis, cantors, educators, congregational administrators and lay leaders as well. The camp system is arguably the finest vehicle for Jewish education ever initiated by the Reform movement, a rich source for the reproduction of new leadership for the movement and a tribute to its strength.

The Reform movement also takes pride in its work on the college campus. As of 1989, there were some one hundred thousand Reform Jewish students on university campuses across North America. Accordingly, beginning in the early 1970s, the UAHC built a network of college field workers, and chapters of Reform youth in various universities joined in seminars, celebrations, religious services and camp programs throughout the school year. The Youth Division of the UAHC reaches out to Israel as well. The number of high school and college students coming to Israel under the auspices of the UAHC has grown geometrically over the years, with the Reform movement now sending more high school and college students to Israel on an annual basis than any of the other major movements in North America. Summer programs, a six-month high school program, year-long college programs and exchange programs of North American and Israeli youth have established the UAHC as one of the great sources of pro-Israel energy within Reform Judaism.

Nor has the impact of the youth division of the UAHC been confined to the young people themselves. In a classic example of what Margaret Mead termed "reverse transmission of culture," the youth of Reform Judaism have brought what they have gleaned from their camp and Israel experiences into their home congregations: Israeli melodies; renewed commitment to religious observances such as Havdalah, the ceremony ending the Shabbat; Israeli folk dancing and a whole new genre of music composed by NFTY members and alumni. Over a period of decades, some of what was once derided as "camp music" has become as beloved and familiar to adults in the context of their prayer and worship as the classic melodies of another age.

From late 1971 through 1973, I was part of this youth phenomenon. Working with youngsters of extraordinary talent and commitment, I and the rest of the NFTY staff created one program after another, combining Jewish learning with participatory program techniques that were subsequently replicated in temples throughout the movement. Those years were most fulfilling on a personal level, particularly in my relationships with the teenagers themselves. They had no ambivalence about their identity as Reform Jews. Born and raised in Reform Jewish households, they rejoiced in their background and felt a genuine sense of mission in reaching out as liberal Jews to the larger society. Indeed, we often spoke together of the future they envisioned for themselves, whether as rabbis or as full participants on a lay level in Reform Jewish life.

The inevitable growth out of high school and on to college and beyond by 'my kids' created a personal crisis in a most unusual way. One night I had a dream in which I saw myself as a sixty-year-old man, pulling out dusty copies of programs I had laboriously developed during my nearly two years of NFTY work and presenting them to incoming tenth graders at a youth group conclave. Sitting bolt upright in bed, I needed a few minutes to understand that my nightmare reflected a disturbing reality. By spring of 1973, the young people with whom I had grown so close were already writing farewell notes. They were on their way to a new stage in their development, far away from me and the programs of the UAHC. It was indeed possible that I could spend the rest of my life investing enormous energy in a group of youngsters only to see them drift off, never to know the impact of the months I had spent with them. Every year, or at most every two years, they would depart and I would remain, welcoming a new group with whom I would have to begin all over again.

That chilling thought led me to Alex Schindler's office the following morning, where I told him that I could not remain in youth work any longer, that I felt the need to move on to another realm of UAHC programming where I might have a chance to work with young people and adults throughout the entire course of their lives. He listened carefully. It so happened at the time that the current director of the department of education was about to leave. The new director, a veteran educator by the name of Abraham Segal, needed a new assistant. Alex asked if I would be interested in going into education. I took a deep breath. At that point in the history of the movement, education enjoyed the lowest possible status in terms of professions within Reform Judaism. While many fine individuals became principals in congregational religious schools, it was generally assumed that rabbis who took such posts were unable to secure positions anywhere else. My first reaction, therefore, was to demur, indicating that I did not wish to ruin my career by going into education. Alex never changed his expression, but reminded me that he had once been director of education. Flushed with embarrassment, I apologized for any implied criticism of a realm in which he had compiled such a distinguished record, but also reminded him of the precipitous national slide in both the quality and prestige of Jewish education since his elevation to the vice-presidency. He asked me to think it over and we left it at that. A few nights later, New York City was hit by a terrible snowstorm. Since Alex lived in Westport, Connecticut, just a few miles beyond Stamford, I offered to drive him home. As we rode up the expressway to Connecticut, Alex began to talk about a career in education. He pointed out to me that many people could work with teenagers, but emphasized that it would take someone special to enter the field of Jewish education at the present time and try to turn things around. A new curriculum had to be structured, new books produced, new technology harnessed and made available, adult education offered for a generation of Jews who would desire it in the not-too-distant future, stimulation of a profession of educators imbued with self-confidence and stature within the congregational family.

After dropping him off at his house, I drove home conscious that he had challenged me. I could remain in NFTY indefinitely, or I could take the risk of moving into uncharted territory, learning under the tutelage of a top-notch educator whose willingness to teach was truly sincere. The next morning I asked to see Alex again and told him that I would like to be considered for the post. He smiled and told me that he would offer my name as one possibility for the position, though he could make no promises. To this day, I am sure that he knew that I would appear in his office the morning after that car ride, and I will always be grateful to him for giving me the nudge I needed to move ahead.

After two extensive interviews with Abe Segal, the product of a Conservative background who had joined the UAHC's education staff under Alex, I was offered the position of assistant director of the UAHC Department of Education. I still had the year to complete with NFTY and the camp season as well, so we agreed that I would work part-time in both departments until the fall, then make the final transfer.

Many other factors were at work in my life as well. My marriage had begun to deteriorate. The pressures of two careers, the confusion engendered by the emergence of the women's movement and the very real changes in two individuals who had married at a very early age eroded the pure and uncomplicated relationship that had begun in our high school years. By the summer of 1973, it had become clear that our marriage was in trouble. Less than one year later, sadly but amicably, Martha and I decided to part and go our separate ways.

By 1973, it was clear that Watergate was more than a simple burglary. Filled with paranoia about the possibility of a McGovern victory in the election, leaders of the Republican Party authorized a break-in to Democratic National Party headquarters in order to secure any information possible about the upcoming campaign. In retrospect, the burglary was totally ridiculous. Nixon was reelected in a landslide victory. But Watergate would not go away. In part because of the tenacity of the press and the public's growing interest in finding out the truth, the circle of guilt rose higher and higher in the administration, reaching into the White House itself. During the summer months, the Watergate hearings ran day and night on television screens across America, revealing the lengths to which the Republicans were prepared to go to get the information they sought so desperately. As I watched these hearings at Kutz Camp, I began to write about Watergate from the perspective of the Jewish values touched upon in the hearings. There were chapters on truth in government, blind loyalty, public vigilance and a number of other Jewish teachings central to the Watergate issues. By summer's end, due in large measure to help from Balfour Brickner and Al Vorspan, I completed my first UAHC publication, *A Jewish Response to Watergate*.

At camp, we rejoiced at the cease-fire in Vietnam. The Reform movement had labored long and hard and at great institutional cost to maintain its opposition to the conflict. Now it was just about over, and Henry Kissinger would soon win the Nobel Peace Prize. How strange that what should have been a day of rejoicing in America was so bittersweet in light of the Watergate scandal. Richard Nixon could have gone down in history as one America's greatest presidents, the leader who opened a door to China, a president who brought peace. Instead, he was now fighting for his very political existence.

Another writing project occupying my time during the summer of 1973 was a series of articles designed to respond to an intense effort by religious fundamentalists to garner massive numbers of converts, including Jews, to Christianity. The campaign, dubbed "Key 73," crystallized in Washington at a hotel adjacent to the Francis Scott Key Bridge. A group of Christian ministers determined to make the year a staging ground for a battle to save souls— Jewish souls among them. As a consequence, street corners, airports and even synagogues had 'visitors,' accosting passersby, challenging them to become "completed Jews" by accepting Jesus as their savior. Expending millions of dollars on literature, pamphlets and audio-visual presentations, the "Key 73" corps distributed many totally distorted depictions of Judaism and the Torah. I saw many of our young people confused and in pain over the overtures of missionaries to their fellow students and friends, and decided to initiate a series of articles that would expose the most blatant misrepresentations of the proselytizers. In time, the articles, written in tandem with Balfour Brickner, were distributed to tens of thousands of families across North America. We composed them with a heavy heart, realizing that Jews and many Christians now stood at arm's length, reversing so much history and so many ties of decency and common aspiration.

The summer concluded, and I said goodbye to many of the NFTY young people who had touched my life. Together we had participated in the furtherance of efforts that made many men, women and children proud to be Reform Jews. Now, however, it was time for them to move on to college and for me to move on to another program division of the UAHC.

As I began my work in the department of education, I also set out on another experiment that I had long hoped to implement. While I opted not to enter the congregational rabbinate, I still felt a need to serve Jews in that sort of setting. Coincidentally, a small group in Stamford had just formed a group that termed itself a *chavurah*, the Stamford Fellowship for Jewish Learning. This collection of some thirty-five families, most of them commuters, and most of them also affiliated with one of Stamford's local congregations, felt a need for something a bit more personal and intimate in the way of Jewish learning and celebration. Having joined together in pursuit of those general goals, they now sought a rabbi to work with them. The rhythms of their lives were not consistent with the program schedules of most congregations. What they really wanted was

173

serious adult study, Shabbat services every other Friday night, Jewish education for their children, and a congregational mechanism that did not require a building but rather met in homes. One of the members heard about me and called to see if I might be interested in meeting with the group. I immediately agreed to do so, and after one such evening, expressed my enthusiastic willingness to work with them within the limits of my professional responsibilities at the UAHC. Further, I specified my personal agenda, which was to make myself unnecessary. I wished to equip them to function as a community with me as a teacher, but with the members themselves leading services, conducting rituals in their homes and for the chavurah as a whole. I told them that I would stay only until they were self-sufficient, after which I would move on.

In pursuit of that ultimate goal the adults became teachers, and we developed a variation of a religious service that I used with college students in prior years. The service, broken down into alternating short sections for individual readers and the entire congregation, had no assigned parts. If the service was to continue, members of the congregation had to read the parts for individuals. I would not do that. If no one read, the service stopped. We decided to use the service for the upcoming High Holidays. For music, I invited the leading NFTY song leader of that era, a young man named Doug Mishkin, now an attorney in Washington and a successful composer of songs on themes of social justice and peace, to serve as the cantor. The group embraced the service enthusiastically, and before long it was all that we could do to keep several members from reading the same part at the same time. There was a sense of investment in the service, very exciting to me, and I realized that this sort of service could only have taken place in a Reform Jewish environment, where risks and innovation were a way of life. For Yom Kippur, we paused at certain points in the service so that individuals could read a poem or a personal composition they themselves had written.

The enthusiasm at the service lasted only until the early afternoon, when we learned that Arab armies had launched a preemptive strike against Israel on this holiest day of the Jewish year, beginning the Yom Kippur War. Memories of Israel's lightning victory in 1967 at first led us to assume that the attack would be met with a stunning counterblow. But as the hours moved on, it became apparent that Israel once again was fighting for its very existence. Egyptian President Anwar Sadat picked his time to attack shrewdly. While every sign of potential invasion might have been anticipated, Israel did not mobilize sufficiently. Now it faced total annihilation. Our services came to an end on a somber note.

To the relief of the entire world Jewish community, and in spite of his growing problems with Watergate, Richard Nixon launched an immediate airlift of military supplies to Israel, which may have spelled the difference between victory and defeat. Despite enormous casualties, and with brilliant military tactics on the part of General Ariel Sharon, the Egyptian armies were driven back, surrounded and forced to surrender. In contrast to the exuberance following the 1967 war, however, Israel and world Jewry fell into despair. A witch hunt ensued in an effort to fix blame for the army's lack of preparation. Unfairly, perhaps, Israeli public opinion found two of Israel's greatest heroes culpable—General Moshe Dayan and Prime Minister Golda Meir.

These terrible circumstances clouded what was to have been a gala celebration of the UAHC's 100th anniversary, culminating in its 1973 Centennial Convention in New York City. It was here that we were to mark the first ten decades of Isaac Mayer Wise's dream. It was also to be the last biennial convention at which Maurice Eisendrath served as UAHC president, thereafter passing the mantle of leadership to Alexander Schindler. The convention would be held, the festive events would proceed as scheduled, but there would be little joy. Too much Jewish blood had been spilled, and the biennial would thus also serve as a time in which to rededicate Reform to the preservation of Jewish continuity and Israel's survival.

CHAPTER XXVII

The Torch is Passed

*T*he UAHC biennial of 1973, marking the 100th anniversary of Isaac Mayer Wise's creation, was plunged into mourning by the death of Rabbi Maurice Eisendrath at age seventy-one. Just prior to the Friday night service at which he was to deliver his last convention sermon as president of the UAHC, Eisendrath suffered a massive, fatal heart attack over Shabbat dinner in his hotel room.

News of his death spread swiftly through the convention, and delegates wept openly in the halls and corridors of Manhattan's Hilton Hotel. Just over an hour later, the Shabbat service intended as a joyous celebration of 100 years of UAHC history became instead a time of solemn reminiscence and mourning for a giant of a man who had brought the Union to a position of national and international prominence. Rabbi Alexander Schindler, Eisendrath's designated successor, delivered the text of Eisendrath's speech at that service, a powerful call to action for the future rather than a mere rehearsal of the past. It called Richard Nixon to account for the Watergate coverup. It demanded renewed commitment to social justice, to the war on poverty and to civil rights. It articulated renewed dedication to the full equality of women, both within Reform Judaism and society as a whole, and challenged the delegates to make Jewish learning and study a greater priority in their lives, so that the Reform imperative of choice based upon knowledge might reassert its primacy as a criterion for constructive change and growth.

176

Eisendrath had reserved a special word for the one hundred or so young people of NFTY attending the convention:

'Beneath the expensive second-hand blue jeans of our young people, beneath the long hair and the bare feet, there lurks a banked but hot coal fire of passion for a world still to be created. It awaits only the opening of the damper, and the damper has been opened for many through our camps and other youth programs that capture their idealism and put it to work. Our youth are restless and rebellious, rebellious even against religion—but only false and fake and hypocritical religion. I believe they burn with a fever for genuine faith and fellowship with their fellow Jews and fellow men. We dare not let them down.'

Sitting with the youth delegates at the service, I watched their faces as these words were uttered. Not a single one of them had ever met Rabbi Eisendrath, let alone known him, but their expressions made clear their insight that the president of the UAHC, separated in age from them by some fifty years, nevertheless had intuited the feelings that lay deep in their hearts. After the service, we assembled the teenagers in a private room so that they could talk about the tragic events of that night. I encouraged them to write down their feelings, so that they might be shared with the Eisendrath family as a source of comfort. Early the following morning, one of the NFTY members, a young girl from Texas, brought me a poem entitled "The Last Shabbat," so simple, so sensitive and so beautiful that I took it to Alex Schindler, suggesting that it might be published as part of the convention proceedings. Instead, Alex included it in his eulogy the next day at Eisendrath's funeral, a final tribute from a young person whose life had been touched by this man, this rabbi, this Jew:

> Glasses filled with wine,
> smiles and candles and laughing,
> and sharing Shabbat.
>
> Suddenly—a hush,
> Maurice is gone, the Rabbi said.

I watched tears,
shocked glances,
sorrow,
gaiety fled the room, irreplaceable.

I never knew him
I never smiled at him,
never talked to him.
I saw him only once,
a shadow,
upon a stage of other shadowed faces.

I heard his voice, his humor.
his happiness that day, his sadness at leaving.
The visitors about me whispered.
His achievements, his accomplishments,
spoke softly their respect.
I listened from the balcony.

I heard history.

Who was not touched by him?
Who did not learn?
Who remained empty after hearing his final words
read by another,
filling that silent room with his hopes and dreams,
his defeats and his victories?

Shalom, Maurice.
I am glad that you were given
one last Shabbat to place among the rest.
We will try to continue what you have begun.

But today—we sit and whisper your memory.
Even I, who did not know you,
I will remember you. L'hitraot.

Maurice Eisendrath was gone, but in his place came a new leader for a new era, destined to lead the Reform movement just as boldly, just as courageously into realms undreamed of at that time.

On November 12, 1973, Rabbi Alexander Schindler became the new president of the UAHC.

Schindler began his administration with the full support of the entire UAHC family, including a number of lay affiliates whose programs had helped to build the movement, and which now constituted a solid foundation for the attainment of new goals and dreams. Perhaps the most powerful and certainly the largest affiliate was, the National Federation of Temple Sisterhoods, founded in 1913. The women of Reform Judaism, key to the formation of NFTY, builders of the homes of many Reform institutions, played a central role in the life of the synagogue and in the movement even before women gained full recognition as leaders in their own right within the national structure of the organization.

A second group, established in 1923, was the National Federation of Temple Brotherhoods. Originally formed to join all the men's clubs of UAHC congregations into a national body, NFTB also subsequently assumed the sponsorship of the Jewish Chautauqua Society. By providing Jewish books and scholars in residence to universities throughout the world, and via the medium of television and film production, the Jewish Chautauqua Society has built stronger bridges of understanding between the Jewish community and those of other faiths.

Finally, the World Union for Progressive Judaism joined North American Reform Judaism with liberal Jews in foreign lands, and included congregations in Israel, Australia, New Zealand, South Africa, England, Switzerland, Brazil, Argentina, the Netherlands and France.

Together with the professional associations of Reform rabbis, cantors, administrators and educators, and sustained by the strength of almost seven hundred congregations, there was every reason to believe that the Reform movement had the potential to become a predominant force in Jewish life. My job was to help the Union attain that distinction in Jewish education.

CHAPTER XXVIII

On the Cutting Edge of Jewish Education

*I*f 1973 marked the beginning of a new era in Reform Judaism, it also was a time of frustration among professional Jewish educators. Declining student enrollment, inadequate funding and the low priority of education among Jewish institutional concerns created a downward spiral in educator morale in all movements. This malaise fed upon itself and created self-imposed barriers to new initiatives.

My new boss, however, had other ideas. Abraham Segal was in many ways a visionary, and refused to accept the inevitability of current circumstances. He set about changing reality, rather than sitting back and allowing it to change him. His philosophy, which I internalized, was a simple one. Our task was to rekindle an enthusiasm for Jewish education within Reform Judaism. Through new books and teacher training workshops, through intense involvement with the educators themselves and through the medium of an entirely reconstructed, lifelong curriculum, he felt that we would reverse the tide and restore the centrality of education in UAHC congregations.

In the space of two years, we laid the groundwork together. Abe functioned as the careful, methodical planner and teacher, while I introduced the informal educational techniques that had worked so well in NFTY, traversing the country, garnering support for the impending innovations. In just twenty-four months, the UAHC published over a dozen new textbooks and, under the aegis of the

Commission on Education, instituted new programs of teacher and principal certification. Most importantly, we developed a master plan for what would ultimately become the new UAHC curriculum, a road map for developing a new Jewish literacy, extending from preschool through adult years in both formal and informal settings. Along the way, Abe worked to mold me into an educator, giving my youthful exuberance free rein but infusing it with the pedagogic foundation that he so selflessly provided. This was expertise that I could not have acquired from any text or in any school, the product of decades of his formidable life experience.

In early 1975, Abe became ill, and several months later concluded that he could no longer continue as director of education. The news left me both saddened and unsure of my personal future. Though I had seen to the day-to-day operations of the department during Abe's absence, I was just twenty-nine, with only eighteen months of on-the-job training. In my heart I knew that I could handle the department, but even my most optimistic thoughts were tempered by the realization that the odds were not in my favor. I shared my thoughts with Alex Schindler, who told me honestly that he could make no promises and named a search committee from every segment of the movement to make the ultimate decision.

On the day the committee convened, I felt helpless. This decision was completely out of my hands. After work that day, I went directly to my apartment in New York and remained by the telephone throughout the evening. When no call came by ten o'clock, I prepared for bed, certain that I had been passed over and, though not surprised, still deeply disappointed.

Suddenly the telephone rang, and I raced to pick it up. It was Alex, calling to inform me that I had been named acting director of the Department and Commission on Jewish Education for a period of two years. He congratulated me and assured me of his confidence in me and willingness to help. I placed the phone back on the hook, sat silently for a moment then yelled aloud in happiness. After calling to inform my family, I lay awake all night, dreaming of the challenges to come and how I would address them. I wanted Reform Jews to be proud of their Department of Education, and I wanted Jewish educators to regain the stature that had eroded so badly during the early 1970s. Those would be my two overarching goals.

Shortly thereafter, I decided to visit my family in Detroit, prior to the beginning of the religious school year and the High Holidays. I especially looked forward to seeing my younger brother, Michael, who had just moved back to my parents' home from Little Rock, Arkansas. Now that we had both reached adulthood, it was time, I felt, to make up for the many years we had spent apart.

Michael was a true musical genius. He played twenty instruments, though he had never learned how to read music. He played guitar with John Lennon and flute with Frank Zappa. He won a four-year violin scholarship to a prominent music conservatory after teaching himself how to play the violin and auditioning for that scholarship—all in a period of six weeks. He was a fine actor and a promising artist. Everyone predicted a brilliant future for him.

And yet, on August 30, 1975, Michael committed suicide. To this day I cannot fathom why, but in the aftermath of Michael's death, I promised myself that I would personally do whatever I could to spare other families the paralyzing trauma of loss by suicide.

Nine years later, the Union of American Hebrew Congregations established a Task Force on Youth Suicide. By 1984, suicide had become a national epidemic, the second leading cause of death among those fifteen to twenty-four years of age, with close to five hundred thousand young people attempting suicide each year and six thousand completing the act. The new task force afforded us an opportunity to combat this largely preventable tragedy in an aggressive fashion. As of 1989, through books and program kits, videotapes and training programs, the UAHC and Reform Judaism have spared dozens of families unspeakable tragedy. My brother Michael's memory lives on through the program that his loss helped to create.

Jewish tradition teaches that one who saves a single life is credited as though he or she saved the entire world. The Reform movement continues to save the lives of young people today, another reason why I and many others are proud to be Reform Jews.

During the shivah period following Michael's death, a woman whom he had been seeing named Nancy Shayne, came to the house to express her condolences. She was accompanied by her sister, Debbie, and the two of them returned to the house every night of the shivah week. Since very few people of my own age were at our home for more than a half hour or so, I sat with Nancy and Debbie when my parents did not require my presence and, joined by my brother David, we talked about Michael long into the night.

Debbie was as kind and sensitive a woman as I had ever met. Moreover, she also made her career in education, but in a world totally different from mine. Debbie held a masters degree in special education and worked with learning-disabled adolescents. In 1975 this was a relatively new field, with early diagnosis and sophisticated testing techniques just beginning to gain widespread acceptance. Debbie's students included boys and girls for whom public consciousness had come too late. Unable to read, write or spell adequately through no fault of their own, and in the absence of a recognition of their very real problems, they had been labeled as 'lazy' or 'troublemakers.' Stripped of self-esteem by both parents and teachers, they 'lived down' to expectations, skipping school, using drugs and even becoming embroiled with the law. Debbie rebuilt their shattered egos, patiently spending hour after hour with them on an individual basis, typing papers for students who were once embarrassed to hand in their work, gradually enabling the dyslexic to read, generating self-pride and new self-respect.

During the months following Michael's death, I saw Debbie often, visiting her classroom on a regular basis, watching her touch and transform lives. She opened my eyes to the whole field of special-needs education and the importance of the UAHC attention to these young people. By 1989, the UAHC Department of Education had a framework in place that will ultimately afford a full and complete Jewish education for young people and adults who are learning disabled, physically or mentally disabled, hearing impaired or sightless, in part as a result of Debbie's influence. As we spent more and more time together, our relationship deepened into love, and in March of 1977 we were married by Alex Schindler in the UAHC chapel.

The twelve years I spent in Jewish education coincided with a remarkable revival of interest in and enthusiasm for Reform Jewish learning and study, which continues today. Certainly a major factor in the renaissance lay in the burgeoning growth of the movement's schools of education at HUC-JIR in Los Angeles and in New York.

From tentative beginnings, in which both students and positions had to be negotiated city by city, the schools now boast a combined alumni roster well in excess of one hundred masters degree graduates as well as a recently instituted doctoral program. Graduates serve in congregations, day schools, Jewish organizations and on the faculty of HUC-JIR itself. They have professionalized the field and elevated the status of the educator in the process.

The UAHC's accomplishments also drew many Jews into the Reform orbit. Central to our new direction was the gradual emergence of the new curriculum with literally hundreds of educators and teachers involved in writing, field testing and implementation, the document was hailed by the Israel-Diaspora Institute of Tel Aviv University as the finest model of curriculum development in all of world Jewry at that time.

The growing Department of Education staff set new directions in teacher training, sharing practical, upbeat classroom strategies for immediate use rather than the theoretical constructs—so often shared and quickly forgotten—of the past. During that same period, the Union regularly published ten to twelve new texts each year.

At Alex Schindler's urging, the department initiated a vigorous program of television production, which had its genesis in a genuine serendipity occasioned by a reunion with my old high school friend, Ze'ev Chafets. Ze'ev had served Menachem Begin faithfully for close to a decade during the lean years of Begin's political career. In the aftermath of Begin's electoral victory and ascension to the office of prime minister of Israel in June of 1977, Ze'ev was an obvious choice for a post in the new administration. Begin entrusted him with the directorship of Israel's Government Press Office. This is no small responsibility, for Israel has an impressive number of resident foreign journalists.

Ze'ev assumed this new post a few months short of his thirtieth birthday—and only five months prior to Anwar Sadat's journey to

Jerusalem during the fall of 1977! As his first major assignment, the still inexperienced Chafets coordinated world coverage of the Sadat visit. As the army of media descended upon Israel, Ze'ev was in the public eye every hour of every day. With virtually no sleep but enormous energy, he got the job done and within two weeks became a celebrity within Israel and a valued colleague and resource for every television, radio and newspaper figure in the world journalism corps.

In September of 1981, Menachem Begin scheduled his first visit to Washington after the election of Ronald Reagan to the presidency. Ze'ev and another of Begin's closest advisors, General Ephraim Poran, known affectionately as Froika, arrived in New York a few days prior to Begin's scheduled arrival to finalize a number of details. I was delighted to learn that Ze'ev was in Manhattan, and we arranged to meet at a small West Side restaurant. Over dinner, part of our conversation centered on the proposed UAHC television project. I discussed various possibilities with Ze'ev and Froika, including a series I envisioned of videotaped interviews with great Jewish personalities, focusing on their Jewish identity, education, values and their message to this and future generations. Many great leaders of Judaism would have had much to say to Jewish young people and adults. David Ben-Gurion, Albert Einstein, Golda Meir and Louis Brandeis were all gone. But others, Menachem Begin included, could be recorded on video as a permanent piece of Jewish history. Froika responded at once. He asked if I would be interested in doing a program with Begin the following Monday, Labor Day. At first I thought he was joking, then realized that this was a real offer.

We began to talk seriously. How could this be done? We needed a crew. No problem, said Ze'ev. We called Justin Friedland, another old high school MSTY friend of ours, then a producer at ABC News in New York. Intrigued by the notion, he immediately agreed to secure a crew on a free-lance basis and direct the show personally. Froika suggested that since this was a UAHC production, Alex Schindler should handle the interview. We spent the next half hour developing a set of questions that would elicit important answers from Begin. By the time we left the restaurant, we were set to go. In

185

the space of two hours, I had become an executive producer and was about to produce my first television special!

On Labor Day, 1981, the UAHC entered the field of television production as Alex Schindler sat with Menachem Begin and asked him a series of personal questions. Begin was wonderful. He spoke openly about his early years, his Jewish education, his personal theology, and above all, his hope that Jewish young people everywhere would take pride in their Judaism and consider coming to Israel to help build the Jewish state. As the interview concluded, there was spontaneous applause from many people who stood in the back of the room just to listen. It was one of those perfect days, and a triumph for the UAHC.

After all the equipment was packed up, Ze'ev and I walked to the Plaza Hotel for a drink. We discussed the postproduction work still to be done, the photographs and possible newsreel footage that should be inserted into the show, and the vast amount of material readily available through the Government Press Office in Israel. We agreed that I would come to Israel as soon as possible to do the necessary follow-up research. Suddenly, both of us began to laugh. Without saying a word, the same thought occurred to both of us at the same time. Here we were, two kids from Detroit, Michigan, who had grown up together, one of whom was now a major international press official, the other an executive in a national Jewish organization, who had just finished doing a television show with Israel's prime minister!

That was the beginning. Today, the UAHC Television and Film Institute has a library of close to two dozen titles, including interviews with leading Jews of our time, as well as programs relating to conversion, interfaith marriage, cults and missionaries. The video medium will continue to be an increasingly significant tool with which to convey the message of Reform Judaism.

During the 1980s, with twelve Reform Jewish day schools in operation and a dozen more on the drawing boards, the UAHC biennial at last endorsed Reform day schools as an option for families seeking an intensive Jewish education in a liberal setting for their children. The Department of Education also launched new efforts in parent and family education, and today stands poised to take on the new frontier of systematic formal and informal adult education. The inertia of the 1970s has been replaced with a dynamism whose momentum will extend well in to the 1990s and beyond.

The UAHC remains on the cutting edge of Jewish education, another reason why I am proud to be a Reform Jew.

CHAPTER XXIX

Reform Takes Center Stage on the International Scene

*N*ineteen seventy-six was a watershed year for both the United States and the Reform movement. For America, it brought the Bicentennial, the 200th anniversary of a nation standing as a beacon of freedom, justice and opportunity for the entire free world. The year-long celebration, highlighted by massive displays of fireworks and other historic July 4th commemorations, reminded the citizens of the United States and the larger community of nations what America had meant to peace and hope over the twenty decades of its existence. In a sense, the Bicentennial helped to ease some of the pain of Vietnam by offering an opportunity for healing and a fresh start.

The Central Conference of American Rabbis marked this year by issuing a new platform for Reform Judaism on the occasion of the centennials of the UAHC and the Hebrew Union College. The new statement, entitled "Reform Judaism—A Centenary Perspective," both reinforced the past and broke new ground for the present and future. It affirmed that tradition must interact with modern culture, that ethics and observance were both essential to a full Reform Jewish existence, that women must have full equality in Jewish life and that the free exercise of informed choice still obtained as the right and responsibility of every Reform Jew. The 1976 statement praised diversity within Reform, accepting differences in approach to specific rituals and observances as valid and yet contributing to a larger unity. It also urged, however, that modern Reform Jews move beyond an exclusive emphasis on the ethical teachings of

Judaism to an examination of the attractive aspects of increased ritual observance. It spoke of the *State* of Israel within a movement platform for the first time, affirming the bonds of Reform to Israel, its stake in building Israel, assuring its security and defining its Jewish character. In a dramatic departure from past official statements the centenary perspective also stated:

'We encourage *aliyah* for those who wish to find maximum personal fulfillment in the cause of Zion.'

This was truly revolutionary, demonstrating once again the capacity of Reform to grow and mature in the light of history and experience. While the document reaffirmed the validity of Jewish life in every land, and the essential partnership of the State of Israel and Jews in other countries, the Reform movement was now on record as having committed itself to providing an opportunity for those Jews who wished to do so to settle in Israel and be part of a strong liberal Jewish community.

For the Reform movement, however, the year 1976 will be best remembered as that time in its development when Reform Judaism came of age in the Zionist world and on the stage of international politics, through the election of Alexander Schindler to the chairmanship of the Conference of Presidents of Major Jewish Organizations. This powerful coalition came into being in the late 1950s, when Secretary of State John Foster Dulles, frustrated and angered by the number of requests from Jewish organizations for meetings with him and President Dwight D. Eisenhower, summoned Dr. Nahum Goldmann to his office. Dulles told Goldmann, a prominent Jewish leader of the era, that unless the Jewish community established a single group to speak with one voice on matters of Jewish concern, he would henceforth refuse to schedule any such appointments with him or with the president. Goldmann, with the help of Maurice Eisendrath and a few other Jewish leaders, acted quickly, and in 1959 the Conference held its first meeting. As of 1989, the group included forty-six constituent organizations and was still recognized in both the United States and Israel as the single most authoritative voice of American Jewry. The Conference was built and guided quietly and effectively by its first executive director, Yehuda Hellman. Hellman always placed the chairman of the Conference center stage, but everyone knew that it was he who worked day and night to assemble facts, create what he felt would be consensus statements, smooth over potential disputes and enable a group that could easily have been fragmented by controversy to function effectively on behalf of the State of Israel.

By 1976, seventeen years after the Conference was established, the respect earned by Alex Schindler during the first years of his presidency of the UAHC, combined with the Reform movement's growing involvement in Zionist activities, led to his election as chairman of the Conference of Presidents. He held this post for an unprecedented two and a half years, guiding American Jewry through many difficult crises in both the United States and Israel, and becoming in the process an acknowledged spokesman for all of American Jewry. Schindler had a unique capacity for discerning consensus in the Conference. He never imposed his own political views or represented them as the will of the body. Moreover, for the duration of his Conference presidency, he refrained from speaking publicly on uniquely Reform concerns, particularly those of a religious nature. As chairman of a group that specifically eschewed discussion of religious questions in order to preserve its unity, he felt bound to refrain from any statement that might have been perceived as parochial or self-serving. At the first UAHC board meeting after his election, however, he made clear that his own limitations should never lead the UAHC to hold back from expression of its concerns:

> 'I do not want the fact that I am the Chairman of the Presidents' Conference to be in any sense a constraining force on the Union. I want the Union to be what it has always been, a fearless spokesman for the truth as it perceives it, both within the Jewish community and the larger American scene.'

At that same meeting, the UAHC board of trustees, echoing the sentiments of CCAR's plank on *aliyah* in the Centenary Perspective, endorsed its own resolution on the matter:

> 'The land of Israel, which is Zion, and the children of Israel who constitute the Jewish people and the God of Israel, are all bound

together in a triple covenant. As Reform Jews, we perceive the political entity of the State of Israel, together with the Jewish people the world over, as constituting a means for the continued evolution of this convenantal relationship.

Our movement has a unique and critical role to play in shaping Israel's future as a Jewish state. We can do this both by enriching Jewish life in our community and by participating in the fabric of Israeli society. Hence the Israel Commission affirms the value of *aliyah* as a valid option for contemporary liberal Jewish commitment and self-fulfillment. A Reform *aliyah* will expand our role in Israel and further our rightful contribution to the life and religious expression of the State and the Jewish people.

Therefore, be it resolved: We affirm a special duty to encourage and assist those Reform Jews who, individually or in groups, wish to participate more fully in the development of the State of Israel and in the development of Progressive Judaism in Israel by making *aliyah* and settling there.'

In November of 1976, Jimmy Carter became president of the United States, defeating Gerald R. Ford. In his capacity as chairman of the Conference of Presidents, Alex Schindler traveled to Washington frequently, engaging in candid, sometimes critical dialogue with Carter and high administration officials on tensions in the Middle East and possible constructive steps in the direction of a peaceful solution to the ongoing conflict and bloodshed. In spite of the daring raid on the airport in Entebbe on the very July 4th of the Bicentennial, in which Israelis rescued a planeload of hostages taken by Palestinian terrorists, there was no desire on the part of Israel or the United States to have to wonder what brutal act or disaster lay ahead.

With the resignation in early 1977 of Yitzhak Rabin as Israel's prime minister, new elections in Israel were called, and most observers assumed that the Labour Party would once again take control of the government as it had since 1948. Shimon Peres, the Labour candidate, seemed almost assured of defeating Likud leader Menachem Begin once again in what was apparently Begin's last run at public office. When Debbie and I were married in New York in March of 1977, part of the discussion at our wedding reception centered on what the chances might be of peace in a new

Labour government. Politics, however, always brings surprises, and never more so than on June 20, 1977, when the election results in Israel became clear. In a stunning upset, Likud and Menachem Begin won the election, and this lifetime oppositionist, known almost exclusively for his role in the anti-British underground prior to the establishment of Israel as a state, was suddenly the prime minister of Israel.

The world media reacted swiftly, with many journalists declaring that a terrorist now headed Israel's government. Virtually no major world leader knew anything about Begin. Most American news agencies had clippings on Begin solely from the 1940s and early 1950s. In the face of this Begin-bashing, there was a clear possibility that the new government in Israel would come into office under a dark cloud. Compounding the difficulties, Begin was hospitalized soon after the election with a mild heart attack.

It was at this point that Alex Schindler rose to international prominence. On his own, Alex flew to Israel to express his endorsement of the Begin government. Privately and publicly, he stated that any lover of Israel also had a duty to support the democratically elected leader of that country. After arriving in Israel, Schindler went to Begin's hospital room to visit him. Though the two differed on many issues, the chemistry between them was such that they became friends almost at once. During his stay in Israel, Schindler saw Begin several times and thus became the first American Jewish leader to engage in extensive discussions with Begin following the election. Returning to the United States, Alex was asked to come to Washington to meet with officials of the Carter administration, who knew nothing about Begin. Thus the president of the UAHC became one of the initial intermediaries between the United States and Israeli governments.

As Begin returned to health, he became aware of a planned attempt on the life of Egypt's president, Anwar Sadat, and instructed Israeli intelligence to inform Sadat of the plot. Shortly thereafter, perhaps out of gratitude to Begin, perhaps because of the security and support he enjoyed within Egypt as a result of his surprise attack on Israel in the Yom Kippur War, and in part perhaps because of his fear that President Carter's call for an international peace conference might reintroduce the Russians into the

Middle East after he had struggled so mightily to rid Egypt of them, Sadat gave a stirring address in which he offered to come to Jerusalem if that would bring peace. Some observers reacted with skepticism, considering the statement political hyperbole. Not Begin. He responded at once by inviting Sadat to Israel.

As fate would have it, the visit to Jerusalem took place during the UAHC's biennial convention in November of 1977 in San Francisco. In his presidential address, Alex Schindler sounded a word of caution:

'The news which emanates from Cairo and Jerusalem these days is intriguing. Sadat's offer to come to Jerusalem constitutes, in effect, an acceptance of Israel's right to exist and gives visible demonstration of his desire for peace. I applaud Sadat's offer, as well as Begin's ready acceptance of it. I admire their courage and pray for the success of their historic encounter.

Still, we should not wax too euphoric. Such a visit can enhance the climate for peace, but it cannot bring peace itself. Complex issues remain to be resolved, and others than Begin and Sadat are required to solve them.'

Later in the convention, the three thousand delegates watched in wonder a delayed videotape of Sadat's actual arrival in Jerusalem. Here was one of Israel's sworn enemies, the architect of the Yom Kippur War, stepping off a plane onto Israeli soil and shaking hands with those whom he had once vowed to destroy. In spite of all the cautions, then, no Jew could be blamed for declaring that a major breakthrough was at hand. For the first time in Israel's history, the possibility of true peace was on the horizon.

The sequence of events made the formal announcement of Reform Judaism's first kibbutz, Kibbutz Yahel, even more exciting, and virtually guaranteed the passage of a resolution creating a new affiliate under the aegis of the Union, to be known as ARZA, the Association of Reform Zionists of America. It declared as well the establishment of a Canadian counterpart, Kadimah. The essence of both organizations was and is to enable the Reform movement to participate in the political sphere of the World Zionist Organization. They are charged with the responsibility of serving as a political entity through whose membership votes power might be wielded in behalf of progressive Judaism in Israel's complex political structure. Until 1977, Reform Judaism, though by now strongly pro-Israel, remained outside the organizational framework of Zionism. The establishment of separate UAHC affiliates, would enable those who wished to express their *political* Zionist commitment to do so within Reform Judaism, joining these affiliates as individuals without imposing a political Zionist status upon the UAHC as a whole. Though many anticipated a long and bitter debate, the opposition to the creation of ARZA and Kadimah was surprisingly small. The resolution passed by an overwhelming majority and thus set into motion a new era in Reform Jewish history of formal engagement with the Zionist world.

Less than one year later, in September of 1978, ARZA held its first national assembly in Washington, D.C. Delegates to that founding assembly proceeded to pass a platform of values upon which ARZA would base its work, then set out to foster the growth of this newest member of the UAHC family. Though its early years held many bitter disappointments, the 1987 World Zionist Congress constituted a tribute to ten years of hard work. After just a decade of existence, ARZA garnered the second largest vote total of any United States group in the Zionist elections and thereby secured the directorship of the World Zionist Organization's Department of Education and the chairmanship of its Actions Committee, the Vaad Hapoel. In that same year, ARZA founded the Israel Religious Action Center in Jerusalem, patterned after the Washington RAC, to fight aggressively for religious rights for Reform Jews and all Israelis. Today, the center initiates and finances legal action on behalf of those who have suffered discrimination, including Reform converts who have immigrated to Israel and been refused registration as Jews under Israel's law of return. The center also educates government officials about Reform Judaism, conducts polls on religious attitudes and plays a vital role in bringing Jewish values to the larger Israeli public.

Fate had more in store for Alexander Schindler as 1978 began. Though he had made the dramatic gesture of coming to Israel to declare his desire for peace, Sadat was chagrined by the failure of many Americans, specifically American Jews, to accept the sincerity of his purpose. He therefore determined to underscore his dedication to peace by inviting a prominent American Jew to Egypt. The individual whom he selected was Rabbi Alexander Schindler. On two separate occasions, and with the blessing of both the United States and Israeli governments, Alex traveled to Egypt to meet with Sadat in one of his palaces. At Sadat's request, he conveyed certain private communications to both Carter and Begin. When the Camp David Peace Accords were signed in March of 1979, more than one analyst speculated that Schindler played a significant role during the early stages of negotiations. Even though his term of office as chairman of the Conference of Presidents had concluded, Alexander Schindler was now an undisputed spokesman for all of American Jewry, establishing Reform Judaism as an increasingly visible and assertive force on the international scene. On July 3, 1978, at ceremonies held on Mount Scopus at the Hebrew University of Jerusalem, he received the Solomon Bublick Prize, honored as the person who, during the two years preceding the award, made the most significant contribution to the progress and development of the State of Israel. He thus joined figures such as David Ben-Gurion and President Harry S. Truman as an individual not merely associated with a single movement but enshrined within the annals of Jewish history.

In light of his unqualified success as chairman of the Conference of Presidents, and in view of the extraordinary growth of Reform Judaism since the beginning of his tenure as president of the Union, Alex Schindler might have been expected to step back for a bit and allow some of his initiatives to take hold before advancing new and more dramatic proposals. Those who anticipated a respite, however, were due instead for another challenge.

CHAPTER XXX

Outreach

A few months after the signing of the Camp David Accords, the UAHC board met in Houston, Texas. Speculation had grown that Alex Schindler was considering a proposal regarding the proselytizing of non-Jews to Judaism. Variations on this theme had been advanced by individual rabbis from time to time, but only in their local communities and often in response to the growing intrusions by non-Jewish missionary groups and cults. The board, therefore, anxiously awaited what would become one of the most famous speeches in Reform Jewish history.

Schindler began by reviewing the most recent statistics on intermarriage, estimated at over 31 percent between the years 1966 and 1972, and then continued:

> 'However much we deplore it, however much we struggle against it as individuals, these are the facts: The tide is running against us. This is the reality and we must face it.
>
> However, facing reality does not import its complacent, fatalistic acceptance. It does not mean that we must prepare to sit *shiva* for the American Jewish community. Quite the contrary! Facing reality means confronting it, coming to grips with it, determining to re-shape it.'

Expressing his concern at the refusal by many Jews to accept those who converted to Judaism, and the tendency to question their motives, Schindler asked that a task force be established to develop a sensitive program of welcoming converts to Judaism, recognizing that those who choose Judaism in good faith are as authentic in their Jewish identity as those who are born Jewish. He also asked that the board endorse the imperative of seeking out those couples who had married without conversion and drawing them into synagogue life. By doing so, he said, we would have a chance of helping to assure that at least the children of those marriages would be reared as Jews. He urged that ways be found to allow the non-Jewish partner of a mixed marriage to join in Jewish ceremonial and life-cycle events, and raised the possibility of considering the patrilineal line as valid a genealogical determinant of Jewish identity as that of the mother.

Finally, he called upon the board to endorse a dignified outreach program to the unchurched, men and women with no religious preference and in search of a meaningful faith, for whom Judaism might provide the ideal spiritual home:

'Judaism offers life, not death. It teaches free will, not surrender of body and soul to another human being. The Jew prays directly to God, not through an intermediary who stands between him and his God. Judaism is a religion of hope, not despair, it insists that man and society are perfectable. Judaism has an enormous amount of wisdom and experience to offer this troubled world, and we Jews ought to be proud to speak about it, frankly, freely and with dignity.'

The response was electric. One board member after another stood up to praise the speech. The resolution was adopted, and the Task Force on Outreach authorized.

The program might have remained an internal UAHC project had it not been for an accident of history. A New York *Times* reporter, having received an advance copy of the speech, was sufficiently impressed to submit it to his editors as a feature story for the following morning's paper. The article on Outreach wound up on the front page of the Sunday New York *Times*, and thus was disseminated throughout the world. This fortuitous circumstance may well have changed the course of Jewish history. Over the weeks and months that followed, thousands of letters flooded UAHC headquarters in New York, including offers of help, words of thanks, pleas for urgent action and expressions of heartfelt appreciation for this initiative.

Among those who studied the contemplated program was a prominent Iowa attorney named David Belin. Belin, a longtime member of the Reform congregation in Des Moines, had served as counsel to the Warren Commission investigating the assassination of President John F. Kennedy, and as counsel to the Rockefeller Commission, investigating the covert activities of the CIA. He called Alex Schindler, so enthusiastic about the program that he volunteered to serve as its chairman. After meeting with Belin, Schindler concluded that he was exactly the right person for the task. Over the next two years, Belin guided the group through its deliberations. Juggling the sensitive agendas of lay leaders, rabbis and UAHC staff, he forged a consensus on a report for the 1981 UAHC biennial. At the same time, he encouraged pilot programs, books and materials and the production of a videotape featuring Jews by Choice, in order to strengthen and reinforce the substantive proposal to be brought to the convention.

Key to the progress of Outreach, however, was securing the preliminary assent of the 1979 biennial plenary in Toronto, Canada. In his presidential address, Schindler repeated the essence of the Houston speech, but then surprised the convention by pressing forward on the issue of patrilineal descent, presented solely as a matter for reflection in Texas:

'I would like you to initiate a decision-making process—led by the CCAR, but involving our entire Movement—which will culminate in the validation of Jewish lineage through the paternal, and not just the maternal line. The status of Jews should be conferred on any child, either of whose parents is Jewish, provided they both agree to raise their child Jewishly and do so. To put the matter somewhat differently, I want the child's rearing and being and, ultimately, his self-definition to be on a par with genealogical factors in determining Jewishness ... adherence to the matrilineal principle confronts us with a dreadful anomaly: the offspring of a mixed marriage, whether reared as a Jew or not, no matter, is automatically a Jew so long as the mother is Jewish; but if the mother isn't, the offspring must ultimately undergo formal conversion, even if he was raised as a Jew and lived in an intensely Jewish home. This is nonsensical, absurd! Surely the father counts for something when we affix his child's religious identity!

'A tradition spanning millennia should not be altered lightly. I agree. We must have a reverence for so time-honored a usage. Yet those circumstances which gave birth to that usage simply no longer obtain. It reflects a polygamous society in which the children of the various wives lived with their mother; but we no longer live in such a society—in conformity with Jewish law. The matrilineal tradition was reinforced by brutal persecution, when Jewish women were impregnated by force, ruthlessly raped, and a compassionate law permitted their children to be deemed Jewish, though they could not know just who the father was. But such a persecution is not rampant still. Moreover that millennial tradition itself provides ample justification for a paternal as well as a maternal yardstick. It invokes the God of our *fathers* in prayer. It rules that we be summoned to the Torah by our *father's* name. It reminds us that we live by *zechut avot*, by the merit of our *fathers*. Indeed, in matters of inheritance, and in some aspects of genealogy, only the paternal line is held relevant; for instance, whether one is a Kohen or a Levi depends on the father's priestly claim and not the mother's. Thus does tradition offer a way to heal itself . . . Please don't shrug this matter off as an academic issue. It is of the gravest moment to us. What we do or fail to do will affect us profoundly. Remember that the intermarriage rate is approaching forty percent, and that the preponderant majority of such marriages involves Jewish men. Their right to determine the religious character of their children must also be secured. Here, then, is still another way to make certain that our grandchildren will be Jews, that they will remain a part of our community and share the destiny of the people of Israel.'

The delegates sat, stunned. The rabbis present were particularly upset, for they believed that such a proposal fell exclusively within the purview of the Central Conference of American Rabbis. But, as was his custom, Alex Schindler spoke his mind, clearly and assertively, to the entire Reform movement. Reaction to the speech was quick in coming, especially from the Orthodox community, who attacked it vehemently, in particular the section on patrilineal descent. They proclaimed that implementation of such a proposal would irrevocably split the Jewish people, and indeed would create an entire new religion. They urged that such a step not be taken, and condemned Alex Schindler for raising it.

While endorsing most of the provisions of the Outreach resolution, the biennial delegates asked that the segment relating to missionizing activity be held in abeyance. They further instructed the task force to return to the 1981 convention with a detailed report and proposal. As for the patrilineal issue, the delegates concluded that the matter should be referred to the CCAR for decision, with a recommendation that it be studied with great care. Two years thereafter, at the 1981 biennial convention in Boston, the detailed report of the task force on Outreach was overwhelmingly approved, and after four years of discussion and debate, the CCAR affirmed and endorsed the principle of patrilineal descent. As of 1989, the Outreach program had become a commission, a joint instrumentality of the UAHC and the Central Conference of American Rabbis, a formal part of the UAHC program.

As it celebrated its tenth anniversary, Outreach could safely lay claim to having fulfilled the lion's share of the tasks entrusted to it a decade earlier. In the first instance, Outreach brought conversion out of the closet, no longer a matter for embarrassment or shame, but rather an important life-cycle event. Albert Einstein once stated that he was sorry he was born a Jew, for that deprived him of the opportunity of choosing to be one. Thousands of men and women have done honor to Judaism by dedicating their lives to its principles and, in the process, opening the eyes of born Jews to the many blessings that are their birthright.

Secondly, the Outreach program successfully raised the consciousness of hundreds of congregations to the need for more intensified efforts to bring those new to Judaism into the community and make them a part of it. A fast-proliferating program called The Times and the Seasons has sought out and brought to the synagogue intermarried couples as well as interfaith unmarried couples. These men and women discuss the potential for their involvement in congregational life, as well as the very real problems and conflicts inherent in their relationship. Furthermore, the Commission has begun to explore ways in which to attract the children of intermarried couples to the temple, whether or not the non-Jewish partner in the marriage chooses to become a Jew.

The issue of patrilineal descent continues to be a controversial one. Prophets of doom still predict that there will be two Jewish communities within a single generation. Others, however, are hard at work, seeking to find a way in which both to affirm the role of the father in determining Jewish identity and preserve Jewish unity.

One thing is certain. The Outreach idea has had a profound impact on North American Jewry. Every major movement, Orthodoxy included, has now developed some program in this realm within the boundaries of its own ideological considerations. Every major movement has studied the models developed by the UAHC. Most have sent representatives to UAHC Outreach conferences, carefully studied UAHC books and materials and films, then either adopted or adapted them for their specific goals. As a result of Outreach, the Reform movement has again found a way not just to save Jews but to make Jews—whether they were born into Judaism or chose Judaism at a later stage of life.

CHAPTER XXXI

The Conversion of Caitlin O'Sullivan

*T*he single event that exemplified the impact of the Outreach program for me in its early years was a religious service on January 10, 1981. On that day, Caitlin O'Sullivan became a Jew. The conversion ceremony took place during a Shabbat morning service at New York City's Stephen Wise Free Synagogue, perhaps the first public conversion ceremony ever in Manhattan. I was there as her rabbi and as her friend.

My first meeting with Caitlin O'Sullivan was an accident. The then-embryonic task force on Reform Jewish Outreach sponsored a weekend program at UAHC headquarters in New York. Registration for the program, originally intended solely for recent converts to Judaism, lagged somewhat behind expectations. Accordingly, I was asked to recruit participants from the Introduction to Judaism classes in the UAHC's New York conversion course. I spoke to one class and distributed flyers for the weekend. No more than ten minutes after completing my 'pitch' I had one application in hand. Caitlin O'Sullivan had made a decision to examine Judaism a little more closely. I remember how struck I was at the time by her confidence, her enthusiasm, her candor. During the Outreach weekend itself, however, Caitlin O'Sullivan spoke very little. She participated knowledgeably in Shabbat services, and even offered a spontaneous closing prayer. But mostly she listened intently to the statements of others, absorbing, concentrating. Finally, on Saturday night, Caitlin shared her personal story. She was raised as a Catholic in a community on the West Coast. After a deeply disillusioning

202

family trauma during her high school years, Caitlin and others in her family fell away from the church. Caitlin, especially, began to examine other religions, particularly Judaism. Now, as an adult, after studying on her own for many years, she had taken a second step in the direction of Judaism by enrolling in the UAHC's conversion course. She made it clear that her mind was not yet made up, that she was still thinking and learning and doing Jewishly. In effect, she was trying Judaism on, seeing how it felt. There was no sense of urgency to her search. After all, conversion was more than a casual decision. It represented a major commitment.

She concluded her remarks. No one in the room moved. No one coughed. No one yawned or stretched. We all knew that in a very real sense, we were witnessing the formation of a Jewish soul. We were deeply moved and touched by this young woman who knew herself so well and who was so determined to maintain her intellectual and religious integrity.

The weekend came to a close. Caitlin left us, but I continued to receive reports of her progress. She called from time to time, just to say hello. Mutual friends told me of her frequent presence at Manhattan's Stephen Wise Free Synagogue. Then, just after the High Holy Days in 1980, Caitlin appeared in my office. She had decided to embrace Judaism and—though it is not required within Reform—to visit the mikvah, the Jewish ritual bath, as a prelude to the service. Most significantly, however, Caitlin O'Sullivan seized upon an idea first expressed at the New York Outreach weekend. She wanted a public conversion, and asked me to participate and offer a blessing on her behalf.

The notion of conversion to Judaism in the presence of the entire congregation was discussed in the Outreach task force as one way to bring conversion out of the closet. The logic was inescapable. Born Jews had never been made privy to the process of conversion. Indeed, conversion at the time was something no one spoke about, most often consigned to the rabbi's study or a deserted chapel. That, many felt, was a mistake. The community needed to be part of conversion, to see thinking, caring men and women choosing Judaism with no ambivalence, no embarrassment, no hangups. What a boon to Jewish pride we felt that would be! What a spur to adult Jewish learning! What a weapon against stereotypes and ethnic prejudice! And what a support to the new Jew; a community bearing witness to this powerful moment with openness and out-stretched arms of welcome. Caitlin O'Sullivan heard this idea at the Outreach weekend and decided to bring it to fruition.

I told Caitlin that I would be honored to be part of her conver-sion and suggested that we talk further about how best to structure the service and set a date. To my amazement, I then learned that Caitlin planned on putting the entire service together: assigning parts to the rabbis, conducting a major portion of the service herself utilizing her newly acquired Hebrew reading proficiency, selecting the music, delivering the sermon. Everything was to be carefully planned and sensitively done. She found a date when no bar or bat mitzvah was scheduled. That Shabbat would be hers alone.

In mid-December of 1980, the Outreach task force sponsored a second New York weekend. Caitlin attended, along with four other 'alumni' of the earlier program. In contrast to her quiet, almost reserved manner eight months earlier, Caitlin now had become a confident, articulate "Jew-in-process." Though her formal conver-sion was still a month away, there was no doubt that many weekend participants looked to Caitlin as a model, a resource, a friend. She issued a blanket invitation to the group to attend her conversion ceremony, and many said they'd be there.

On New Year's Day, 1981, as I watched the various college football games, I suddenly realized that Caitlin's service was a week away and that I had not the slightest idea of what I intended to say to her in front of all those people. My rabbi's manual was no help. This had to be totally personal. Eight hours later, I had a first draft. Over the next several days, I shared it with at least a dozen col-leagues and friends. Each made suggestions, changes and addi-tions. At last, by Thursday I felt I was ready. That night, Caitlin and I spoke by phone. She outlined the service. We talked through her personal declaration and the blessing itself. Then Caitlin dropped the bombshell. She was having second thoughts. She wasn't sure she was doing the right thing, and she was scared. Her parents were coming, along with dozens of other friends and acquaintances she had invited, and the pressure was a little frightening. I did my best to reassure her that her feelings were normal and natural. This was, after all, a life-altering step. After thirty minutes on the phone, we agreed that Caitlin should call another friend who had chosen Judaism, just to talk. The call was made. By Friday morning, Caitlin once again felt confident about her decision.

That Friday night, I couldn't sleep. I kept going over my remarks, pacing the floor, making sure that I had done as much as I could to make the next morning's service as meaningful and moving as possible. I finally drifted off to sleep at about 3:00 A.M., but was up again at 6:00. I kept thinking about how much insight the Torah has. Wherever in the Torah it says "And he got up early in the morning," it indicates that the person is facing an important and somewhat frightening task—Abraham preparing to take Isaac to sacrifice him, for example. I finally gave up on sleep and left for the synagogue at 8:00 A.M.

When services don't begin until 10:30 A.M., most temples are locked at 8:15 in the morning. The Stephen Wise Free Synagogue was no exception. There I was, dressed, ready for services, standing outside in the cold and feeling very silly. Finally, a compassionate security guard let me in, and I sat inside for almost two hours. About ten o'clock, Caitlin arrived. Together with everyone participating in the service, we went over the order one last time. Before I knew it, it was time for the service to begin.

Those participating in the Shabbat worship walked up onto the bimah. Looking out at the congregation, I was surprised and pleased. There were members of the temple, faculty and students of the Hebrew Union College-Jewish Institute of Religion in New York, numerous alumni of the New York Outreach weekends, men and women who had been part of Caitlin's conversion class, people from my apartment building in New York who were intrigued by my description of what was to happen and, of course, Caitlin's family seated in the very first row, eyes riveted upon her every move, giving silent support and encouragement. The sanctuary was full.

Rabbis Edward Klein and Balfour Brickner, the latter my former UAHC colleague and now a rabbi at Stephen Wise, conducted the first part of the service, explaining the history and significance of certain blessings for the benefit of all in attendance. Caitlin read a number of sections as well. Then came the Torah service. Caitlin chanted the blessings, after which Rabbi Brickner read and commented on the sedra, the weekly Torah portion. Caitlin read a section from the Book of Ruth, that classic account of conversion to Judaism, with the blessings before and after chanted by her conversion course instructor.

At last the magical moment arrived. The congregation waited expectantly. There was not a sound in the sanctuary. Caitlin and I stood at the bimah. My hands were shaking, and I decided to share my feelings with Caitlin.

"Caitlin," I said, "I want you to know that I'm scared to death. I've never done this before."

"That's all right," she replied, "neither have I."

The congregation roared. The tension broken, I continued:

'Caitlin, in the presence of your family and friends, before this open ark and witnessed by this entire congregation, your journey begins. Every Jewish experience until this moment has been only a prelude to the challenge you are about to accept. All the searching, all the study, all the doubts and fears, the joy and exhilaration of discovery and decision culminate in this instance of re-creation. You are about to become a Jewish newborn, entitled thereby to an extra measure of love and caring from the Jewish community. We are obligated to nurture and nourish you.

But you in turn take on new and awesome responsibilities. You have committed yourself and your future to Jewish living and to the creation of a personal Jewish past. You will continue to study and do, learn and experience, growing each day as a unique and special person. We are also now dependent upon you for our physical and spiritual Jewish survival. You will influence generations of Jewish children and adults. You will teach them by your example and invest them with Jewish identity. From this moment on, then, Caitlin, our destiny is inextricably bound up with yours.

As a rabbi, as one who cares deeply about Judaism, the Jewish people and the Jewish future, but above all as a friend who has come to admire and respect you, it is now my privilege to recognize your formal entry into Judaism.'

We walked to the open ark. Caitlin took the Torah in her arms and cradled it as I spoke:

"In the presence of this congregation I ask you to hold this Torah and to recite the Shema, the watchword of our faith."

Caitlin recited the Shema in a strong, clear voice, then sang it with her eyes closed, wrapped in a tallit. A chill ran up my spine. I spoke to her again:

"In the presence of this community, I ask if you freely cast your lot with that of the Jewish people from this day forth."

She replied: "I do."

I responded: "In accordance with Jewish custom, I give unto you the Hebrew name you have chosen as your own, *Elisheva*—'God is my oath'—Elisheva bat Avraham v'Sarah. May it become a name honored in the household of Israel."

I then asked Caitlin to stand at the bimah and to declare her acceptance of Judaism. The congregation leaned forward, eager to hear this woman who had already moved and touched them so. Caitlin began:

'I, Caitlin O'Sullivan, at this moment embrace Judaism into my being. I do this freely, openly and with great joy before the assembled congregation as a pledge to God and humanity. I cast off the necessity of intercession and undertake the responsibility of a direct, active and immediate relationship to the Power of the Universe. I honor and thank my parents and my heritage for giving me life and the strength to commit myself to a belief that is my fulfillment, but different from theirs. I approach the Jewish people with deep love and ask their acceptance of me as a member of the Jewish community. I commit the totality of my strength and loyalty to support and defend the Jewish people amid all circumstances to the absolute limit of my being. I pledge to live each day within a Jewish framework, to create and maintain a Jewish home. To observe the traditions and customs of Judaism within my home and in public worship to the extent that these practices further and enhance my love of God and the Jewish people. To spend time in study and the pursuit of Jewish learning, developing the deepest possible understanding of Jewish law, language, thought and culture in order to contribute to my spiritual development and to the future of Judaism. To love and serve other people, always striving to understand the meaning of commitment to another human being. To develop my individual gifts and talents to their highest potential as a fulfillment of the promise of creation. To allow beauty, harmony and peace into my awareness alongside the struggle for achievement, remembering that joy and celebration are as exalted and beloved of God as study, work and prayer.'

Caitlin looked at me. She was finished. I looked out at the congregation. Many were in tears. I led Caitlin back to the ark, and spoke both to her and to all in attendance:

'We who bear witness to this moment have, like you, been eternally transformed. We will never be the same again. We have been blessed through our participation in this, your moment. I therefore ask this entire congregation to join with you and with me in affirming the uniqueness of this day by reciting the Shehecheyanu.'

The congregation stood as one and recited the Shehecheyanu, that special prayer which Jews recite at a unique moment. It may have been my imagination, but I can't remember ever hearing it said quite so enthusiastically. A new Jewish soul had come into the world, and the spiritual parents rejoiced. Caitlin bowed her head, I offered a blessing and then we gave one another a big hug. It was a moment that changed at least two lives.

Later in the service, Caitlin delivered the sermon. She spoke of the sort of experience to which every Jew might aspire:

'One Friday evening, I decided I wanted to light Shabbat candles. I asked my friend if it was all right—was there anything wrong with it if I wasn't Jewish? He assured me that lightning would not strike me, nor an earthquake swallow me up. He helped me learn the blessing and we talked about the various customs involved in the physical act of kindling the light. I picked something that seemed to work with my personality and I did it. As I opened my eyes and beheld the light I had created, I was moved as I had never been moved in my life. In that moment, I understood the concept of mystery, of spirit, of invoking a power greater than myself, through myself. I understood that by activating something very deep and personal, I could also touch something as incomprehensible as the light of the stars in the universe. In that moment, I was changed forever, changed utterly.'

She concluded:

'My discovery of Judaism as a Jew has just begun. Judaism is multi-ethnic, multi-cultural, multi-national. The only limits to an expression of Jewish identity must necessarily be self-imposed. My explorations may take me far, far afield. I know not where. I have reached, I have struggled for knowledge and understanding, and now I am ready to begin.'

No matter where life takes me as a rabbi, I do not believe I will ever again feel as I did on that Shabbat morning. The moment and the community met in perfect union, electric, powerful, Jewish. Only within Reform Judaism could such a moment have taken place. For me, it constituted total validation of the entire Outreach concept. History has shown that there are many others who, like Caitlin O'Sullivan, wish to embrace Judaism. Our Reform movement, at least, will always welcome them, providing a point of entry into a Jewish lifestyle of their choosing and helping born Jews to see Judaism through new and fresh eyes.

CHAPTER XXXII

Joshua's Guarantors

*J*ust one week after Alex Schindler's historic Outreach address in Houston, on December 15, 1978, my wife Debbie gave birth to a child, our son Joshua. Though we completed a Lamaze class together, the doctors at New York Hospital decided that a Caesarian delivery was necessary, and I was not permitted in the operating room. As I sat in the hospital waiting room, I wondered whether the baby would be a boy or a girl. Having been raised in a family of boys, I felt a bit apprehensive at the thought of having a daughter, fearing that my lack of experience with little girls would somehow make me deficient as a father. As with all parents, however, all I truly hoped for was a healthy child. When the doctor emerged from the operating room to inform me that we had a son and that Debbie was all right, my first reaction was one of relief. Almost immediately, however, that feeling was replaced with an overwhelming sense of awe and wonder at what had transpired. I thanked the doctor, then walked to the window of the waiting room, looked out at the falling snow and uttered a silent prayer of thanks to God for having allowed me to live to see this day.

It was a Friday night, Shabbat, just after sundown, and I could not help but call to mind an ancient Jewish legend. Jewish tradition teaches that on Shabbat, every Jew is granted an additional soul for the duration of the Sabbath. On this Shabbat, at least, I knew that the legend was true. Debbie and I had been bequeathed an additional soul for the duration of our lifetimes, a little boy for whom we would sacrifice and strive, for whom we would work to provide every opportunity, a son whom we would do our best to raise as a Jew.

When the nurse brought Joshua out of the operating room, she stopped and asked if I would like to hold him. I looked down at his tiny form and was honestly afraid to pick him up for fear I would break him! I told the nurse that I would wait for Debbie to return to her room, and she simply smiled and returned Joshua to the nursery. I called my parents and Debbie's parents to give them the news. Debbie's parents were home and they were, of course, ecstatic. My parents, however, were already at the synagogue for Friday night services. I phoned the temple and asked that someone get a message to my parents that they had a grandson. According to the account of someone who was present, my father received a note on the bimah of Temple Israel just as he was about to lead the congregation in reciting the Shema, the declaration by Jews of their faith in one God. I can only imagine what that particular affirmation meant to him on that evening in 1978.

It is true, I have come to believe, that every child who comes into this world is a little miracle, a piece of tangible evidence that God wishes the world to continue, a reminder that what we do here on earth is not simply for the sake of our own self-gratification, but part of an historical continuum which is our sacred task to preserve, protect and improve for those who come after us. Our children are living messengers we send ahead on a path to the next generation; they testify to our successes and our failures, and bring to their world much of what we have given—or not given—them. In New York Hospital on that Shabbat, I resolved to do what I could to assure that Joshua's world would be more kind, more decent, more caring and more substantive in its Jewish commitments than the world in which I lived.

Joshua's world will be all these things in part as a result of the Reform movement's continued commitment to social justice. In the course of Joshua's young life, the UAHC has already championed a number of causes critical to the future of his generation.

In the early 1980s, the Union combatted the so-called 'Moral Majority' and the Christian Right and their goal of "Christianizing" America. Their political agenda included prayer in public schools, censorship of textbooks and curricula, a refusal to grant homosexuals civil rights and a determination to outlaw abortion. Through the Commission on Social Action and the Washington Religious Action Center, the UAHC will always resist staunchly any breach of the wall of separation between church and state, and any challenge to our constitutional rights. Both are essential to religious freedom, and together with coalition partners of all faiths the Reform movement will remain in the forefront of that constant struggle.

Joshua's Reform movement will also continue its historic role as the champion of those who have no champion—the homeless, the poor, and the hungry, whether in America or in faraway lands. In 1984, for example, the world learned of a terrible famine in Ethiopia and the deaths of thousands in that nation. Almost at once, the UAHC established a program called Project Reap, intended to raise funds to feed the hungry and to send doctors to provide medical assistance for the suffering citizens of Ethiopia, both Jew and non-Jew.

Urging the UAHC on was an old friend, a free-lance humanitarian and maverick fundraiser Abie Nathan. Nathan—born in Iraq and raised in India, and an Israeli fighter pilot during the War of Independence—was once dubbed "the world's smallest peace organization" for his often singlehanded attempts to bring peace between Israel and her neighbors. He made a daring flight in an old biplane to Egypt during the tense period preceding the 1967 War with a peace proclamation signed by 60,000 Israelis, but President Nasser refused to see him. Abie earned enough money to finance his activities when he introduced hamburgers to Israel in his once-famous California restaurant in Tel Aviv, just off Dizengoff Street. He raised hundreds of thousands of dollars from his fellow Israelis to provide relief to starving Nigerians in Biafra and the victims of war and hunger in Cambodia. He operates a "peace ship" staffed entirely by an international crew of volunteers that broadcasts music and peace messages in Hebrew, Arabic and English from international waters off the coast of Israel.

Over the years, Abie's efforts fired the imagination of members of NFTY and engendered strong bonds of friendship between Nathan and the youth of Reform Judaism. In 1984, Abie Nathan decided to do something about the Ethiopian famine. He broadcast an appeal from his peace ship, and almost overnight some one hundred thousand dollars was raised from Israeli citizens in every walk of life. He flew to London, and persuaded Ethiopian consular authorities to grant him a visa to Ethiopia, which did not recognize Israel. Landing in the Ethiopian capital of Addis Ababa, he peeled off $5,000 from his own funds and said simply, "I want to help." Ethiopian officials granted his request for a plane to fly him to the drought-stricken areas where he could see what had to be done. He came and saw the human need, the gentle people, the starving children. Nathan promised to return with help, and in partnership with the UAHC, he did. Abie called NFTY director Rabbi Steve Schafer, who in turn spoke to Alex Schindler and Charles J. Rothschild, Jr., then-chairman of the UAHC Board of Trustees. Nathan's plan—to build tent cities with hospital facilities, food and water—was immediately endorsed by UAHC leadership.

During Chanukah of that year, the UAHC placed a full-page ad in the Sunday New York *Times*, calling upon all American citizens to celebrate the Jewish Festival of Lights by providing a light of hope to Ethiopians in need. The response was overwhelming. In just a few short weeks, close to $200,000 came to UAHC headquarters in hundreds of envelopes, one-dollar bills, ten-dollar bills, thousand-dollar checks from young people and adults of every religion and from every walk of life. Again, the Reform movement had shown its sense of responsibility, not just to Reform Jews, not just to the Jewish community, but its sacred determination to reach out to the world with love and hope.

In November of 1988, seventy leaders of the civil rights movement of the sixties gathered in Atlanta, Georgia, to reminisce and rededicate themselves to restoring bonds of friendship and mutual dedication to common values between blacks and Jews. For two days, they shared memories of a time when the two communities marched shoulder to shoulder in common resolve.

Carolyn Goodman, mother of slain civil rights worker Andrew Goodman, was present. Former President Jimmy Carter was there, along with Andrew Young, Julian Bond and NAACP Director Ben Hooks. As the conference came to a close, Al Vorspan came to the podium to wrap up the proceedings and to speak on behalf of the Jewish veterans of the civil rights struggle. More than three decades after he first helped lead the Union and its members into significant involvement in black-Jewish relations, Vorspan candidly acknowledged the deep differences between the two groups on a variety of issues, but concluded his statement with this declaration:

'I think without a special connection between blacks and Jews, social justice is impossible in the United States of America. That's how important I think blacks and Jews are. When blacks and Jews are at each others throats for whatever reason, social justice is an impossible dream. We've got to transmit this message to young people. It must be their dream as well as ours, that same vision that has given so much meaning to our lives.'

Joshua's generation will, I know, accept that charge as a result of his Reform movement.

Joshua's Reform Judaism will fight for the right of every Jew to live in freedom and with dignity, whether in Israel, the Soviet Union or in any land where Jews are imperiled or subjected to discrimination.

Joshua's Reform movement will never shrink from condemning injustice, whether apartheid in South Africa or heartless cutbacks in food stamps, welfare or housing programs for those in need.

I will do my utmost to help preserve those commitments, and many others, now as a vice-president of the UAHC, for Joshua's sake, for the sake of the Jewish people and for the sake of America as a whole.

Not too long ago, Joshua asked me if I believed in God. I told him the story of my personal journey, including the fourth miracle of my life. In 1984, when Josh was just five years old, my father began to exhibit disturbing symptoms of some physical ailment. The doctors performed a battery of tests but found nothing until multiple sophisticated scans showed evidence of a possible tumor in his abdomen. I received word of this in New York and rushed to Detroit to be with him on the night prior to surgery. I arrived at the hospital after visiting hours but, as a rabbi, was able to go to his room. Dad and I were all alone, and for almost an hour we spoke as we had not spoken for many years. Dad was certain that it was a tumor and was already preparing for the inevitability of a terminal condition. He spoke to me about his hopes for my future and for

Joshua's as well. After listening silently, I told him that I wanted to say a prayer for him. Then, without waiting for his response, I rose and walked to the side of his hospital bed. I placed my hand on his forehead and recited the traditional Misheberach. As I concluded the blessing, I stood in silence with my eyes closed and suddenly felt a strange sensation. A feeling of total calm and assurance filled me. It was an experience I had never had before and have not had since. Opening my eyes, I said to my father with complete confidence: "You do not have a tumor. You are going to be all right." My father laughed until he saw the look in my eyes as I gazed directly into his. "You're serious, aren't you?" he asked. I repeated once again: "There is no tumor. You are going to be all right."

We sat and spoke for another hour, and I realized that our roles had been reversed in this moment of crisis. My father often taught me that our relationship with our parents goes through three stages. When we are young, they protect us. When we reach adolescence, they prevent us. Then, if God grants us both enough years, we as children have the privilege of ministering to our parents in the same way that they cared for us. On that night in 1984, there had been just such a role reversal. Even as my father had sat at my bedside some eighteen years earlier, reassuring me that I would ultimately be all right, here I was now in that same position.

I left the hospital and returned to my parents' home, praying for my father throughout the night as he must have prayed for me prior to my cancer surgery. Every time I closed my eyes, I felt that same mysterious calm. To this day, I am absolutely convinced that I received an answer from God to my personal prayer. The next morning, I walked along the hallway with my father as he was wheeled into surgery.

As the operation began, my mother and I sat and waited. An hour passed, two hours, three, four. Then the doctor entered the room with a broad smile on his face. There was no tumor, he declared. It had been in his words, "a shadow of some sort that led the radiologist to assume that a growth might be present." After all was said and done, all they did was remove my father's appendix. He was fine.

I knew, however, that I had been witness to a miracle. No one can convince me otherwise. At last I understood the conviction my father had felt when my childhood friend had been declared close to death. At last I understood the calm with which he responded to the furious doctors in the hospital. As my father came out of anaesthetic, I reminded him that, like me, he had much more to do.

When I told Joshua this story, he asked me how I knew that God answered my prayer. I replied, "I said a prayer, Josh, and I got an answer. I can't explain it any better than that. One day perhaps you will understand. I just knew."

Then I laughed. I had heard those same words before, long, long ago.

CHAPTER XXXIII

Why I Am a Reform Jew

*A*s I conclude this book, the story of one man's personal
odyssey to Reform identity and pride, the saga of Reform
Judaism continues. In 1989, the UAHC spoke out strongly against
the Supreme Court's chipping away at the historic *Roe* v. *Wade* decision on abortion rights. During the spring of 1989, members of over
two hundred UAHC congregations reinterpreted the ancient Jewish custom of cleansing their homes of leaven in preparation for
Passover, and instead brought those food products to the synagogue
or to local food pantries to feed the hungry. During the summer of
1989, the UAHC's Camp Harlam in Pennsylvania, cooperated with
the Israeli air force in providing a summer camp experience for a
dozen Israeli youngsters whose fathers died in defense of Israel's
security. In September of 1989, the UAHC announced a program
whereby copies of books designed to prevent youth suicide were
distributed free of charge to tenth-grade students in UAHC congregations.

So the work of Reform goes on and, in its impact, can only
continue to intensify. If population experts are correct, the Reform
movement is already the largest stream of Judaism within North
America and by the year 2000 will constitute fifty percent or
more of all affiliated Jews. Growing numbers of men, women and
children join Reform congregations, seeking to be part of this
remarkable manifestation of Jewish optimism, hope, vision and
determination. Critics of Reform wonder aloud how this could
possibly be. They sneer at Reform as "watered-down Judaism," as a

movement with no standards and no expectations of its participants. They deride Reform's liberal stance as naive and even harmful to Jews. They sit, many in ivory towers of splendid isolation from real human concerns, and turn inward as they distance themselves from the overwhelming majority of Jews whom they profess to serve.

I believe that they are wrong. Though I have always condemned triumphalism of any sort, I assert without any reservation whatsoever that Reform Judaism is Judaism's best chance for creative and meaningful survival and growth in a modern world and in a free, democratic society. I believe that Orthodox Judaism is the best form of Judaism—for Orthodox Jews. I believe that Conservatism Judaism and Reconstructionism are the best forms of Judaism—for their adherents. For me, however, the choice is clear, and this is why.

I am a Reform Jew because of the freedom that Reform allows—and indeed commands. It is no easy matter to deal with the responsibility of freedom. Freedom requires choices, and the believing Reform Jew makes those choices based upon knowledge. I am not satisfied with the general level of Reform Jewish literacy, nor with the basis upon which many Reform Jews make their personal decisions. I will work to increase their knowledge, but I will continue nonetheless to affirm that right of choice. There is nothing within Jewish tradition that is inherently alien to Reform, and the right to choose has resulted in a Reform Jewish community of enormous diversity and richness in terms of belief and ritual observance. We learn from one another, we respect one another and frankly, we often attempt to influence one another's Jewish lifestyles. When all is said and done, however, we are joined under a common banner of intellectual freedom, a Jewish way of life that can accommodate the dictates of one's rational and spiritual self without external, uncompromising and unchangeable guidelines. I am a Reform Jew, then, not because I have rejected Orthodoxy, but because I have embraced Reform. I respect and honor those for whom an Orthodox or Conservative or Reconstructionist way of life brings meaning and self-fulfillment, but my Jewish aspirations and dreams find expression in the most profound of ways within the institutions of Reform Judaism.

I am a Reform Jew because Reform is inclusive rather than exclusive, prepared to reach out to the unaffiliated, to those who have come to Judaism through conversion, to those born Jews who currently hover on the periphery of Jewish life, starting where they are, rather than expecting them to approach what for many is an intimidating and strange new environment.

I am a Reform Jew because of the absolute equality accorded to women within our ranks. Close to two decades after the ordination of the first woman within Reform, and the graduation of over two hundred more women rabbis and canters thereafter, no major movement but Reform has extended the full range of rights and privileges in both the synagogue and religious spheres of Jewish life to fifty percent of our Jewish family.

I am a Reform Jew because Reform cares for young people through education, youth groups, camps and college programs and Israel opportunities, always encouraging, always holding out a vision and conveying a clear message that they can make a difference in the world.

I am a Reform Jew because of Reform's passion for social justice, its fearless engagement with the great issues of our time, whether within the Jewish community or in society as a whole, and its courage in confronting even those of the highest office where circumstances warrant.

I am a Reform Jew because of the Reform movement's compassion for the poor and helpless, its readiness to bring those in need, whatever their religion, whatever their color, under the sheltering wings of a caring community.

I am a Reform Jew because Reform Judaism never shrinks from self-criticism, from a constant re-evaluation of its growth and evolution, rooted in a history that allows for creative and constructive change, never demanding blind loyalty to the past, never demanding uniformity in order to achieve unity.

I am a Reform Jew because Reform Judaism is a living faith, stressing action based upon belief and an essential partnership between God and every member of the family of humanity.

I am a Reform Jew because Reform Judaism has never given up on the necessity for bonds of understanding and friendship between Jews and those of every faith, ties often threatened by tension

219

and anger and frustration but nonetheless vital in the struggle for a more decent and compassionate society.

I am a Reform Jew because our movement extends to every corner of the world, bringing the blessings of a liberal Judaism to all those who wish to embrace it; whether in Israel, Europe, South America, the Soviet Union, or in any country where the spirit of a modern Judaism burns bright.

I am a Reform Jew because the Reform quest is never finished. Whatever the challenge, I know that Reform will be there to meet the need.

I am a Reform Jew because of the thousands of men and women who have assumed volunteer leadership roles within Reform, people with their own professions, their own families, who nevertheless devote countless hours to the fulfillment and realization of a dream that they help to create on a daily basis. They are the true builders of Reform, for they have given themselves, their children and their Jewish destiny over to that philosophy and to that Jewish way of life in a sacred expression of trust.

I am a Reform Jew because many decades ago two men, a blacksmith and a merchant, brought their families to North America seeking freedom and a new way of life. I am a Reform Jew because they were wise enough to accept that Judaism might take different forms in that new land, as it had so many times in history, but nevertheless be Judaism at its finest. I am a Reform Jew because two children of these men and their wives met, fell in love and were married, and gradually found their way from an Orthodox upbringing to a deep commitment to the values and teachings of this movement.

I am a Reform Jew because those two children, my mother and father, brought me into this world and raised me and my brothers with openness and with respect for our freedom to choose from among the options they afforded us.

I am a Reform Jew because from early childhood, Reform Judaism has touched my life in every possible way, with learning, with values, with programs, with inspiration.

And I am a Reform Jew because Debbie and I understand that our son Joshua's world will need Reform Judaism more than ever before.

Today my father prepares to celebrate his forty-fifth year in the rabbinate. My mother has attained a reputation as one of the finest teachers of responsa literature, certainly in the Midwest and perhaps in the entire country. My brother, David, an accomplished pianist, performs throughout the world. Debbie still teaches those who need her remarkable skills. Joshua attends a Jewish day school, has already spent two summers at UAHC camps, loves Judaism and is totally secure in his Jewish identity.

And I, I am a Reform rabbi, still waiting to learn, to apprehend my mission. I have not found it as yet, but when I do, I am certain that it will be part and parcel of that Reform movement to which I have committed my life.